Developing Quality in Personal Social Services

T0383971

Public Policy and Social Welfare
A Series Edited by Bernd Marin

 European Centre Vienna

Volume 22

Adalbert Evers, Riitta Haverinen, Kai Leichsenring,
Gerald Wistow (Eds.)

Developing Quality in Personal Social Services

Concepts, Cases and Comments

Routledge
Taylor & Francis Group

LONDON AND NEW YORK

First published 1997 by Ashgate Publishing

Reissued 2018 by Routledge
2 Park Square, Milton Park, Abingdon, Oxon, OX14 4RN
52 Vanderbilt Avenue, New York, NY 10017

Routledge is an imprint of the Taylor & Francis Group, an informa business

Publisher's Note
The publisher has gone to great lengths to ensure the quality of this reprint but points out that some imperfections in the original copies may be apparent.

Disclaimer
The publisher has made every effort to trace copyright holders and welcomes correspondence from those they have been unable to contact.

A Library of Congress record exists under LC control number: 98184146

ISBN 13: 978-1-138-35145-5 (hbk)
ISBN 13: 978-1-138-35149-3 (pbk)
ISBN 13: 978-0-429-43524-9 (ebk)

Contents

Developing Quality in Personal Social Services: Introduction

Adalbert Evers
Riitta Haverinen
Kai Leichsenring
Gerald Wistow

Issues concerning quality have become increasingly significant for the development of personal social services in Europe during the 1990s. However, under the influence of massive privatization programmes and the search for cuts in social welfare budgets, a particular discourse on quality has become increasingly prominent, one which relies very much on a business-based approach.

In reality, the issue of quality has always been intrinsic to social service development. The ways in which it has been articulated, however, have mirrored the essential defining characteristics of personal social services. Thus it has been characterized, on the one hand, by a professional discourse of "good practice", which was based on vocational ethics similar to other occupations. On the other hand, the personal social services have always been marked by legal norms and (bureaucratic) procedures characteristic of the general expansion of public welfare institutions.

The outcome of such influences has been impressive. The public sector not only created employment opportunities and satisfied legal entitlements but it often served as a point of reference for "good quality" in terms of equality and justice, thereby marking a clear demarcation with the market sector.

However, this role and status of statutory personal social services has diminished in recent years, and for a number of reasons:

- First, public services in general have lost their potential to serve as a blueprint for effective organization. In times of harsh technological change and global competition, the private sector has taken over the leading role with respect to efficiency and effective management.
- Secondly, publicly funded personal social services that had hitherto been guided by professional ethics of "good practice" and by the notion of social services as a "public good", were increasingly challenged by economic imperatives as resources became scarcer. Although public services in general have not been prepared to think in terms of efficiency gains by adopting private sector management methods, the search for value for money has become an important ingredient in the widespread efforts to modernize statutory services within the framework of so-called "New Public Management".
- Thirdly, we are witnessing a crisis of professionalism insofar as the users of personal social services are questioning professional expertise. Due to their pluralization and emancipation, specific groups of users are less willing than ever to be patronized by professionals or to accept compromises between their individual aspirations and the views of experts.
- Furthermore – and as a consequence of the latter – the concept of privatizing public services has been increasingly difficult to challenge in the absence of notions of efficiency other than those associated with market mechanisms.

Given these developments, the public sector, in particular the "younger" branch of personal social services, has been forced into a rather reactive role with respect to the development of guiding principles for organization and management. Moreover, one repercussion of the hegemony of the market can be seen in the fact that, today, the concept of quality development is seen as almost synonymous with the introduction of managerial approaches to quality assurance.

But is it really the case that there are no alternatives to Total Quality Management and ISO 9000? Do personal social services have to be organized just like any other investment broker or food retailer? Could there be no values of importance other than efficiency and performance? Could the relationships between providers, controllers and clients of personal social services be regulated differently than by mechanisms of supply and demand?

Our brief introduction would be incomplete without mentioning at least some starting points for identifying characteristics of the personal social services which need to be retained and reconciled with business approaches to quality development.

In this respect, one important concept is that of the social citizen who is entitled to specified services and to public support. This role might be similar to the consumer of private market goods and services, who (in theory) is free to choose according to his or her preferences. However, instead of simply recalling and recording consumer preferences, as business approaches do, personal social services would be well recommended to define user orientation in terms of empowerment, individual and collective participation. In particular, direct involvement in decision-making and other forms of user empowerment need to be clearly distinguished from completing "client satisfaction forms".

This is not to say that business approaches to quality assurance will automatically convert personal social services into private businesses. Indeed, it is possible that the introduction of suitably modified versions of such approaches could enable both a reconsideration of traditional concepts and forms of social services together with a greater willingness to accept change. In this connection we are already witnessing the development of alternative concepts of quality that are complementing business approaches. These concepts are generated by a wide range of interest groups, user and consumer movements. Such groups have an alternative understanding of quality and contribute to a range of counter-discourses in the politics of quality and consumption.

Given this background, the European Centre for Social Welfare Policy and Research in Vienna (Austria) and The National Research and Development Centre for Welfare and Health (STAKES) in Helsinki (Finland) jointly initiated an international debate about quality in personal social services. In spring 1996, a scientific seminar was organized in Helsinki under the title "Developing Quality in Personal Social Services". This seminar was characterized by a broad approach towards quality, the aim being to encompass issues that are not always given prominence in the mainstream discourses about quality development. Starting from presentations about the origins and nature of different approaches to quality assurance, the debate included critical reflections on existing tools and instruments for quality measurement, on the one hand, and opportunities for introducing business approaches as an additional dimension for social service reforms, on the other hand. This broadly-based public debate led most contributors to conclude that different approaches have to be combined and developed. Universal solutions cannot fit the diverse characteristics of personal social services or their users and, therefore, the requirement is to develop approaches to quality which match that diversity.

About this Book

The great success of the seminar "Developing Quality in Personal Social Services" – bringing together more than 40 paper givers and 100 participants from all over Europe – convinced the organizers to also publish a reader under the same title. As this publication should focus on the very confrontation of business approaches with the specificities of personal social services, a new call for contributions resulted in revised versions of selected papers that had been presented at the above seminar.

The publication is divided into three sections. The first section is devoted to the presentation of different concepts with respect to quality in personal social services. Adalbert Evers emphasizes the interdependency between the kind of global concept for personal social services one is oriented to and the attitude one takes towards concepts for quality development – especially business-based ones. He discusses these interlinkages with a view on three key issues in the debate on social service concepts: their "personal" and "caring" quality, the role of "mixed" solutions and diversity, and their role as public goods. Christopher Pollitt compares the business and professional approaches to quality improvement and their suitability to personal social services in a critical way drawing conclusions on the possibilities and drawbacks of these approaches. Mikko Mäntysaari discusses the promises of quality management in the context of Nordic welfare states and especially in the Finnish human services. Tessa Harding, Clare Evans, Suzy Croft and Peter Beresford emphasize user definitions of quality, noting that they are substantially different from those of professionals and suggesting that participation by users can be both a route to quality and also a measure of it.

The second section of the book focuses on different methods by which quality may be enhanced in the personal social services. Marketta Rajavaara's contribution focuses on professional models and values, their compatibility with business models and the impact of quality initiatives on professional cultures and inter-professional relationships. Monica Dowling combines professional social work and user perspectives on quality, while also emphasizing that the observation of practice and the organizational structures in which social workers operate is no less important than the measurement of attitudes, efficiency or outcomes. By contrast with the previous two contributors, managerial concepts of quality and their associated methodologies provide the starting point for Maria Oppen's consideration of whether in Germany Total Quality Management (TQM) can be adapted and transferred to social services contexts. Verbeek emphasizes that, while value for money imperatives underlie the interest in quality in the Netherlands, consumer pressures for responsive, individually-tailored services may also coincide with professional commitments to quality improvements. Barbara Klein examines the role of inspections as a mechanism for quality assurance in residential and nursing homes in Britain and Germany, contrasting especially the emphasis on quality as outcomes for users in the former and compliance with legal requirements in the latter. Rosemary Bland's paper complements the previous one by examining the inspection of domiciliary services in Scotland and, most particularly, reporting on how user-centred standards can be developed and applied within such inspection processes.

Contributions to the final section consist of case-studies selected to illustrate opportunities and problems arising from initiatives to enhance quality in a range of service and national contexts. For example, while the introduction of competitive markets into the personal social services has been widely advocated as a mechanism for improving quality, Brian Hardy and Gerald Wistow demonstrate that the arrangements for contracting in British domiciliary care markets are of a kind which threaten to compromise existing standards rather than enhance them. Sturle Næss and Kari Wærness, from a Norwegian perspective, not only argue that managerial models of quality are inappropriate to public services for older people but they also question whether the two most common criteria of quality – autonomy and independence – are necessarily enhanced by the way domiciliary services are delivered. Steen Bengtsson returns to the role of markets in his study of different forms of user influence on quality in Denmark, concluding that there may be scope to strengthen such influences by combining both exit and voice strategies. Experience elsewhere in Scandinavia, in the City of Stockholm, is shown by Jonas Bjelfvenstam to demonstrate that a focus on improving quality for users can reinforce, rather than conflict with, initiatives to improve cost effectiveness and secure benefits for taxpayers. Christensen also focuses on different perspectives on quality in a study of home care and home nursing services in Norway which demonstrates that while service reorganizations have achieved no change in the subjective perceptions of quality from the user's point of view, some improvements are evident from that of care workers. Carla Costanzi's contribution switches the focus to quality in institutional services and includes an account of how the City of Genoa developed definitions and tools to promote the quality of life for residents in homes for older people. Riitta Haverinen analyses the influences shaping initiatives to improve quality in Finland, emphasizing especially the impact of a number of national initiatives on local professionals and service delivery processes. By contrast, Marja Pijl's case-study reports on a single initiative, the provision of care budgets to service recipients in the Netherlands, and uses it to demonstrate that user-defined quality standards do not sit well with those underpinning either professional or business approaches to quality improvement. Finally, Britt Slagsvold returns the discussion to quality in institutional settings and provides an account of how the measurement of quality may fail to capture user's experiences of services and, indeed, distort the relationship between them and their caregivers.

PART I

CONCEPTS

Quality Development – Part of a Changing Culture of Care in Personal Social Services

Adalbert Evers

1 The Point of Departure: Different Concepts of Assuring Quality in Personal Social Services

Personal Social Services (PSS) have been a major growth industry in all European countries. With the current changes in both quantity and impact, the prevailing views and concepts with respect to quality have changed as well. There have been processes of professionalization; changes in social rights to care; transitions from charity- or state-based systems to mixed markets; changes concerning the readiness of families to use outside help and concerning aspirations when using PSS. If one agrees that caring in the widest sense is the essence of PSS – caring being understood not only as providing material help but also as providing advice and personal and social support – then these changes can be summed up in what I call a "changing culture of care" (Evers, 1995). The same moving forces that operate behind the changing images of care are also behind the changing notions of quality.

In light of this, one ought to distinguish two separate yet related items which are (i) quality measurement (especially for standard-setting and control from the outside) and (ii) quality improvement (as a way for doing better within a given broader framework). The following considerations will revolve around Quality Assurance (QA), which is meant as a label to cover both issues. There are four important types and traditions of QA that can be distinguished (also see the typology suggested by Rajavaara in this book).

- The first comes from the field of professionals and their organizations – these are the traditions of peer reviews by colleagues, standards and ethics given by and controlled within a professional association. This model is linked with the development of the welfare state, which helped to professionalize the field of help, care and social work. It is about both setting and controlling quality standards and about quality improvements.
- The second type is the "inspectorate approach", sometimes executed by people from the same professional field. This model has flourished alongside the welfare state as a provider of universalistic services meant to be highly standardized and uniform, e.g. in the area of schools and hospitals. The inspectorate approach is very much about the processes of laying down what is seen as a general standard and about guidance on quality control (for the diversity of the prevailing styles, see Klein and Bland in this book).
- The legacy of the third type of defining quality and assuring it, basically stems from the late 1960s and the euphoria of being able to construct bottom-up models for new service relationships based on both individual and collective citizen and consumer control and participation (see Harding/Beresford, 1996; in this book especially Beresford/Croft/Evans/Harding).
- The fourth type of quality assurance comes from outside – the business sector – with concepts suggesting reforms in organizational and management structures. These range from top-down models (Kelly, 1991) to comprehensive concepts for constant institutional reform, such as Total Quality Management (TQM) (Deming, 1982). These concepts differ from the first type in many instances but especially to the degree they address the entire body of a firm or organization; some of them try to create, at least for a while, a high level of joint readiness and commitment to question not only inherited structures and routines but also prevailing individual perspectives. Altogether, the business-based models are very much concerned with doing better than the others within a shared culture and environment (see the descriptions and remarks concerning development and purposes in PSS by Mäntysaari, Oppen, Pollitt and Rajavaara in this book).

It is well known that in European public services today, the concepts coming from the market sector clearly prevail (see the picture given in the overview by Pollitt/Bouckaert, 1995). To a large part, this is in line with the fact that the global ideological trends have shifted towards an increasing impact from market liberalism: the majority of the shifts in the "welfare mixes" in PSS have been towards more market values, arrangements and mechanisms (Wistow/Knapp/Hardy/Allen, 1994). This has had a number of positive effects for the culture of care, as well as for the type of QA which is thereby emphasized. Let me enumerate a few:

- The new care culture and business concepts of QA seem to be more prepared to look at the wishes of the people cared for; after a century of client concepts, the idea of serving the consumer has finally given some fresh air to the PSS sector.
- QA business concepts are in line with rearrangements in the service sector towards more freedom of decision at the decentralized level of the single unit, and towards greater possibilities to change routines and to innovate, basically allowing for more diversity. This stands in direct contrast to the hierarchical top-down control model, such as the inspectorate tradition; and it makes a difference in the professional model, one constantly in danger of becoming autistic by using criteria and professional standards which have lost touch with reality in the working environment.
- Finally, the business approach can help to bring a teamwork orientation into settings where hierarchical characteristics marched hand in hand with the inspectorate tradition and where professional rivalry was an obstacle to professional QA models (for similar arguments concerning suitability, especially of TQM, see Rajavaara in this book).

2 The Point of Concern: Defining the Challenge Linked with the Introduction of Business-based Concepts

However, as some of the readers may have already suspected, such an appraisal is just an introduction to a more critical discourse about the role and limits of business-based QA concepts. I will concentrate on them because they currently prevail in both discussion and practice. In fact, the main purpose of this paper will be to collect hints, experiences and reflections concerning the problems of introducing a business approach into the domain of PSS. My argument is, that the respective approaches do not and sometimes cannot grasp some of the peculiarities of the area of personal social services.

At first sight, this means argueing – like many of my colleagues (as well as a number of contributors to this book; for example, Mäntysaari) – that there are problems with business-based QA concepts coming from the outside, and that it is a challenge to adapt them to the specific realities of the PSS sector. In fact, the central argument of this article will be a different one. In order to give the reader an idea of this difference, one can begin with the simple question of what is special in the PSS sector. Usually, the answers will be twofold:

- First of all, there is a structural difference: a personal service is constituted by a personal interaction, in contrast to a material good or product.
- Secondly, there are empirical and perhaps also contingent differences, many of them concerning the fact that the services are state-based and thus seen as *public* goods. Others relate to differences in the economy, such as the prevalence of

small-scale providers and a huge diversity of service organizations and styles in many countries.

However, beyond the basic abstract principle that constitutes the structural difference just mentioned between material products and personal services, there are in fact many different ideas about how to shape the interactions between service providers and consumers. Some tend to minimalize the difference to ordinary consumer relations, e.g. with the idea of a quick and ready-made service – a perspective which helps to take over the market vocabulary. On behalf of the empirical and somewhat contingent differences between the service and market sectors, various standpoints can also be found when it comes to describing their impact. If one is in favour of turning PSS more into private provision rather than treating them as public goods, this will have a clear impact when discussing the suitability of business-based QA; the same will hold true with respect to the question of whether it is better to keep the PSS economy as diverse as it is, with large parts being restricted to local boundaries or allowing for large capital to take over and create standardizing effects.

In other words, the position and vision to which one refers with respect to the future design of PSS, will influence one's judgement not only about the different concepts of QA but also about the degree of changes which a business-based approach has to undergo to make it work. This holds true not only with respect to different interest-based preferences – e.g. on the part of the state, professionals, users or the tax-paying public – detected in deliberations on quality (Munro, 1995; for quality as a plural concept, see Pijl and Rajavaara in this book). The global visions which can be found and have their basis across different (interest) groups are themselves critical. There will obviously be fewer reservations towards business-based concepts of QA if one already envisions a more business-like organized PSS sector. Therefore, the discourse should not be about changes needed in order to adapt business models to *a given reality* of PSS, but rather about changes and challenges for QA in relation to *a specific concept and vision for change* in PSS and its culture of care.

Many present contributions to the debate on the future of PSS seem, however, to lack such a vision or to transport it implicitly. The one orienting the following considerations is different from the business/consumerist vision for future PSS, which in many countries may be already mainstream. In line with former work about the culture of care and the welfare mix in the PSS sector (Evers, 1995), the emphasis will be on the importance of factors which today play a very limited role in usual market places. Here are a few examples:

- the positive contributions to be made by the co-producer and co-decision-making role of family- and community-based networks; and

- the importance of state guarantees and interventions to create social citizenship rights and to represent collective perspectives and common interests as a counterbalance to what are so often praised as individual "preferences".

By emphasizing the importance of such dimensions, these reflections will probably contain more reservations concerning the role of business-based QA than others. Peculiarities associated with QA issues will be addressed in three sections:

- the fact that personal and care services are forms of personal interaction and community-related relationships, different from the usual producer-consumer relations (section 4);
- the fact that these partly belong to a different "local" and "moral" economy (section 5); and
- the fact that questions of public interest and citizen/user concerns are at least as important as consumer preferences (section 6).

From there follows an idea about quality and its assurance which is in a way multidimensional. It should take account of people as co-producers, citizens and consumers (Evers, 1997), which likewise means that there should be a place for each of the four roads to QA sketched above. Within such a policy mix, maybe the third and fourth of them – user involvement as well as market and consumer approaches – are presently both more important and more difficult than others, simply because they have been traditionally so much neglected compared with such professional or social-policy criteria for quality as equality and security.

However, before turning to these points, some observations will be presented concerning the sociopolitical context and the fact that so much emphasis is presently put on QA issues.

3   A Special Point: Quality Development in a Given Sociopolitical Context

Asking how important quality development is, might be of interest in order not to be trapped by the emphasis given to one item, which always means giving less to others. We should not forget that asking parents about the quality of their kindergartens, or a caring relative about the quality of his/her home-care arrangement, means arguing about a part of a much broader question, which could be, "How good is your municipality or your country when it comes to helping you in child-raising or elderly care?" Quality in terms of this broader question no longer revolves around a specific service action to be singled out, but rather about a complex arrangement entailing such questions as the level of obligatory fees, the difficulties in finally becoming entitled for a place in an institution, and many other similar questions. The restricted perspective of the predominant contributions to the present quality debate, however, is exactly one of the reasons behind its attractiveness: it promises clear, quantitative statements on limited issues where vague discussions on broad issues generally prevail. Yet the attempt of "measuring" the quality of a single service arrangement should not make us forget about the broader dimension of quality – one which includes the fairness of our welfare institutions, rights and our culture at large (Hoyes et al., 1992).

In view of this, one should keep an eye on the fact that potential investments in quality development are usually suggested at times when we find an unwillingness to invest in closing care gaps or in better training, and when the emphasis is usually not on better quality but on getting by with less money. Therefore, the boundaries between reorganization processes oriented towards improving quality, and a New Public Management (Naschold, 1993) concerned with doing things more quickly and with less staff, should be kept in mind. Usually there is a link between quality-development items and increasing productivity (see Pollitt in this book); and one should ask about how these might be balanced.

Therefore, in an environment where we presently find little or no concern with what could be called "quality at large", it is indeed questionable if we look most closely at the quality of what single service units deliver: often, the low quality of a service is to a great degree determined by outside decisions which result e.g. in understaffing or wasting of time and resources due to bureaucratic rules imposed from the outside. One could argue that, just as happens in the general rhetoric about strengthening individual responsibility, there is the risk of blaming the victim – here, an individual PSS unit, its care workers or managers – for problems set by the economic or social policy environment. So, an impact investigation might pay off which states the balance of inside and outside factors concerning e.g. the five most important quality items found to be deficient in whatever PSS unit happens to be chosen.

4   The Peculiarities of Service Relationships

It is commonplace that, due to the specificity of a service, its quality is dependent on an interactive process which blurs the demarcation lines between producers and consumers: hence, the speech about "pro-sumers" and "co-producers". But from my point of view, this fact is merely a point of departure for further considerations. Very much depends on the concept of care and service by which the interaction is shaped. This can be done in a way which reduces its differences with the market and product approach, by giving a "full service" and "quick fix" to the consumer in command. For a long time, another contrasting concept had prevailed – a kind of public sector/ professional approach where the client gets something largely predetermined according to professional assessments and detailed social legislation.

Given the fact that in many cases the former clients and ought-to-be consumers must in fact cooperate actively in negotiating and arranging a service relationship, we arrive at a complicated interaction process where the division of labour as well as the outcome and definition of goals and quality can change considerably over time. This creates, on the one hand, problems for professional and inspectorate types of QA to the degree that they are concerned with setting or reinforcing standards and norms: preparing a meal is hard to write down as a routine item on bills and reimbursement systems if the relatives sometimes help in it. On the other hand, it makes any care-service organization especially dependent on their counterparts when they want to produce quality. Difficult contradictions may arise between process quality, which can be high in terms of sensibility to the need for cooperation, and outcome quality, which may be harmed by the leeway for risky decisions by the "prosumers".

A second problem often cited when importing QA is the fact that the quality of a service can only be measured in terms of looking at a chain of acts by different organizations cooperating or transferring responsibility from one to another – e.g. from a hospital to a nursing home. Every institution might be doing well and may be ready to cooperate; but the preconditions and means might be missing. Therefore, creating cooperation for quality between different units and organizations often serving the same clients, is most important. While this is a top quality problem in PSS, nearly all QA concepts have little to offer here. Interorganizational cooperation – something which is more about a system than a unit – has little or no counterpart in the purchaser-provider relations of the business sector.

Less obvious are two other challenges in care. These are situated around the question of what makes personal service relations really "personal".

First of all, this means simply conceiving caretakers as persons who are more than just the impersonal incarnation of professional roles and skills, something which makes them as service-givers to a degree unique and not easily substituted. In all PSS, we see users clinging to the person with whom they are interrelated, as well as the importance they attach to continuity and trust as essential components of a "rationality of caring" (Waerness, 1984). The decision on whether to hire outside help and which service to choose, is very much about trust and empathy. This gives at least some hints concerning the degree to which benchmarks for quality in personal social services should be sought not only in the marketplace – which aims basically at making relationships interchangeable – but also by looking at informal, mostly non-professional helping and caring relationships as a reference model.

Secondly, the speech about autonomy, choice, empowerment and consumer-led services clouds another important characteristic in many areas of care and PSS – they often deal with especially weak and vulnerable groups, such as frail elderly people, children, marginalized and desocialized persons. This creates specific limits for direct consumer control, as well as for simple one-to-one translations of user wishes into professional tasks. Professionals must learn to cope with an undeniable power over their clients. For quality control and development, some original concepts have therefore been created in the PSS sector – models of regular supervision for professionals or advocacy models for vulnerable user groups, e.g. outside persons on the board of a nursing home. Summing up, it could be said that any reflections on the balance between enabling and protecting, between consumer-led and professional-led elements in the social service sector, may quickly bring to the surface the competing visions and perspectives that influence the attitude towards QA concepts.

Finally, there is a third, perhaps most basic problem related to a demanding definition of a "personal" social service: the impact of shared concerns, core values and commitments which help to give a caring quality to a service. With a view to that, the more developed business-based concepts of QA, such as TQM, have developed a special sensitivity (most QA concepts have not; see the instructive contribution of Slagsvold in this book). They concentrate very much on the development of a shared vision, a strengthened corporate identity and commitment on the part of the employees. In the care and personal social service sector, two things seem remarkable in this context.

First of all, the level of explicit reflection of such coherent visions and basic values in the public-service sector is usually very low. This is not only due to such single factors as training; the generally low level of explicit values about the goals and quality of a care service has also to do with convictions deeply rooted in our liberal culture, insisting on values as very much a private, individual affair (this can fall well in line with the "silent presence" of concepts within a service or organization which are never explicitly thematized). One could take the example of an old people's or nursing home (for the following, see Moody, 1993). What most often prevails today is the "autonomy" model, which is part of the unfinished liberal agenda on behalf of the vulnerable. Here, quality will be very much about everyone doing his or her part, while respecting mutual distance, safeguarding individual rights laid down in contracts, etc.

There are, however, very different models of a perhaps more "communitarian" character. Here, fostering an atmosphere of lively exchange and cooperation, as well as strengthening the ethic of caring and human relationships, are most important. Instead of centring on the defence of and respect for individual rights, the emphasis will be much more on creating a supportive context. But this also calls for more responsibility of all parties concerned than in the liberal model; and this is one reason why such concepts are often regarded with mistrust. Anyone who is tempted to ridicule the value-based communitarian approach, should now be reminded that advanced business-based models for re-engineering organizations, such as TQM, are exactly such an attempt to create a corporate spirit of community amongst the workers and members of an organization. Hence, one could perhaps inquire into the silent relationship between the evangelic rhetoric of these business-related concepts for quality development, and the total absence of shared commitment they meet in organizations ruled by rivalry and the message to care about oneself in the first place.

However, it is exactly when taking a positive view of approaches from the business sector concerned with strengthening a shared commitment for quality, that one will notice their limitations and perhaps redetect some positive aspects of the PSS tradition. The presupposition to create a climate of outspoken commitment and to keep it alive, works perhaps somewhat better in small-scale care organizations, as compared to big hierarchical organizations as are found in the global marketplace or the big welfare bureaucracies. However, TQM merely provides the leeway for creating or confirming strong values and a "moral perspective". The really interesting point concerns the process of doing so and the shape of a care culture aimed at upgrading its own values and impact – values which are not only private and which by their very presence might allow for raising the degree of daily interaction in e.g. a nursing home beyond the level of sheer "bed and body work". To what degree can this be the outcome of a single event at the level of one unit where TQM concepts are applied? Perhaps one needs a complementary commitment for such questions at the level of the whole care system. Concepts like TQM can perhaps stimulate that; but they cannot substitute it.

5   The Mixed Economy of Care and Personal Social Services

Usually, the term of the mixed economy – similar as the term "welfare mix" – points to the fact that there are different spheres interacting and competing when it comes to PSS: market providers, public organizations, non-profit and voluntary organizations, and families and households from the non-monetary informal economy (Wistow et al., 1994). However there is an additional and different meaning of "mix" in the ways in which the discourse on new steering mechanisms in the public sector deals with it all (Naschold, 1993), and outside the British debate with respect to the definition of "third-sector" organizations (Evers, 1995). In the framework of concepts for a New Public Management, there has been much discussion about the intertwining of different rationales mixing the logics of state planning and market competition, such as by creating quasi-markets, purchaser-provider splits and compulsory competitive tendering. The other notion of mixes perceives third-sector service organizations as "hybrids" intertwining elements of a public and private economy, such as a voluntary organization with profit centres. This sensitivity for the manifold features of merging different rationales is also shared by other studies which have analysed the manifold links of service organizations with specific local and subcultures and their social and moral economies (OECD, 1996). This kind of "social embeddedness" can have quite traditional features, such as in local church- and parish-based provisions, but it can as well be a hallmark of new community-based initiatives in care and PSS, partly contracted into the local service network (see Taylor, 1994).

The argument is that the sheer existence of these dimensions of a mixed economy and the strategic position one takes towards it, are important when discussing the suitability of QA concepts. Three examples may illustrate this:

The first is about the problems which have arisen with the shift from a closed public system of PSS financing and provision towards different systems of contracting out and compulsory competitive tendering which blur the demarcation lines with the market sector. While these concepts do decentralize decision-making power and responsibility, they nevertheless create new problems of quality control. First of all, such systems often give systematic incentives for the single contracted-in service provider to reach for competitive advantages by making savings through reducing this or that aspect of quality. This again makes quality control a more important and difficult issue. At first hand, one could say that a detailed and clear contract between purchaser and provider might be helpful. However, there are hints from experiences in the UK and The Netherlands that making contracts detailed enough to allow for effective quality control, e.g. by a renewed inspectorate approach, will lead to a bureaucratic impasse which destroys the flexibility achieved by the introduction of the systems themselves. A Dutch study (van der Pennen et al., 1995) about the effects of introducing new steering systems in local PSS, draws an interesting conclusion: enumerating quality benchmarks in a contract will neither give a coherent mission to the organization to be contracted in, nor will it work as the only point of departure for quality control. In order to safeguard that providers act according to the wishes of a public body, it needs a more basic presupposition which helps to safeguard a kind of general mutual understanding and some basic trust – something the authors of the Netherlands study have called a shared "policy vision". Here, a problem already raised before concerning the "corporate spirit of community" comes back to us on the level of a whole policy sector: the significance of a usually very limited pool of goods, values and tasks to be shared. To what degree can it be recompensated on the system level by contract and control approaches? Perhaps this problem is less pressing in the business sector and for the QA concepts developed there: they have only one dominating link, the producer-consumer relationship, in contrast to the more complicated network within the mixed economy of PSS where state institutions, the municipality and a diversity of other organizations related to the field – as well as the customers themselves – can together be "clients" of a service-providing unit.

The second illustrative example is about the fact that, in many countries, PSS units or parts of them are intertwined with local communities, subcultures and networks; they are finely tuned with demands arising from there, as well as by their respective values and aspirations. It is not by accident that at least in my country care services are usually recommended and chosen by word of mouth; the issues of trust and reliability ever come back which are so important for services which invade the private sphere. Furthermore, it should be noted that many small-scale service providers are not led by managers, but rather by professionals; their style of working can be compared with craftsmanship, or with the special commitment of local shop owners. In the French debate, one has called these services "les services à proximité". The hints just given should remind us of the fact that there is a considerable difference between a global and a local economy (OECD, 1996). Preserving a dimension of localism in PSS can be a very controversial issue. Taking a position which does not want to abolish it but prefers to develop it further as part of a rich and diversified landscape of care and PSS providers, will have consequences when assessing QA concepts. Because for this specific local and moral economy, the takeover of models of standard-setting and control coming from the big hierarchical systems – be it something like the public school system or something like big business – will be problematic. The challenge would be to develop methods for quality improvement which respect the peculiarities of this local economy. An interesting example has been presented in a study about reforms in local PSS systems (Evers/ Leichsenring, 1996). The municipality of the city of Delft, for example, runs its own consultancy and developers' unit. Since it is linked to the local field of services for the elderly, it can do consultancy for quality improvement in a different style than external consultancy firms.

The third and last example given here refers to the presence of the moral economy recreated in the most important institution when it comes to personal help and care – the family. A lot of research has been produced about what is called in the German discourse the "specific female working attitude and sensibility" – part of the gender difference (Ostner/Beck-Gernsheim, 1978). It is well known that PSS very much depend on one of its aspects – the readiness to work beyond what is formally agreed in the working contract, due to one's commitment to the people for whom one is caring. Many services are based on this readiness and often even exploit it as a hidden resource used in practice while denied on conceptual grounds. Therefore, trade unionism and many concepts of professionalism have for decades tried to block this potential source of what they see as "self-exploitation". However, this specific female working and caring attitude is basic for a special type of intrinsic motivation; and if one adds other types of cooperation, such as volunteering, one is faced with kinds of employees who are very different from the employees in ordinary enterprises. Here, once again, much depends from the attitude one takes *vis-à-vis* this fact of female predispositions and voluntary commitment. One should examine not only the concepts of structural and outcome criteria but also the ways of proceeding in QA and the modernization of services: whether they are prepared to deal in constructive ways with such types of care work and the working attitudes related to it, interwoven with special ideas about the quality of a caring relationship. The contributions of Næss/Wærness and Christensen in this book both illustrate cases of modernization processes implemented in the name of quality not aware of the enormous impact of the "rationality of caring" (Wærness) and its roots in community and household settings for quality defined from the users' perspective.

6   Care and Social Services as Public Goods

The last point of concern to be debated here refers to the fact that the majority of PSS have traditionally been created as "public goods". This can mean that basically every citizen has a right to the service; and in order to safeguard this, one needs specification procedures and legal norms which concretize, on the one hand, such social-policy related criteria as equality and, on the other, which authorize some professional criteria. For the inspectorate approach, both items can play an important role; control is oriented towards norms which define quality not only in terms of professional standards, but also by the degree of successful implementation of legal rights concerning procedures for entitlement and access. In most European countries, the domain where PSS enjoy the clear-cut status of a public good is shrinking. Nevertheless, there are still many PSS within the public responsibility. This, then, has a number of consequences for the meaning of quality and the ways to define it (see as well Stewart/Clarke, 1987):

(a) Providers have to design their services according to specific social-policy criteria of distributional justice, which are non-existent or far less relevant than in private business.
(b) The public addressed cannot be defined only in terms of consumers and customers but has also to be understood as a public of citizens with specified social rights.
(c) Public services involve a kind of professionalism which has usually to be in line with standards not only agreed with direct recipients of the service, but with a broader public as represented by administrators and legislators.
(d) Public institutions steered by political proceedings can easily become the object of claims for participation and collective forms of user involvement usually unknown in private companies.

Once again, the attitude towards these dimensions is important. One extreme position might be a purely consumerist perspective, wherein – e.g. by offering cash instead of services – any responsibility beyond setting criteria for entitlement is removed both from the state and from the citizens. The items on which the money is spent, the quality of the services chosen, etc., become a private affair. Whatever the position might be towards such trends, there are areas like, e.g. social work where, due to the high level of legal decisions about freedom and resources, public status and the four dimensions of quality noted above will remain important. Let us see, what that means for quality assurance.

(ad a) Public institutions, when designing their "products" – as managerial jargon phrases it – are confronted with social-policy-related questions like fairness and justice which generally do not exist in the private sector, such as whether a local care centre should distribute its limited help resources to many people or give more intense help to a limited number of very frail clients. The problem of defining what is the best quality for a specific group is inextricably linked with the wider challenge of coming to a fair arrangement wherein both the type of service and the size and character of the group are variables. While this example is concerned with providing more space for decisions and evaluating the impact of such additional criteria as social justice when defining a "good product" in PSS, another example is about restrictions. In business, the diversification of a product – e.g. an offer ranging from simple to professional PC equipment – is part of a strategy of constructing a range of "good products" in terms of quality-price relationships. In contrast to that, public services can usually not do this; they have to promise the same rights for different patients even while it takes very different costs and measures to make them effective. To sum up, the narrow question of the quality of what is given when somebody receives something, may marginalize a more important question: how to safeguard that, within the legal framework, there be a democratic process which guarantees a fair decision about who and how many get how much.

(ad b) Correlated with social-policy concerns is the dimension of citizen concerns and rights. This brings in criteria of quality and rationales usually not present in an individual consumer perspective. This is important because the goods brought about by many PSS can be as manifold as the potential negative side-effects: e.g. building a school in a deprived area means not only offering some education to a number of single pupils as direct consumers but can also mean bringing about better conditions for the parents concerned or for local associations that can use the rooms, etc. The full potential quality preserved by the school as a product will not become visible when only taking the perspective of the customers but it will if one also considers that of the other local citizens involved. And therefore, besides the school board, a city district meeting may be welcomed as an additional tool. There, quality-related aspects may be raised which would otherwise be missing. So, instead of playing off public and private solutions against each other, one might conceive mixed "round-table" systems which make it possible to articulate different angles and dimensions of service quality and to come to an agreement about

a concept entailing priorities and compromises. Switching simply from state-imposed systems of PSS towards a likewise unidimensional concept of consumer orientation based on marketing studies or individual preferences, is the utopia of a "democracy without policy" (Montin/Elander, 1995). Why not conceive "exit" and "voice" principles as complementary and overlapping, instead of fixing them as mutually exclusive elements? Why not envision a process which links the different sides involved – producers, public authorities and the people to be addressed – as citizens, members of a community, users and consumers?

(ad c) The way that issues of equality and citizenship rights have been just discussed, illustrates that "keeping the customer satisfied" is a much more central goal in normal business when compared to public PSS. Obviously, concepts of quality improvement which are "customer-led" represent, on the one hand, clear advantages, especially wherever a tradition of declared public concern accompanied a reality of poor and inefficient services. On the other hand, it is the task of a professional and part of one's professional ethos as a member of a *public* service, to make clear why the needs which have been stated by professionals are possibly different from the initial wishes and preferences of the users. It depends on the level and legitimacy of broader agreements between politics and the public on the practices in the respective service sector to what degree service workers can manage to intermediate individual wishes with their professional offers and suggestions.

(ad d) A keyword here will be negotiation; and this directs the emphasis towards the people who are indeed consumers but who are at the same time users to be involved. In the business-based concepts for QA, however, the consumer dimension is the only one taken up with all kinds of market research, etc., to be implemented. This tends to disregard the user perspective on quality assurance and the potential role of forms of direct and indirect participation, such as with representatives of user groups on the board of service organizations or special possibilities for taking part in a negotiation process about designing an individual arrangement for e.g. home care. Furthermore, it should be taken into account that the special economy of services rooted in the local and neighbourhood context (services qualified by Taylor et al. [1994] as run "by us, for us") offers additional possibilities for people at the community level to be involved.

7   Summary and Conclusions

Reflecting on possibilities for QA, especially business-based concepts, three points have been highlighted which are critical for the special nature of care and PSS – the interactive nature of services, the mixed economy in the PSS sector, and their status as public goods. Depending on how these peculiarities are conceptually taken into regard, the judgement of concepts for quality control and quality development will vary accordingly.

- The first critical point identified was the degree to which one can find the presence of strong and explicit shared values and commitments in service interactions which are important for preserving and bettering the personal, caring character of service relationships. Elaborate business concepts like the TQM approach might help in cases where all parties concerned are really willing to engage in a difficult process – defining strong and explicit values as a basis for organizing care in ways that give institutional support to personal commitment.
- The second critical point identified was the presence of a local and moral economy including non-professional contributions in care and PSS, usually balanced in a mix with state-public and ordinary market elements. This special dimension of the mixed economy of PSS calls for ways to define and assure quality beyond the logic of big business and bureaucracies, encouraging diversity and its contributions to it, where a "rationality of caring" can counterbalance the rationality of managerialism and consumerism.
- The third critical point which has been identified was the impact of questions like social justice, social rights and the professional ethos linked with them, counterbalancing the dimension of individual preferences and consumer satisfaction as the central or even sole criterion of business-based approaches.

With respect to the kinds of concepts of QA to be used, or the policy mix to be implemented, it will be important whether these points are taken seriously or are marginalized. Unfortunately, they are seen by many today as impediments and only by a few as points of departure for quality and its improvement. The image of PSS as being deficient and lagging behind, is unfortunately very much constructed by a perspective which takes other market sectors for daily consumer goods and services as a role model rather uncritically.

References

Deming, W.E. (1982) *Out of the Crisis. Quality, Productivity and Competitive Position.* Cambridge: Cambridge University Press.

Evers, A. (1995) 'Part of the Welfare Mix: The Third Sector as an Intermediate Area', *Voluntas* 6 (2): 159-182.

Evers, A. (1995a) 'The Future of Elderly Care in Europe: Limits and Aspirations', in: Scharf, Th./Wenger, G.C. (eds.), *International Perspectives on Community Care for Older People.* Aldershot: Avebury.

Evers, A. (1997) 'Consumers, Citizens and Coproducers – A Pluralistic Perspective on Democracy in Social Services', in: Flösser, G./Otto, H.U. (eds.), *Towards More Democracy in Social Services.* Berlin/New York: de Gruyter.

Evers, A./Leichsenring, K. (1996) *Reduktion oder Redefinition politischer Verantwortung? Modernisierung sozialer Dienste in Delft und Stockholm.* EUROSOCIAL Report 60. Wien: Europäisches Zentrum für Wohlfahrtspolitik und Sozialforschung.

Harding, T./Beresford, P. (eds.) (1996) *The Standards We Expect: What Service Users and Carers Want from Social Services Workers.* London: National Institute of Social Work.

Hoyes, L./Means, R./Le Grand, J. (1992) *Made to Measure? Performance Measurement and Community Care.* Occasional Paper 39. University of Bristol, School for Advanced Urban Studies.

Kelly, A. (1991) 'The "New" Managerialism in the Social Services', pp. 178-193 in: Carter, P./Jeffs, T./Smith, M.K. (eds.), *Social Work and Social Welfare Yearbook,* Vol. 3.

Montin, S./Elander, I. (1995) 'Citizenship, Consumerism and Local Government in Sweden', *Scandinavian Political Studies* 18 (1): 25-51.

Moody, H.R. (1993) *Ethics in an Aging Society.* Baltimore and London.

Munro, R. (1995) 'Governing the New Province of Quality: Autonomy, Accounting and the Dissemination of Accountability', in: Wilkinson, A./Wilmott, H. (eds.), *Making Quality Critical: New Perspectives on Organizational Change.* London and New York: Routledge.

Naschold, F. (1993) *Modernisierung des Staates. Zur Ordnungs- und Innovationspolitik des öffentlichen Sektors.* Berlin: edition sigma.

OECD (ed.) (1996) *Reconciling Economy and Society. Towards a Plural Economy.* Paris: OECD.

Oppen, M. (1995) *Qualitätsmanagement.* Berlin: edition sigma.

Ostner, I./Beck-Gernsheim, E. (1978) 'Frauen verändern – Berufe nicht? Ein theoretischer Ansatz zur Problematik "Frau und Beruf"', *Soziale Welt* 29: 257-287.

Pollitt, C./Bouckaert, G. (eds.) (1995) *Quality Improvement in European Public Services. Concepts, Cases, and Commentary.* London and New Delhi: Sage.

Stewart, J./Clarke, M. (1987) 'The Public Service Orientation: Issues and Dilemmas', *Public Administration* 65 (2): 161-178.

Taylor, M./Langan, J./Hoggett, P. (1994) *Encouraging Diversity: Voluntary and Private Organizations in Community Care.* Aldershot: Gower.

van der Pennen, A.W. et al. (1995) *Welzijnsbeleid in de lokale samenleving.* Rijswijk/Den Haag: Social and Cultural Planning Office.

Waerness, K. (1984) 'On the Rationality of Caring', *Economic and Industrial Democracy* 5: 185-211.

Wistow G./Knapp, M./Hardy, B./Allen, C. (1994) *Social Care in a Mixed Economy of Welfare.* Buckingham and Philadelphia: Open University Press.

CHAPTER 2

Business and Professional Approaches to Quality Improvement: A Comparison of their Suitability for the Personal Social Services

Christopher Pollitt

1   Aims and Approach

The present paper is ambitious in scope, and therefore, inevitably, somewhat wanting in detail. The central objective is to explore the potential of various approaches to quality improvement for the world of the personal social services and community care (hereinafter abbreviated to PSS). The approaches under scrutiny can be classified into two main groups, business approaches and professional approaches. The "business approaches" are those which, during the last two decades, have become widely used and widely discussed in private sector manufacturing and services. They comprise ISO 9000/EN 29000, Total Quality Management (TQM), benchmarking and Business Process Re-engineering (BPR).

The "professional approaches" are those which have long characterized public services in a number of European and North American countries, namely peer review and inspection (with registration as a status that may be coupled to either approach).

Instead of taking each approach and analysing it *ab initio* this paper adopts a rather different strategy. It will be *assumed* that all these approaches have something to offer (that their models of quality improvement possess some validity) and instead the question will be asked:

> *What would be required to ensure that these approaches to*
> *quality improvement actually led to behavioural change?*

By thus examining the requirements of each approach we may gain a measure of its "realism" or appropriateness for the contemporary world of personal social services. Of course the answers we derive from such an intellectual exercise may not be the same for each country and context. It is beyond both the scope of this paper and the competence of its author to comment on the contemporary circumstances of the PSS in every European country. Clearly, it is possible that the requirements (or "key success factors" as they might be termed in management speak) for a given technique to succeed may be present in one country but not necessarily in another. The paper concludes with a brief reflection on the different kinds of quality gains likely to be yielded by the different approaches. It points to problems with both business and professional models and identifies issues where considerable adaptation will be needed for the PSS.

2   Business and Professional Approaches Identified

To identify which approaches we are talking about is not entirely simple. Both business and professional approaches have a tendency to take on local names so that essentially the same approach may be called something different in different places or institutions. This tendency is exacerbated by the understandable wish of management consultants (who are frequently active in the field of promoting quality improvement techniques) to label or "patent" their own distinctive system. With some business approaches such as Total Quality Management (TQM) or Business Process Re-engineering (BPR) even the "founding fathers" or "gurus" seem to avoid detailed definitions and provide instead only broad philosophical proclamations or descriptions of what the approach will do rather than what, analytically, they are (Joss/Kogan, 1995: 12-15).

Having issued these definitional warnings we will not delay the main business of this paper by making a large detour into semantic questions. Instead we will immediately commence an examination of the conditions for success for each main approach. An attempt to summarize the main practical features of each approach is made in appendices 1 (business approaches) and 2 (professional approaches). Hopefully these appendices will provide some clarification for readers who are still unsure about the defining features of any particular approach (Appendix 1: ISO 9000, TQM, benchmarking, BPR; Appendix 2: peer review and external inspection).

3   The Prerequisites for Behavioural Change

Assuming that the business and professional approaches identified in the preceding section embody some real wisdom and understanding of the nature of service quality improvement, what requirements need to be in place to enable the application of these approaches to bear fruit? Or, to put it more crudely, what do we need to do to make them work?

This question can be answered at a number of different levels. At a detailed level the answers will vary with the approach or technique itself. The answer for, say, TQM, will be somewhat different from the answer for peer review or inspection. At a more general level, however, the answer may not vary so much. If one examines the extensive research and experience gathered in the health care sector, for example, certain generic conditions for behavioural change appear to emerge (Harrison, 1994). Prima facie these would seem to apply to the world of personal social services also. They are as follows:

(a) The professionals and/or other staff involved need to understand the approach they are being expected to implement.
(b) The resources, equipment, facilities, time and skills for implementation must be available.
(c) (a) and (b) above must be true for every link in the implementation chain: the more links the more difficult it will be to satisfy this requirement.
(d) The professionals and/or other staff must be motivated to use the approach in question. Where services are "co-produced" (Brudney, 1995: 205-208), the service users involved in the "prosumption" of the service must also be motivated, or at the very least accepting, towards the approach.
(e) Any significant disincentives to use the approach in question must be reduced or removed.

Each one of these prerequisites can now be examined in relation to the business and professional approaches referred to above. Finally, we will reflect on the different kind of quality gains that the different approaches are likely to yield.

4   Professionals and Other Staff Need to Understand the Chosen Approach

A blatantly obvious requirement, one might have supposed, yet there can still be problems with it. An evaluation of the attempt to introduce TQM in the UK National Health Service noted that two commercial companies examined as "controls" displayed "a higher level of senior management commitment and understanding" than most of the NHS pilot sites (Centre for the Evaluation of Public Policy and Practice, 1994: 3). There is still, perhaps, in some parts of the public sector, a perception by the most senior public officials that new management techniques can be introduced "lower down", and that they themselves either do not need to or cannot afford the time to familiarize themselves thoroughly with the details. In so far as this kind of attitude persists it is likely to handicap business approaches such as TQM and BPR more than professional approaches such as peer review or inspection. This is because TQM and BPR are more "totalitarian" (Pollitt/Bouckaert, 1995: 4-7) in the sense that they embrace the whole organization and require a sense of corporate/collective commitment that is less essential in the case of the familiar processes of professional self-improvement.

This point can be developed further. Whereas mono-professional forms of peer review such as medical or nursing audit mainly require the understanding and participation of the professional group concerned, the more ambitious business approaches (TQM and BPR) seek to obtain not just the understanding but also the motivational support of all staff. This is part of a wider trend within human re-source management. As Storey (1989: 20) says, the objective is "to elicit the commitment of employees and not merely secure their compliance". Clearly, therefore, the training requirements for TQM and BPR are likely to be greater than those for professional approaches. The hypothesized quality pay-off (see final section on benefits) is correspondingly more dramatic (Hammer/Champy, 1995: 32). But the training requirement is also quite dramatic, given that some of the main public sector services tend to be extremely labour-intensive (teaching, health care, personal social services) and that therefore potential trainees are great in number.

For the personal social services there is a further level of difficulty in meeting the prerequisite that all the staff involved need to understand (and be committed to) the chosen approach. Not only are the staff groups involved in PSS extremely diverse; not only are many part-time and/or volunteers, but the effectiveness of the delivered services frequently depends upon a degree of active cooperation from the citizens who are in receipt of those services. For example, the probation serv-ice depends upon gaining some level of acceptance from the offenders it serves; if the "clients" are constantly trying to evade and deceive their probation officers "success" is unlikely. Equally, programmes for mentally-ill or disabled people depend to a considerable degree on gaining the trust and consent of the groups they serve. These are, in fact, examples of "co-production" or "prosumption".

Thus services of this kind are particularly suitable for "constructivist" approaches to quality definition, where service users play a major role in defining and valuing the dimensions along which quality will be sought, measured and assessed. In such approaches "quality" is defined as the degree of alignment between, on the one hand, the *expectations* of service users (along whatever dimensions they deem most important) and their *perceptions of actual service* along the same dimensions (Pollitt/ Bouckaert, 1995). However, in the UK at least, there has as yet been quite limited research into what the users of some social and community service want. What is more there is only modest understanding of how to take the prior step of construct-ing fora in which the users can begin to *express* their wants. The relative effective-ness of alternative mechanisms for giving users "voice" has not received as much attention as it requires (Pollitt, 1995). Yet without this kind of understanding *any* quality improvement technique will risk being perceived as imposed from above, and will be less likely to gain the cooperation of the user/co-producers (see, e.g. Barnes/Prior, 1995; Youll/McCourt-Perring, 1993). The absence of mutual understanding of this kind may not be a huge handicap to professional approaches which are in any case founded on the assumption that the professionals will set the standards because they know what is needed. For business methods such as TQM and BPR, however, the absence of an articulate body of consumers, specifying their requirements, unhinges the philosophical underpinnings of their whole approach.

5 The Resources, Equipment, Facilities, Time and Skills for Implementation Must Be Available

Again, this seems both obvious and inescapable. But again it is not hard to find examples where management (or professionals) apparently wanted the ends (quality improvements) but were not prepared to will the means (time, training, etc). Consider, for example, the picture of medical audit meetings conjured up in one piece of fieldwork research – doctors arriving late and leaving early from a brief, lunch-time meeting, pagers constantly buzzing during the discussions and some of the relevant medical staff not present at all (Kerrison/Packwood/Buxton, 1993). Or, in the case of a business approach – TQM – we may note the observation of a recent evaluation of TQM applications in the UK NHS:

> More generally, across all the sites, there had been little or no training for any personnel involved in designing and carrying out customer satisfaction surveys, or for analysing problems in processes and developing systematic responses ... there had been a tendency to rely on one or two people who had gained experience in research methodology ..." (Centre for the Evaluation of Public Policy and Practice, 1994: 5-19).

Similar problems have been found in the application of another business approach – benchmarking – in the NHS (VFM Update, 1995).

It is worth noting that, even where extensive resources *are* invested in the introduction of TQM and BPR, success is far from guaranteed. The business literature makes it quite clear that these are controversial and (especially in the case of BPR) high-risk strategies even within the world of big business. The list of dramatic corporate successes is balanced by a parallel list of expensive disappointments (see, e.g. Howe et al., 1992; Grint, 1994). Consider these two quotations, the first from one of the leading figures in TQM and the second from the founding fathers of BPR:

> As far as measuring the TQM results that have been achieved, there's a big information vacuum out there (Juran, 1991).

Our unscientific estimate is that as many as 50% to 70% of the organizations that undertake a re-engineering effort do not achieve the dramatic results intended (Hammer/Champy, 1995: 200).

In the past the PSS sector has not been noted for its willingness to invest heavily in training and information systems. On the contrary, it has been an arena in which many of the "players" lack formal training and even more lack any kind of certification. In the UK it is also well known for the poor state of its information systems (e.g. Audit Commission, 1992). Although recently efforts have begun to try to remedy this state of affairs there is still a long way to go. One might therefore suggest that it will be hard for most UK SSDs to meet the requirements of a full-blooded application of ISO 9000, TQM, benchmarking or BPR. Selectively employed, perhaps, benchmarking would be the least demanding (though still quite challenging) member of this family. The basic idea is so simple, and initially particular processes could be chosen for limited experiments and to gain confidence in employing the techniques. There is also a sense in which benchmarking is less evangelical than TQM or BPR, and therefore raises fewer cultural hackles, whilst on the other hand it does not degenerate into endless form-filling quite as easily as the ISO 9000 approach can sometimes seem to.

6   The Two Preceding Requirements (Understanding, Resources) Must Be Met for Every Link in the Implementation Chain

The conceptualization of programme implementation as a chain of decisions and actions, no stronger than its weakest link, was made popular more than 20 years ago in an influential book by Pressman and Wildavsky (Pressman/Wildavsky, 1973). More recently the notion of approaching issues of quality improvement by conceiving of organizations as collections of "processes" has been one of the corner stones of both TQM and BPR (see Appendix 1). In the cases of health care and personal social services (and, to a lesser extent, education) the chain is often a long and complicated one. For example, when the patient enters hospital for a hip replacement operation, his or her attention may be focused on the doctors and nurses on the ward and in the operating theatre. The actions of these staff are certainly vital in the achievement of patient satisfaction and effective and efficient treatment. But many others also contribute to these desired outcomes, and failures among these other "links" can easily "spoil" the episode of treatment to a greater or lesser degree. Porters move the patient around. Technicians in the imaging department handle his or her X-rays. Ancillary workers keep the ward clean. Cooks prepare the food. Medical records staff endeavour to keep track of the patient's records and have them quickly available whenever clinical staff call for them. And so on.

Consider a (real) set of events from a hospital where a variant of BPR was being implemented. Considerable work was put into reducing the "cycle times" for conducting tests in the pathology laboratory. This work was successful to the extent that test results began to be delivered back to the doctors much more quickly. It was then discovered, however, that once the tests had been returned they frequently sat around in the doctors' offices for some time before being acted upon. So overall there was no improvement in the time it took to treat patients – an improvement in one link in the chain had been neutralized by the failure to extend the analysis right through all the other links.

These problems are particularly germane to the personal social services. In the PSS the "professionals" are only one group among many working in the "chain of care". Home helps come in to clean the houses of the infirm elderly. Other staff deliver meals to the doorstep or receive clients who are arriving for their appointments. Increasingly, also the provision of social services is a "mixed economy" in which many commercial and charitable organizations, voluntary groups and informal carers play indispensable roles in the supply of care (Warner, 1992, gives a good overview of the position at the commencement of the recent community care reforms in the UK). Furthermore SSDs are obliged to work in more-or-less cooperative relationships with a variety of other statutory agencies, most obviously the police (in respect of child care and work with young persons) and health authorities (in respect of community care).

One implication of this state of affairs may be that mono-professional approaches to quality improvement are seriously inadequate for the PSS because of their narrow scope while at the same time the latest business approaches, though more ambitious in this respect, are extraordinarily difficult to apply because they would entail bringing together so many disparate organizations, groups and individuals into a single, culturally homogeneous learning process. The suggestion, sometimes heard, that these latter problems can readily be solved through writing contracts which specify quality assurance procedures must be deemed optimistic indeed. As the British have discovered during the current period of community care reforms, the business of, say, inspecting contracted (registered) residential homes to see whether or not they achieve adequate quality is far from straightforward. First, there is the considerable intellectual challenge of devising appropriate standards for a relational, co-produced service such as residential care. Second, there is the practical problem that the inspection burden on social service departments may be huge – there were many instances where SSD inspectors fell short of the statutory requirement under English law to inspect registered homes twice per annum (Central Council for Education and Training in Social Work, 1992: 20). Third, there is a parallel problem for the providers of care – the operators of small residential homes may find it extremely difficult to adapt to a bureaucratic regime of detailed record-keeping, questionnaires, inspections, etc. Fourth, the whole process may become something of a charade anyway, because both inspector and provider may be aware that there is no credible alternative source of supply in that particular locality, or it may be that the inspector is a long-standing professional colleague of those running the home (Central Council for Education and Training in Social Work, 1992: 14).

7   Staff Must Be Motivated to Use the Approach in Question

It is at this point that cultural and value-based differences between professional and business approaches become significant. There is no doubt that sometimes professional groups have regarded quality improvement techniques from the business world with considerable scepticism, if not cynicism. TQM and BPR, with their characteristic jargons and catchphrases, can easily be seen as alien implants. On the other hand the TQM literature does at least address problems of staff motivation, whereas the assumption lying behind peer review and inspection often seems to be that professional staff are so well-motivated anyway that they will need no further incentive than information in order to enthusiastically adopt the best professional practices.

One may divide questions of motivation into two broad categories, intrinsic and extrinsic. In the business world the stress is often on extrinsic motives, especially the desire to earn more money, gain more status or wield more power and influence. These personal objectives tend to be frowned upon in the PSS sector, where pay is often low, status seldom high and the prevailing culture emphasizes intrinsic values such as the satisfaction to be gained from helping people in need. It would be hard to convince most PSS staff that improving the quality of their services would soon bring high salaries and public esteem in its train (and they would be right to be sceptical!). Nor does individual performance-related pay (PRP) fit very easily into a pattern of services where so much depends on cooperation between different agencies and groups, and on co-production.

There remains, therefore, a real question for both business and professional approaches, which might bluntly be formulated as : "What do the staff get out of it for their extra efforts to take on new approaches?". If the answer is that in the PSS the satisfactions are principally intrinsic, in that staff will see that service users really are getting a better deal, then those benefits will need to be visible within a reasonable timescale. Some of the tactical advice in the business texts may be useful here: TQM, benchmarking and BPR experts not infrequently recommend going for some "quick wins" right at the beginning. This means choosing particular processes where rapid quality improvements will be both visible and winnable without too much pain and disruption. Early success then helps create a climate of trust around the particular technique being applied, and boosts self-esteem among staff. The more difficult areas can then be tackled with this sense of greater confidence.

Another useful motivator, frequently mentioned in the business literature, is the sense of greater autonomy that the decentralization of authority which often accompanies TQM and BPR can bring. Some of the case-studies of TQM in health care settings make it very clear that increased discretion can help convince staff that something worthwhile is happening (Joss/Kogan, 1995; NHS Management Executive, 1993). Professional approaches may also point to the value of decentralization, but, generally speaking, the professional literature tends to be more focused on appropriate procedures and less concerned with organizational issues than are business and management texts.

8   Removing Disincentives

The most common disincentive to changing behaviour is probably fear, followed closely by disbelief in the likelihood that the change will actually produce results. We will examine each of these two disincentives in turn.

In the case of professional approaches the fear may be that the individual will be "caught out" – seen as incompetent, or performing less well than his or her colleagues. In the case of business approaches this may also be a factor, but frequently there is an additional fear that TQM, BPR (or whatever) has been introduced as a screen for efficiency cuts, "downsizing" and therefore redundancies. Both specific fears can be hard to allay. Anxiety about being seen to be professionally below par can be reduced by surrounding peer review and/or inspection with confidentiality guarantees. But such guarantees have their own costs. Clearly they reduce transparency and public accountability. Furthermore they diminish the possibilities for team or group learning (and therefore improvement). In the case of business approaches the fear of redundancy may be removed by top management making it clear that no compulsory redundancies will occur within a given period – if indeed they are in a position to make such a commitment.

Disbelief in the effectiveness and/or legitimacy of the approach is the second major disincentive. Why put oneself out for something that isn't going to work anyway? Such negative attitudes are likely to be particularly prevalent in organizations that have experienced a succession of management "quick fixes" (including restructurings) that have failed to solve underlying problems. In the UK a number of NHS hospitals and local authority departments (including SSDs) may fall into this category. Under these circumstances a whole culture of disbelief has taken root, and can be very hard to dislodge (Metcalfe/Richards, 1987: 18-19). A few "quick wins" (rather than "quick fixes" which then become unstuck) may help, but some sort of more general programme of organizational development could be needed over a longer term. It is too much to expect a single approach such as TQM or benchmarking or ISO 9000 to achieve great success when the organization into which it is injected is itself in a state of general decay.

9   Summary Reflections: What Kind of Quality?

To oversimplify somewhat, the two sets of approaches we are here concerned with are directed at the realization of two different kinds of quality regime. Professional approaches are mainly concerned with *producer quality*, that is services that are technically of a high standard in terms of prevailing professional aspirations. Business approaches are concerned with *consumer quality* (or "user quality"), that is services which are tailored to satisfy consumer requirements and expectations (and which, by so doing, increase the probability that the customer will remain loyal). These notions of producer and consumer quality are developed at greater length elsewhere (Pollitt/Bouckaert, 1995: 16-19).

Each type of quality regime has its own characteristic form of decay or pathology. Producer quality can degenerate into a situation of cosy connoisseurialism in which senior members of a profession or expert group exercise great influence without having to justify their judgements in terms of any transparent or evidence-based criteria. An alternative professional pathology occurs where peer judgements are made but there is little effective follow-through to see if behaviour has altered and no sanctions for those who persist in ignoring peer advice.

Business approaches, by contrast, can quite easily decay into a form of managerialism where managers manipulate consumers in order to enhance their own control over other staff. This can sometimes be achieved through superficial exercises in "consultation" with consumers and/or by means of carefully crafted satisfaction questionnaires where the agenda is set by managers and not (as would be the case with a genuine consumer quality approach) by consumer requirements.

So, to return to our fundamental question, what are the prospects for using professional or business approaches to achieve real quality improvement in the PSS sector? First we must take note of "the bad news". *Neither* professional *nor* contemporary business approaches to quality improvement appear to fit easily into the mould of the contemporary personal social services. The professional approaches seem inadequate for several reasons. First, "professionals" are actually in a minority among the deliverers of such services. Second, such professionals as there are (in the UK case mainly the social work profession) lack the kind of quasi-academic, self-evaluating cultures that have grown up around teachers and doctors. Indeed, some social workers continue to be deeply critical of the very notion of professionalization. Third, the pluralist and "co-produced" nature of many social services means that approaches based on the assumption that a profession possessed of the necessary expertise can unilaterally set technical standards for its own practice are fundamentally inappropriate anyway.

The business approaches may be found wanting for a rather different set of reasons. First, they tend to assume the existence of a form of executive line management that is capable of driving through changes in systems and procedures.

This assumption does not conform to the empirical reality of everyday social and community care. Second, the more evangelical business approaches such as some variants of TQM and BPR posit such sweeping changes as to call in question their own validity, even in the commercial circumstances of their origins (Hammer/ Champy, 1995: 40; Howe et al., 1992). These are high-risk strategies which *may* work dramatically well sometimes, to stave off commercial failure, so long as there is determined management, and often a willingness to contemplate extensive redundancies. But these are far from the circumstances in which such approaches would usually be applied in the personal social services sector. Third, both TQM and BPR place a high priority on accurate measurement and the creative use of performance information, whereas the PSS have tended to be notorious for their lack of precisely such information. So the PSS are, so to speak, coming from a long way behind.

The "good news" is less obvious, and requires some interpretation. We may distinguish certain general trends, manifest – to different degrees – in both professional and business approaches, from other elements that are more specific to particular approaches.

At least two positive general trends are readily visible. First, there is a very widespread move *away* from purely connoisseurial evaluation and towards much clearer and more specific definitions of quality (Henkel, 1991; Pollitt/Bouckaert, 1995). Whether or not one agrees with the particular definition of quality adopted in a given set of circumstances, the greater transparency and self-consciousness that accompanies this tendency is surely to be welcomed in the PSS, as elsewhere? Both peer review and inspection have been evolving in the general direction of closer specification of protocols and standards, while the business approaches reviewed here are all insistent on the need to construct a clear operational definition of quality rather than leaving it to "feel" and "experience". Of course these more impressionistic approaches may be used to help build up the operational definition, but, because the latter has to be explicit, it should also be much easier than in the past – at least in principal – to link quality to democratic accountability.

The second general tendency is to pay more attention to the end-user of the service. Again, this is much more obvious in the business approaches (with the partial exception of ISO 9000), but in a less strident way it is also creeping into inspection and even peer review. When teams from the UK Higher Education Funding Council visit universities to assess the quality of teaching they automatically expect to meet and talk to students as well as staff, and they will also want to see evidence that the staff regularly and systematically sample student opinion. This in itself is no longer a matter of much controversy, which shows that there has been a considerable cultural shift over the last 10-15 years. Similarly, when the SSI inspects the community care arrangements of an SSD it will want to see proof of systematic consultation with users.

Turning to more approach-specific benefits one might argue that the advantages of the professional approaches were mainly cultural ones whereas the business approaches were stronger on analysis. As we have seen, a quality improvement drive which comes from within the staff's own professional community may command greater initial credibility than one which is suspected of being from the alien world of commerce. Initial credibility is important, but not all important. Business approaches gain from their stronger emphasis on measurement and on establishing as precise as possible an estimate of customer requirements. All the business approaches discussed here are also more emphatic than most professional approaches in stressing the need to "close the loop" by constant monitoring and feedback of results. Some – especially TQM – have also been fruitful in developing relatively non-hierarchical, generic ways of working, such as quality circles and job enrichment teams. The stress on multi-disciplinary working, cutting across traditional professional and departmental boundaries, often proves an early benefit from the use of such approaches (e.g. NHS Management Executive, 1993: 12). With some modification these techniques may prove suitable for trying to draw together the multiplicity of workers who are involved in the delivery of social and community care. Professional approaches tend not to have been so fertile in this respect, partly because in a professional context commitment tends to be assumed to exist rather than being regarded as something that needs to be built up and then sustained.

To summarize, neither professional nor business approaches to quality improvement are tailor-made for the PSS sector. Both will require considerable adaptation. There is a sense in which business approaches, especially TQM and benchmarking, promise more but also require greater changes within the service delivery organizations. They offer a more-than-incremental shift to higher quality but at a higher price (greater need to invest in training and new information systems) and with a greater risk of disappointment. In addition it may be considered that TQM is an especially promising import to the PSS because of the stress that is laid on placing the customer's demands at the heart of the process of quality definition, and because of the promise that techniques such as SERVQUAL hold out for measuring the perception/expectation gap (see Appendix 1).

The required adaptation is, however, considerable. To begin with, the notion of a "customer" needs to be converted into that of a citizen, endowed with rights and responsibilities as well as wants and preferences (Pollitt/Bouckaert, 1995: 4-14). Beyond this a second modification will often be needed. For it cannot be assumed that the users of many social services are just waiting, able and willing to voice their needs as soon as the authorities consult them (Pollitt, 1995). On the contrary, many of these users are frightened, alienated and/or disabled in a wide variety of ways. "Consultation" – and even more "participation" – may be the foundation stone of quality improvement in the PSS, but considerable ingenuity will be called for if the necessary base of trust and communication skills is to be built. Precisely how this is done is likely to vary from one context to another, but that it *is* done may be the crucial "additional ingredient" necessary to enable real quality improvement to take place among that kaleidoscope of activities and groups that constitutes the social and community services sector.

Acknowledgements

One part of this paper is based on work done during a series of international seminar programmes financed by the Economic and Social Research Council. Another part draws upon a project financed by a grant from the British Council and the Flemish Research Council. In both projects I worked closely with my colleague and friend, Professor Geert Bouckaert of the Catholic University of Leuven. The intellectual borrowings between us are now too complex to be summarized here, but I am certainly in his debt, as I hope he is in mine.

References

Association of Finnish Local Authorities (1995a) *Total Quality Management in Municipal Service Provision*. Helsinki: Association of Finnish Local Authorities.

Association of Finnish Local Authorities (1995b) *Quality in the Procurement of Municipal Services*. Helsinki: Association of Finnish Local Authorities.

Audit Commission (1992) *Community Care: Managing the Cascade of Change*. London: HMSO.

Audit Commission and Social Services Inspectorate (1995) *Joint Reviews of Social Services Authorities: Consultation Document*, April. London: Department of Health.

Barnes, M./Prior, D. (1995) 'Spoilt for Choice? How Consumerism Can Disempower Public Service Users', *Public Money and Management* 15 (3): 53-58.

British Standards Institute (1987) *Quality Systems Standard*. London: BSI.

Bullivant, J./Naylor, M. (1992) 'The Best of the Best', *Health Service Journal* 27 August: 24-25.

Brudney, J. (1995) 'Volunteer Programs in the Public Sector: Benefits and Challenges for Public Management', pp. 199-219 in Halachmi, A./Bouckaert, G. (eds.), *The Enduring Challenges in Public Management*. San Francisco: Jossey-Bass.

Camp, R. (1989) *Benchmarking: The Search for Industry Best Practices that Lead to a Superior Performance*. Milwaukee: Quality Press.

Central Council for Education and Training in Social Work (1992) *Exploring Competence in Registration, Inspection and Quality Control*, CCETSW Paper 24.1. London: CCETSW.

Centre for the Evaluation of Public Policy and Practice (1994) *Total Quality Management in the National Health Service: Final Report of an Evaluation*. Uxbridge: CEPPP, Brunel University.

Clinical Benchmarking Company Ltd. (1995) 'Creating Comparisons and Setting Standards', *VFM Update* 17: 6-7.

Conti, R./Warner, M. (1994) 'Taylorism, Teams and Technology in Re-engineering Work Organization', *New Technology, Work and Employment* 9: 93-102.

Freeman-Bell, G./Grover, R. (1994) 'The Use of Quality Management in Local Authorities', *Local Government Studies* 20 (4): 554-569.

Gaster, L. (1995) *Quality in Public Services: Managers' Choices*. Buckingham: Open University Press.

Hammer, M./Champy, J. (1995) *Re-engineering the Corporation: A Manifesto for a Business Revolution* (revised edition). London: Nicholas Brearley.

Harrison, S. (1994) 'Knowledge into Practice: What's the Problem?', *Journal of Management in Medicine* 8 (2): 9-16.

Hart, M. (1995) Quality Improvement in NHS Outpatient Clinics, Ph.D Exposition Document. Leicester: De Monfort University (submitted December 1995, Ph.D awarded March 1996).

Henkel, M. (1991) *Government, Evaluation and Change*. London: Jessica Kingsley.

Henkel, M./Kogan, M./Packwood, T./Whitaker, T./Youll, P. (1989) *The Health Advisory Service: An Evaluation*. London: King Edward's Hospital Fund.

Howe, R./Gaeddert, D./Howe, M. (1992) *Quality on Trial.* London: McGraw Hill.

Hyde, A. (1995) 'Quality Re-engineering and Performance: Managing Change in the Public Sector', pp. 150-176 in Halachmi, A./Bouckaert, G. (eds.), *The Enduring Challenges in Public Management*. San Francisco: Jossey-Bass.

Johansson, H./McHugh, P./Pendlebury, A./Wheeler III, W. (1993) *Business Process Re-engineering: Breakpoint Strategies for Market Dominance*. New York: Wiley.

Joss, R./Kogan, M. (1995) *Advancing Quality: Total Quality Management in the National Health Service*. Buckingham: Open University Press.

Juran, J. (1991) Speech to the General Accounting Office. Washington DC.

Kerrison, S./Packwood, T./Buxton, M. (1993) *Medical Audit: Taking Stock*. London: King's Fund.

Kerrison, S./Packwood, T./Buxton, M. (1994) 'Monitoring Medical Audit', pp. 155-177 in: Robinson, R./Le Grand, J. (eds.), *Evaluating the NHS Reforms*. London: King's Fund Institute.

Leicestershire General Hospital NHS Trust (1995) 'Putting Theory into Practice', *VFM-Update* 17: 23-25.

Loffler, E. (1995) *The Modernization of the Public Sector in an International Comparative Perspective: Concepts and Methods of Awarding and Assessing Quality in the Public Sector in OECD Countries*, Speyer Forschungberichte 151. Speyer: Foschunginstitut fur Öffentliche Verwaltung.

McGowan, R. (1995) 'Total Quality Management: Lessons from Business and Government', *Public Productivity and Management Review* 18 (4): 321-331.

Metcalfe, L./Richards, S. (1987) *Improving Public Management*. London: Sage.

Millar, B. (1995) 'Time Machine', *Health Service Journal*: 11.

NHS Management Executive (1993) *Quality in Action: the St. Helier NHS Trust: A Case Study*. Leeds: NHSME.

Pollitt, C. (1993) 'The Politics of Medical Quality: Auditing Doctors in the UK and the USA', *Health Services Management Research* 6 (1): 24-34.

Pollitt, C. (1995) 'Improving the Quality of Social Services: New Opportunities for Participation?', Paper presented to the 12th International Symposium, University of Bielefeld, October 1995.

Pollitt, C./Bouckaert, G. (eds.) (1995) *Quality Improvement in European Public Services.* London: Sage.

Pollitt, C. (1996) 'Business Approaches to Quality Improvement: Why They Are Hard for the NHS to Swallow', *Quality in Health Care* 5: 1-7.

Power, M. (1995) *Audit and Decline of Inspection.* London: CIPFA/Public Finance Foundation.

Pressman, J./Wildavsky, A. (1973) *Implementation.* Berkeley: University of California Press.

Social Services Inspectorate (1995) *How Well Are Children Being Looked After? Agendas for Action Arising from the National Residential Child Care Inspection, 1992-1994.* London: Department of Health.

Social Work Research Centre (1995) *Is Social Work Effective? Research Findings from the Social Work Research Centre.* Stirling: Social Work Research Centre, University of Stirling.

Storey, J. (1989) 'Human Resource Management in the Public Sector', *Public Money and Management* 9 (3): 19-24.

VFM Update (1995) 'Trouble-shooting Benchmark Activity', *VFM-Update* 17: 20.

Warner, N. (1992) 'Changes in Resource Management in the Social Services', pp 179-193 in Pollitt, C./Harrison, S. (eds.), *Handbook of Public Services Management.* Oxford: Blackwell.

Whittle, S. (1992) 'Total Quality Management: Redundant Approaches to Cultural Change', *Quality of Working: News and Abstracts* 110: 8-13.

Wilmott, H. (1994) 'Business Process Re-engineering and Human Resource Management', *Personnel Review* 23: 34-46.

Youll, P./McCourt-Perring, C. (1993) *Raising Voices: Ensuring Quality in Residential Care.* London: HMSO.

Zeithmal, V./Parasuraman, A./Berry, L. (1990) *Delivering Quality Service.* New York: Free Press.

ISO 9000

The ISO 9000 series is a set of generic international standards for quality. The UK equivalent (and progenitor) is BS 5750 (British Standards Institute, 1987). BS 5750, in turn, had its origins in attempts to set standards for the supply of equipment to the Ministry of Defence. Under the ISO 9000 approach an organization seeks registration for particular processes or systems. It pays a fee and then, after a period of preparation, the chosen process/system is assessed by an approved (external, third party) assessor. If the assessor decides that the process meets the requirement of the standard then the organization can display its accreditation on its products and literature. The requirements of the standard are complex and lay heavy emphasis on the creation and control of appropriate documentation. The standard tends to assume a contractual relationship between producer and customer. The main emphasis is on controlling procedures rather than satisfying customers, and as such it has a somewhat bureaucratic character relative to later developments such as TQM (see below, and Loffler, 1995). The procedures for designing the product/service, controlling documents, purchasing key inputs, rendering the product identifiable and traceable, inspecting and taking corrective action all have to be set down in considerable detail. For example, in relation to document control the standard requires the organization to be able to:

a) Identify which documents need to be "control documents" (e.g. manuals, handbooks).
b) Only issue control documents which have been checked by designated staff.
c) Ensure availability of control documents to everyone who needs them.
d) Ensure removal or updating of out-of-date control documents.
e) Maintain a master list of those who are to receive control documents.

ISO 9000 standards were originally written with manufacturing industry in mind, and interpreting the requirements in such a way as to fit the provision of services rather than goods was not always straightforward. However, in 1991 an additional part of the standard which was specifically designed for services (ISO 9004-2) was introduced. ISO 9000 was adopted by the European Union as EN 29000.

ISO 9000 does not itself set numerical standards. It does require a system for accurately identifying customer requirements although it does not specify how this should be done. It has been criticized for failing to afford a more salient role to user satisfaction. It has also been said to be rather an expensive and essentially bureaucratic process which, of itself, does little to motivate or involve rank and file staff (Freeman-Bell/Grover, 1994; Gaster, 1995). Nevertheless it does offer the service user assurance that the service-providing organization has been through a strenuous process of focusing on the fine details of its systems for ensuring a consistent, well-controlled service.

ISO 9000/BS 5750 has been widely implemented in public service settings. In Finland, for example, five municipalities took part in a pilot project entitled *Quality and the Community*. One of these (Espoo) concerned a social welfare and health centre. All five produced quality manuals and published the findings of their early explorations. Booklets were produced summarizing the results of this programme (Association of Finnish Local Authorities, 1995a and 1995b). In the UK BS 5750 has been sought by both health authorities and local government. By the autumn of 1992, 106 quality management certificates had been awarded to local government services, mainly in construction and civil engineering (Freeman-Bell/Grover, 1994). Social Services Departments had not played much part in this first wave. In the NHS a few general practices (primary care) and biomedical engineering departments had achieved accreditation, but it could not be said that enthusiasm for BS 5750/ISO 9000 was widespread within the health service. TQM (see below) was much more popular (Joss/Kogan, 1995).

TQM

TQM is probably the best known contemporary approach to quality improvement. It is not easy to provide a definitive summary because there are actually several major variants, each with their own guru (Gaster, 1995: 75-77; McGowan, 1995; Whittle, 1992). Nevertheless it is possible to identify certain general elements which are common to most or all of the major texts describing TQM:

a) It is a corporate perspective – indeed, an entire management philosophy – that "should be central to the organization's goals and should not be viewed as a tangential activity" (McGowan, 1995: 322).
b) Accordingly, TQM frequently entails the production of an organization-wide plan embodying specific quality goals.
c) It is necessary to generate real commitment and enthusiasm for quality all the way down the "line" from top management to the "shop floor".
d) Because many quality problems typically arise across departmental and disciplinary boundaries within organizations, TQM seeks to transcend such internal divisions, usually by following "customer-provider" links right across the internal workings of the organization concerned.
e) When first applied TQM usually requires a substantial investment in training.
f) The commitment is to continuous improvement. TQM emphasizes an ongoing process rather than a once-for-all setting of quality standards.

g) TQM emphasizes the avoidance of mistakes and defects before they occur, rather than correcting them retrospectively (and often expensively).

This approach is encapsulated in the catchphrase "right first time". Thus TQM is a much broader approach than ISO 9000, though there is no reason why a TQM system could not incorporate the use of ISO 9000 as a way of guaranteeing the integrity of subsidiary processes within the larger approach. TQM has been quite widely adopted within some European public sectors. In 1989 a number of pilot TQM projects were launched within the UK National Health Service (NHS – for an evaluation of these see Centre for the Evaluation of Public Policy and Practice, 1994; for an official account of one of the more successful pilots, see NHS Management Executive, 1993). It has also been widely used in the public sector in the USA.

The European Quality Award is founded on TQM principles. From 1996 this will be explicitly open to public sector applicants (Loffler, 1995: 44-45) It is administered by the European Foundation for Quality Management (EFQM), which was set up by a number of large private sector companies in 1988. Applications are built around organizational self-assessments based upon the European Model for Business Excellence. This model accords specific point scores or weightings to different elements, as follows:

Enablers

Total weighting	50%
Leadership	10%
People management	9%
Policy and strategy	8%
Resources	9%
Processes	14%

Results

Total weighting	50%	
People satisfaction	9%	(in this case "people" means principally the organization's workforce)
Customer satisfaction	20%	
Impact on society	6%	
Business results	15%	

SERVQUAL is a particularly interesting variant of TQM. Developed by Zeithmal, Parasuraman and Berry (1990) it conceives of service quality problems as consisting of a number of "gaps" in the performance of the organization which need to be closed. The most important of these is often the gap between what the customer expects of a particular service and what they perceive themselves as actually experiencing when they receive the service. In their research Zeithmal et al. carried out an extensive factor analysis of different dimensions of service quality from which they identified five aspects which they suggested were those along which most customers would judge most services. These were as follows:

a) Tangibles: the appearance of the physical facilities, equipment, personnel and communication materials.
b) Reliability: the ability to perform the promised service dependently and accurately.
c) Responsiveness: the willingness to help customers and provide prompt service.
d) Competence: the knowledge and courtesy of employees and their ability to convey trust and confidence.
e) Empathy: the caring individualized attention the organization provides its customers.

Questionnaires were developed by which the gap between perceptions and expectations could be measured along these five dimensions. The weight of each dimension varies according to the particular circumstances of the service in question – this is a matter to be determined empirically in each case. This kind of gap analysis has begun to be applied in a number of public sector settings. British Railways have used it to assess levels of passenger satisfaction on certain train services. Academics have begun to use SERVQUAL to measure patient satisfaction with the quality of service in NHS clinics (Hart, 1995).

Benchmarking

Like TQM, benchmarking was imported from the United States. The basic idea is straightforward. An organization identifies one or more of its processes where it wishes to make quality improvements. It then looks for one or more other organizations that appear to have achieved high degrees of excellence in that same process. A careful and detailed study is made of how the other organization – the market leader or "benchmark organization" – carries out the process in question. On the basis of that comparative study the first organization then designs and implements a plan for raising its own performance up to or beyond the level of that of the benchmark. Many large private sector corporations have made successful use of benchmarking. A best-selling book about the experience at the Xerox Corporation helped to make the technique fashionable (Camp, 1989). Other firms that used it included British Telecom, Eastman Kodak, the Trustees Savings Bank and ICL. In a loose sense benchmaking appears to have been quite widely adopted within the UK public sector, although thorough applications of the technique appear, thus far, to have been infrequent. In the early 1990s a National Health Service

Benchmarking Centre was set up and various attempts to benchmark were begun across the service (Bullivant/Naylor, 1992). In the autumn of 1995 a clinical benchmarking company was set up to advise NHS trusts on clinical applications of the technique (The Clinical Benchmarking Company Ltd., 1995).

There are a number of key features which appear to be necessary for benchmarking to work effectively:

a) The process to be benchmarked should be an important one to the organization concerned.
b) It is vital to achieve a deep and detailed understanding of the nature of the process as it currently operates. Benchmarking therefore requires detailed research, both within the organization adopting it and within the benchmark organization that is being taken as the standard. This takes time and effort, and benchmarking is therefore not a "quick fix".
c) If benchmarking is taking place in a competitive environment then there must be something of value in the benchmarking comparison for the best practice ("benchmark") organization as well as for the aspirant organization.

Because of (c) attempts to benchmark a key function in a direct competitor may well encounter access problems. To avoid this "functional benchmarking" is often rec-ommended as a good way to begin. In functional benchmarking a comparator may be chosen that is unlikely to fear direct competition from the organization wishing to benchmark, e.g. a hospital concerned with out-patient booking efficiency may seek to study a receipt booking process operated by a successful airline. Large organiza-tions with many different delivery units may be able to benchmark internally, by comparing one sub-unit with another and asking the question of why some sub-units manage to produce a higher quality performance than others. "Benchmarking clubs" of several firms have sometimes grown up in the private sector, with regular meet-ings to examine how certain functions are performed.

Unsurprisingly, the success of benchmarking efforts cannot be guaranteed. Typi-cal problems include choosing an inappropriate process to benchmark (e.g. an un-important one); failing to implement change when monitoring data shows that improvement is possible; failures by senior management to invest sufficient time, resources and support in the benchmarking process; attempts to benchmark too many measures or processes all at once, and inaccurate or meaningless data (VFM Update, 1995).

Business Process Re-engineering (BPR)

BPR became very popular in the US private sector in the early 1990s. Subsequently it spread to the US public sector (Hyde, 1995) and pilot projects have now begun to appear in the UK public sector. Like benchmarking BPR entails tight focus on the details of key organizational processes. In some respects it appears to be a combination of Operations Research and Contemporary IT, though usually with a much more strategic and challenging manifesto than either of these "parents" usually claims. Indeed, the claims made for BPR tend to be extremely radical:

> Re-engineering, we are convinced, can't be carried out in small cautious steps. It is an all-or-nothing proposition that produces dramatically impressive results. Most companies have no choice but to muster the courage to do it.
> (Hammer/Champy, 1995: 5)

Definitions of BPR tend to be quite elusive, or to be cast in extremely general terms, e.g.

> Business Process Re-engineering is, by definition, the means by which an organization can achieve radical change in performance as measured by cost, cycle time, service and quality, by the application of a variety of tools and techniques that focus on the business as a set of related customer-oriented core business processes rather than as a set of organizational functions. (Johansson et al., 1993: 15-16)

Like TQM (the principles of which BPR to a considerable extent incorporates) re-engineering tracks major organizational processes across the vertical, functional divisions that still characterize most organizations. Following re-engineering these processes are radically simplified and speeded up and, in consequence, many jobs within these organizations are themselves redesigned. One common feature of BPR applications is that different tasks are combined in new generic roles within the organization. In the UK both central government and the NHS have expressed interest in BPR. Two major hospitals have launched large-scale BPR programmes and many others have smaller experiments (Leicestershire General Hospital NHS Trust, 1995; Millar, 1995).

It is too soon for many systematic evaluations of public sector BPR projects to be available. However, perhaps partly because of its radical claims, BPR has been the subject of a good deal of criticism. Grint (1994) has characterized it as more a utopia than a set of practical recipes for immediate success. More concretely, BPR's model of organizational change is said to be both deficient (particularly in respect of human resource dimensions) and vague. In its private sector applications it seems frequently to have been associated with extensive "downsizing" (redundancy) among the workforce (Conti/Warner, 1994; Willmott, 1994). The early experiences of the two large-scale NHS hospital applications certainly point to the difficulty of any broad-scope embedding of BPR principles in multi-professional organizations that already possess their own strong notions of service and professional excellence.

APPENDIX 2: SUMMARY OF PROFESSIONAL APPROACHES
           TO QUALITY IMPROVEMENT

Peer Review

The fundamental notion behind peer review is that the work of an individual professional or group of professionals will be assessed by a group of fellow-professionals. Often (but not necessarily) these peers will be chosen as particularly senior or experienced members of the profession (as in the traditional external examiner system in English universities). It is thus a collegial approach to quality improvement.

In traditional peer review the assessments made tend to be holistic and non-formulaic, and are offered in an essentially formative mode – that is in a supportive way, with a view to encouraging improvement. However, peer review can be – and increasingly is – conducted in a variety of ways, some of which may become more judgemental/summative and/or much more closely constrained by explicit standards, guidelines or protocols.

Thus there are a number of key questions one can ask about any particular system of peer review in order to identify its particular character. First, are the peers *internal or external* to the organization under review? In the UK National Health Service medical audit is usually a form of internal peer review, whereas in the US Medicare programme peer review is external (Pollitt, 1993). External peer review tends to be less "cosy", especially if it is done "blind" (see below).

A second question is whether the peers doing the reviewing know the identities of those whose work they are examining. Where neither side can discover the identity of the other (as in the refereeing of papers submitted for publication in high-quality academic journals) the process is termed *"double blind"*. Where the reviewer knows the identity of the reviewed but the latter does not know who is reviewing his/her work then the process is *"single blind"*. In other cases (e.g. where site visits to universities take place to review the quality of teaching) the peers are *"mutually sighted"*. It is generally believed that the double-blind process minimizes bias, but it is not always a practical possibility. Also mutually sighted review may have a definite advantage when empathic support over time may be needed in order to raise performance – the double-blind relationship may produce less bias but it is by definition impersonal and cold.

A third question is whether the process is conducted according to *specific standards or guidelines* (such as a clinical protocol specifying the optimal procedure for managing a particular condition) or whether it is more open-ended/impressionistic. Refereeing articles for academic journals, for example, used to be fairly unstructured but, increasingly, journal editors are now asking their referees to make their comments under fixed headings and according to closely specified criteria.

Fourth, there are a set of practical questions concerning the *frequency* of review and whether it is *voluntary or mandatory*. Also, are there *sanctions* associated with "failure" to reach the standards set by peers or with refusal to offer one's work for review? And are the outcomes of the review process *confidential or freely available within the public domain?* All these factors can affect the power of the review to raise quality (and the aspects of quality it is likely to influence). For example, in the UK doubts have been cast on the effectiveness of occasional, confidential, internal, unsanctioned medical audit to make much impression on the general quality of clinical care (Pollitt, 1993; Kerrison et al., 1994).

An illuminating analysis of some of the strengths and weaknesses of one particular kind of peer review can be found in Henkel et al., 1989. This takes the form of an evaluation of the UK Health Advisory Service (HAS).

Inspection

There are many forms of inspection, and it is probably impossible to cite any single defining characteristic which both defines them all and simultaneously excludes other types of assessment and review. Inspection may rather be thought of as a role partaking of a "cluster of characteristics" (Power, 1995: 6). Judging by the (extensive but scattered) literature the key characteristics seem to include at least the following:

a) Inspectors are *independent* of those they inspect.
b) Inspectors base their assessments on some claim to *specialist expertise* (and in this respect inspection is therefore similar to peer review). Recruitment to inspector posts is characteristically from the ranks of the most senior and experienced professionals.
c) The prime responsibility of inspectors is to report to some higher (usually state) authority – *to give summative assurance to the wider society or its representatives* that appropriate standards are being met (Henkel et al., 1989: 6). Inspectors may also attempt to provide useful support to those they inspect (formative mode) but this must not be at the expense of their prime responsibility.
d) The characteristic mode of expression of inspectors is that of *a narrative report which critiques existing service processes and outputs.*

In the UK most public service professions – teachers, social workers, the prison service, the police – are subject to inspectorates. The medical profession has succeeded in resisting the creation of an inspectorate, but since 1989 some parts of it have been subject to visitation by a Health Advisory Service that has acted as an uncomfortable mixture of inspection and peer review (for a fascinating account of its origins and practices, see Henkel et al., 1989). However, the various inspectorates have conducted themselves in widely varying ways. For example, some inspectorates have operated with fairly loosely defined ("connoisseurial") criteria whilst others have developed much more detailed and operationalized checklists and standards. There is room here to do no more than give a very brief summary of inspection within the social services sector.

Although in the UK inspection has been a local government function for more than 50 years very little college-based training and no formal qualifications have been available until relatively recently (Central Council for Education and Training in Social Work, 1992: 22). Since the late 1980s, however, inspection has become a much more prominent element in the world of social and community work. This shift has taken place for a number of reasons, including the general decline of political trust towards professions in general and social workers in particular (see Henkel, 1991: chapters 5-7), the huge expansion of provision for the elderly in private residential homes and the specific requirements of the Community Care Act, 1991 (which formalized a type of purchaser/provider split in community care). Local authorities have had to create independent inspection units to regulate standards in both their own residential facilities and in independent homes. And at a national level a Social Services Inspectorate (SSI) was created in 1985 (Henkel, 1991). By the mid-1990s it was working in tandem with the Audit Commission to carry out reviews of local authority SSDs (Audit Commission/Social Services Inspectorate, 1995) and had begun to produce a series of special reports and models of good practice (e.g. in the field of child care – Social Services Inspectorate, 1995). Despite these tangible achievements, however, the development of the SSI has not been an easy road. As Henkel (1991: 210) commented at an earlier stage:

> The problems for the SSI in establishing a coherent value position are huge. The professional identity of social work has never been secure and challenges to it have been internal as well as external.

CHAPTER 3

Quality Management in Finland – Problems and Possibilities

Mikko Mäntysaari

1 Quality Management

When quality is envisaged as the main objective of a whole organization, we are speaking about the concept of quality management. Total Quality Management (TQM) is one of the schools of quality management and is in fact a set of relatively mature methods. The concepts of quality control and quality assurance were created in the 1920s, with statistical quality control presented by the mathematician Walter Shewhart in 1924 (Gitlow et al., 1989). The main figure in TQM, W. Edwards Deming, first presented his methods to a Japanese audience in 1950. Armand V. Feigenbaum presented in writing the principles of TQM in his 1951 book *Total Quality Control* (Feigenbaum, 1961).

Quality assurance became more prevalent in health care services from the 1960s onwards, and it has been further developed especially in the sphere of nursing science. Quality management is rapidly becoming popular also in social welfare services. From the Nixon era at the beginning of the 1970s, quality control received special emphasis in the U.S. social care system (Mäntysaari, 1993). Quality control issues are still important in AFDC delivery (Camasso/Jagannathan, 1994), although it might not be popular in TQM circles since it is considered as an "outmoded" way of thinking. Quality control means concentrating on the mistakes, "picking up the bad apples" as it is often called in TQM literature, and is seen as somewhat obsolete; but the fact is that this kind of concentration on mistakes seems to be necessary in last-resort economic assistance programmes everywhere.

At the present time, there is a worldwide effort going on to actively establish quality management systems for social services. Deming (Deming, 1994: 6) and others (Grönroos, 1989; Martin, 1993a: 17) agreeing with him think that quality management is at home in service and manufacturing enterprises alike. Services receiving public revenue enjoy no special position with regard to quality management. It is fair to say that I agree in many ways with Deming, but I also see problems in applying the TQM philosophy[1] to human services. This paper addresses those problems.

2   The Promises of Quality Management

TQM is a part of an extensive surge of reforms sometimes called "New Public Management" or "New Managerialism" (Kelly, 1991). There have been several waves of reforms in recent years in Finnish public administration. First came planning-programming-budgeting, then management-by-results, and now finally quality management (Martin, 1993a: 1). The ideas of self-learning organizations, teamwork, shallow hierarchies, self-guiding working groups, and other similar concepts are shared not only by the various forms of quality reform but also by other novel means to organize human work (Tegethoff/Wilkesman, 1995; Nüssle, 1994: 435). The fashionable terms "reflexivity" and "self-monitoring" are parts of the same phenomenon, as is the highlighting of evaluation. Considering all these waves, quality management in-the-making may raise doubts as to what new contributions this wave might have to offer. Someone has even suggested, in a serious frame of mind, that these waves are in fact purposely produced by the consulting firms themselves in order to create demand for their services. Apparently that explanation is too simplistic.

The roots of these changes in the management ideologies lie in the more and more international economy which forces the traditional welfare states to react to changes in the global economy a lot faster than they used to. The modes of providing human services have been characterized as having made a transition from a Fordian means of production to a post-Fordian model of production (Arnkil, 1991). The Fordian model – or the model fashioned after industrial mass production (big organizations, standardized products) – has been replaced by one where services are eagerly being converted to a flexible and demand-driven mode of production. The split between service purchaser and service provider is happening in all welfare states, even in Nordic countries where most of the personal social services are still produced by public providers. Quality reform is almost compulsory after a purchaser-provider split: purchasing services with public money means that there have to be at least some quality standards for the services provided.

Compared to the interest in quality management, there are surprisingly few in-depth analyses about the problems and possibilities for applying TQM in the personal social services. Martin has written a stimulating and well-argued book about

TQM in social services (Martin, 1993a: 2). He sees four good reasons for quality management (I will return to these statements again on page 56):

- Especially concerning human services, quality management (or quality reform) means a new opening which must be taken seriously, because it is a worthwhile attempt to answer the crisis regarding the quality of public services. This crisis has been created by the fact that the demand for services now exceeds the supply, while the conditions for service production are becoming more restricted everywhere.
- Quality management means creating customers loyal to the public services.
- Quality is free.
- Quality management, unlike some of the former administrative waves of reforms, is in accordance with the traditional values of providing human services.

3   Quality Management in the Nordic Welfare States

According to Martin, TQM is fairly widespread in organizations providing human services in the U.S. (Martin, 1993a). In the Nordic countries, quality management is being much discussed nowadays; but regarding the production of public services, thinking is generally still clearly at the stage of quality assurance. In Finland, especially in the field of social care, it has not advanced yet very far beyond the starting point.

This article is based on experiences gathered from a quality development project within the Finnish national social and health care services. Our project commenced at the National Research and Development Centre for Welfare and Health (STAKES) in 1993. Quality development is ongoing and has in fact gathered quite some momentum in developing Finnish social services. Our project "Quality of Social Services" has had TQM philosophy as its conceptual frame, albeit a loose one. Applying it has not, nevertheless, always been without problems in social care settings. My intention is to indicate some of the reasons behind these problems.

4   Quality Management in Finnish Human Services

In Finland, the most important service producers in human services are the municipalities. Although the number of private service producers has been growing during the last few years, the role of private or voluntary service production is still quite marginal. The same concerns state-produced services: these are almost nonexistent.

Finland has 455 municipalities in all, and most of them are quite small, with only a couple of thousand inhabitants (57% of the municipalities have less than 6,000 inhabitants). Most Finns live in fair-sized cities, although we have only six cities with populations over 100,000 inhabitants.

It is obvious that quality management has developed further in health care services than in social welfare.[2] According to a nationwide survey done in 1993, there was a relatively large number of quality development projects going on in Finnish health care, and only 18% of all health care organizations did not have some kind of quality-assurance work going on at the time (Perälä/Räikkönen, 1994: 49).

Another more recent study (Voutilainen et al., 1994: 18) confirmed these results. Hospitals (both general and psychiatric) had more quality-assurance projects than local health care centres: 84% of all general hospitals and 88% of all psychiatric hospitals had ongoing quality-assurance projects, and 66% of all health care centres had an active quality-assurance project. It is interesting to notice that there is a certain difference between hospitals and primary health care centres where most of the Finnish general practitioners are working. I can see two different explanations for this difference: the first concerns the size of organizations. It might be easier to establish a quality project in larger organizations. The other possible explanation concerns the role of professions: in organizations where professionalization has gone further, quality assurance can be management's strategy to control professional work – or it can be the profession's strategy to fight back against bureaucratic control.

Whatever the reasons might be, it seems that the quality-assurance model of developing work has established itself as a main strategy in health care. However, there is still little evidence on the real effects of this strategy: what really happens in those health care organizations that implement quality management strategies (Makela, 1994: 4)? The final criterion is, of course, the improving health of the patient. Marjukka Mäkelä has reviewed the literature on quality assurance in primary health care. She found altogether 256 articles: of these, only five cases fulfilled all the inclusion criteria (randomized controlled trial, a setting of either primary or ambulatory care, and a full quality-assurance cycle implemented) (Makela, 1994: 11). The results of these cases showed moderate improvement in the outcome measures, but the research settings were often "weak" (small samples, no control groups) by the standards of clinical research.

5 Quality Management in Social Services

The evidence from the above studies seems to suggest that it is a lot easier to establish a quality management project in a big organization – such as a hospital – than in smaller units, such as primary health care centres. This is not surprising, because even at the starting phase quality assurance draws a lot of resources from an organization, not to speak of gearing it into full speed.

When it comes to social services, we do not yet have a nationwide survey of the scope of the use of quality management. Only a couple of years ago, quality management was quite an unfamiliar way of thinking in developing Finnish social welfare

Table 1: Finnish Municipalities and the Sample

Inhabitants	Municipalities in Finland		Sample	
	N	%	N	%
Small municipalities < 6,000	259	56.9	18	36.7
Middle-sized municipalities 6,001-20,000	149	32.8	26	53.1
Cities > 20,001	47	10.3	5	10.2
Total	455	100	49	100

organizations. Because of this, it is difficult to give a complete and entirely trustworthy analysis of the situation of quality management in Finnish social services.

To get information on the scope and also on the difficulties in implementing quality management, I conducted a set of thematic interviews in March 1996. I systematically picked (every fifth case) a sample of 25 Finnish municipalities and phoned the responsible manager. Another round of 24 interviews was conducted by Ms. Katja Aarrekoski in June 1996. The final size of the sample was 10.7% of all municipalities.

As Table 1 shows, the municipality sample was not representative in that it overrepresented middle-sized municipalities.

The interviews were rather unstructured, but everybody was asked

- if there were any quality management projects going on in the organization;
- whether they had seen the Quality Management Policy document prepared and sent to the municipalities by STAKES;
- if they had read our document about quality management in personal social services and, if so, whether there was anything worth commenting on in it; and
- what kind of hindrances and problems they see in quality management with respect to their own organization.

Of these four themes, it was especially the first and last that were of interest for the purposes of this paper.

Table 2:   Quality Management in Finnish Social Welfare

| | The Size of the Municipality | | | | |
	Small (N=18)	Intermediary (N=26)	Large (N=5)	Total	%
Any quality project	9	17	5	31	63
Quality-management project	1	6	5	12	24

As Table 2 shows, there is a fair number of quality management projects going on at present. More than 60% of the municipalities had some type of quality development work going on. The result is quite similar as with primary health care centres, where 66% had some kind of quality-management project running in 1994 (Voutilainen et al., 1994: 66). However, these projects focused more on the big Finnish cities, and the inclusion criterion is rather loose – we accepted, for example, small-scale seminars on quality-oriented themes as an example of quality work. More demanding projects following more or less strictly the quality-management type of thinking are not so common. Only 24% of the municipalities had something which could be described as a quality-management project in the strict sense of the concept. Many of these projects have just commenced or were just about to start. In any case, it is possible to claim that the Finnish social welfare system has adopted the ideas of quality management, and that there are surprisingly many development projects going on.

One of my main interests was connected to the factors that may hinder quality development. The respondents mentioned a number of factors, of which the most prominent were

- the lack of time, hurry, and stress at work, where daily routines consume all the available time;
- lack of resources, fiscal austerity in the municipalities, lack of competent staff, all related to the general societal framework of quality management;
- negative attitudes, unwillingness to change working habits, a lack of general commitment to quality thinking and of commitment on the part of managers or politicians, coupled with difficulties in getting the staff committed; and
- problems in quality-management philosophy, in measurement, difficulties in defining the whole concept of quality, and the lack of evidence for the real benefits

of quality work. However, the majority of the interviewees did not mention any of these factors.

The problems in applying quality management seem to be quite similar in both health care and social services. Table 3 presents all the problems mentioned in the large-scale survey about quality assurance in health care (nursing) (Perälä/ Räikkönen, 1994: 59) together with problems mentioned by the social administrators interviewed. Although the data and methods are quite different, it is interesting to see not only the similarities between the responses, but also the differences. It seems that social service managers clearly tend to stress the lack of resources as the main hindrance in the implementation of quality management more than health care professionals do. On the other hand, health care professionals put more stress on the lack of knowledge as a main hindrance for quality development.

Table 3:   Main Hindrances for Quality Management in Social Services and Nursing (in %)

Hindrance	Health Care (nursing), %	Social Service %
Lack of time	55	43
Lack of resources	14	41
Attitude	32	33
Daily routines	-	20
Current insecurities at the workplace	3	18
Lack of knowledge and skills in quality assurance	53	10
Difficulties in implementing quality assurance or management	12	2
Difficulties in assessing quality	12	6
Lack of coordination in quality assurance	8	2
Lack of quality teams or coordinators	7	8
Problems in multi-professional teamwork	6	-
Others	8	6

6   Bureaucratic Resistance?

Despite the fact that there were surprisingly many quality-management projects starting or already going on, I think there are more profound reasons for the relatively slow start which quality management has had in the human services than the abovementioned lack of resources and difficult working situation. My thesis is that a more fundamental phenomenon is involved in this delay: the basic philosophy of TQM is not as self-evidently supportive of the traditional values of human services (as seen by Martin, 1993a, b: 2-7).

Although I do not wish to totally counterclaim Martin's point, advancing quality management is by no means as simple as he suggests. Scientific discussion on quality management is ambivalent in an interesting way. Many think that those interested in quality management are in a sort of religious trance, and that dealing with issues of quality is not necessarily conducive to benefits that would justify such enthusiasm (Schiff/Goldfield, 1994; Pollitt/Bouckaert, 1995: 5). Berman especially regards the discussion on TQM to be anecdotal. It seems that many of those who are enthusiastic about TQM at the same time belittle the resistance-effect of bureaucracy: developing quality in public administration is not as simple as one might expect (Berman, 1995: 56).

I will outline each of Martin's arguments from the Finnish perspective. Below are some of the factors that, at least in Finland, limit the usability of the TQM philosophy in the context of human service management.

7   Responding to the Crisis in Quality

The current economic depression has strongly increased the need for social services, while resources have remained the same. Thus, we will necessarily have to face a quality crisis. The first argument by Martin in favour of quality management was that implementing quality management means an articulated response to the present quality crisis of the welfare state.

That might well be the case, but what type of response are we dealing with? Quality management has been seen as a sort of "third way" between Taylorism and the human relations school. It has been influenced by both (Martin, 1993a: 10). I think that TQM can also be implemented in both ways: in either the Taylorian or the human-relations spirit (Schiff/Goldfield, 1994).

The vital point is how changes in working life are met. According to Kai Ilmonen (1995), the number of conflicts of interest in organizations has been on the increase. The hierarchical top-down model, basing itself on a strict professional sectoring, has proven itself to be dysfunctional. The essential thing is, however, that people's attitudes towards their jobs have changed. The paycheck is not necessarily the main source of job satisfaction. One is more likely to seek reliable employment of some personal significance. At the same time, it is in the best interest of employers to make their employees further commit themselves to the goals of the organization, and to furnish an atmosphere of "greed" for work. Ilmonen thinks this can be striven for basically in two ways very distinct from each other: authoritarian paternalism and responsible autonomy.

Authoritarian paternalism has been primarily applied to Tayloristic mass production and mass service productions ("Macdonaldization") and to small-scale businesses. Any visible signs of discipline capable of provoking resistance are hidden in technology, ways of organizing it, a strict sequencing of working time, more subtle ways of punishment, and rewards.

The other possible way of reacting is "responsible autonomy". The employee is given relative freedom and autonomy in his or her work, but for the employer there is also a certain "business" risk involved. Responsible autonomy is based on the credibility of the employee's professional skills in the eyes of the employer. To emphasize autonomy means amplifying it; moreover, reflexivity is involved. Thus, the subdued authoritarian control is replaced by the employees themselves becoming increasingly occupied with monitoring themselves and their actions.

Quality reform can be undertaken either in the vein of authoritarian paternalism or that of responsible autonomy. Schiff and Goldfield, two American medical doctors with personal experience in Continuous Quality Improvement (CQI), give interesting examples of how "Tayloristic" quality reform can actually be. The rhetoric does not meet the reality, and vice versa (Schiff/Goldfield, 1994).

One might therefore ask whether "Tayloristic" quality reform can really lead to an authentic response to the quality crisis, or whether the reform is becoming part of the problem.

8　Creating a Loyal Clientele

Quality reform means a more customer-oriented way of producing services.

In this respect, I agree with Martin. A loyal clientele is undoubtedly necessary, although one might claim that the Finns are quite happy about the quality of social services. In Finland, people are in general very satisfied with the level of welfare services. An investigation by Lindgvist and Sihvo (1994), based on an extensive sample, indicated that the level of satisfaction has in fact risen during the recession, counter to conventional expectations.

However, there are still people who do not consider the quality of social services to be very high.[3] In the summer of 1995, our project team (Mäntysaari et al., 1996) asked the users of social services to give feedback on service quality. In 14 days, our team answered 279 calls, of which 82% contained negative remarks, part of them quite notably so. Although the majority of Finns are, it seems, satisfied with personal social services, the callers were generally very dissatisfied, especially with last-resort economic benefits and social care services. The effects of cost-cutting were also evident in the quality of care for the elderly.

Although it would be natural to assume that discontentment could derive solely from the fact that the customer did not get what he or she expected from the service, this was not the case. The Finns seemed to be especially discontent with the way in which services are provided. It seemed that the manner in which services are produced was not in accordance with the Finns' notions of social justice.

Quality in social services means full citizenship. This has been nicely put in the following quotation from a service user (Priestlay, 1995: 19):

> I am not asking for better service because I have a disability; I am asking for equal service because I am equally a citizen.

9   Is Quality Free, After All?

I mentioned above that the main obstacle on the way to quality management is the fact that quality is being discussed at the same time as cost-cutting, even if a dismantling of the welfare state is not taking place.

The much-touted notion "quality is free" is based on estimating the cost of poor-quality services to be so high that the cost of producing similar high-quality services or products always remains lower, and improving quality thus becomes essentially free.

Unfortunately, the formula contains an error: one cannot take it for granted that those financing the services are ready to invest in the service process to the extent that corrective actions would be facilitated. Quality is thought to be free only in the sense that the burden on the employees can be increased "free of cost" by promoting the type of quality management where the employees will commit themselves without any extra cost increase.

When I asked the interviewees to name the main impediments to quality development, haste and the lack of time were the most recurring answers. The extra time for work development could only be allocated by recruiting more staff, especially in the smaller work groups. Otherwise, the increasing need for services can only be satisfied by increasing the pace of work. In this situation, the request for developing quality can only be seen as an act of deliberately putting more pressure on personnel. It is therefore no wonder that many staff groups have assumed a passive or hostile attitude towards quality management.

From stray information, it can be deduced that the situation outside Finland is similar to the Finnish case in this respect. Although most writers regard the effects of quality management to be positive as far as both users and producers are concerned, the side effects of quality management are increasingly addressed: the hastening pace of work, increasing emotional workload, etc. (Schiff/Goldfield, 1994).

Because of these reasons, the slogan "quality is free" is inapplicable in the case of human services. I would prefer to clearly state that quality costs more effort and even some money (Grosser, 1995: 170).

10 Values

I agree with Martin on the fact that the basic principles of quality management and human-service production appear by and large similar. This parallelism is perhaps not to be overestimated, though. Despite the apparent beauty of principle, it may well be that even in quality-managed human-service organizations, the customers experience feelings of being socially labelled or controlled for no good reason, or they feel that their needs are not being responded to in a proper way.

One central problem is, of course, the fact that the question of the customer is a complicated one. As we know, the apparent user of the service is not necessarily the sole nor even the most important actor in defining the criteria of quality (Nüssle, 1994). Because social services are publicly financed and depend on political processes, it is important that the process of production be widely accepted. Defining the quality of human services needs to be carried out together with political decision-makers. The TQM philosophy speaks about customers as the one and only group to be allowed to define the quality of the services provided. Political decision-makers are not human-service professionals, and often they are not customers, either. Of course it is possible to see the politicians as customers, although this would be wrong even in the frame of the TQM philosophy.

Customers or not, it is ultimately these people who have the final say in defining quality, although this can lead to serious problems regarding both the social service professionals and service users. At least in Finland, this problem was not evident when quality management was introduced into our health care services; but in social welfare services, the role of political processes in defining quality soon became apparent. It is possible that the troubled relationship of democratic decision-making with the human services is creating one of the biggest problems in implementing the TQM philosophy into human services.

Perhaps Martin is right precisely in his claim that the "background values" of TQM and that of welfare services are parallel. That is to say, it is possible to claim that their underlying values are internally incoherent in the same way.

TQM's conception of needs is inconsistent. As far as enterprises go, they hardly have to ponder the extent to which a service provider is entitled to define the way in which a service user satisfies his or her needs. It is presumed that services satisfy the needs of the customer in general, but the question of to which extent service production will shape needs beforehand, or create them, is not necessarily raised. Controlling needs is a tricky thing in producing human services (Mäntysaari, 1991). On the one hand, the general legitimacy of producing services requires the control of need satisfaction; but on the other hand, advancing the self-determination of the user is a generally-accepted goal.

11 Discussion

After a relatively long period of time, it now seems evident that quality management has made its way into the Finnish social welfare administration. Finnish society is still in very bad shape – we have a very high unemployment rate, and the workload of service producers has been at an extremely high level since the economic crisis began. Especially social workers are under heavy strain. Because of this, it is quite understandable that many professionals are rather suspicious about this new managerial reform. This scepticism is, however, not the only permissible attitude towards quality reform. Many people are placing great hopes on quality management.

The development of Finnish quality management is at the crossroads. There is much to be gained from the TQM ideology but, on the other hand, there might also be problems. In the above, I have brought forward the following problems in the application of quality management to human social services:

- Quality management is one possible way of responding to the so-called "quality crisis". Although the majority of Finns are quite content with personal social services, there are also indicators telling of quality problems in providing the services. One of the strategies followed by TQM concentrated on standardizing services. When this is done straightforwardly, it may lead to MacDonaldism, which may not be good for the clients and certainly will not be good for the staff.
- Quality is not free. Producing social care services is strenuous, and a demand for quality management without proper resources may only be fulfilled by demanding more from the workers.

It seems clear that the TQM philosophy *per se* is not suitable for human-service production in the way its proponents suggest. It has to be modified to better suit the special nature of welfare services.

Notes

1   I am perfectly well aware of TQM's nature as an ideology rather than a "philosophy" in the German sense of the word. However, there are grounds for calling it a "philosophy", too: see, for example, Martin (1993a) and Deming (1994).
2   At least, quality management as an ideology has had wider support in health care than in social services. To what extent there really is a big difference in the day-to-day practice between social services and health care services in applying quality-management models, is a question too difficult to answer with the existing data.
3   The connection between quality and customer satisfaction is anything but unclear: "High-quality services do not guarantee desirable client outcomes or client satisfaction; but practitioners believe, based on the best available knowledge, that using certain technologies and arranging services in specified ways will in all likelihood benefit the client" (Ezell et al., 1989).

References

Arnkil, E. (1991) *Peilejä. Hypoteesejä sosiaalityön ristiriidoista ja kehitysvyöhykkeistä*, Volume Tutkimuksia. Helsinki: Sosiaali- ja terveyshallitus.

Berman, E. M. (1995) 'Implementing TQM in State Welfare Agencies', *Administration in Social Work* 19 (1): 55-72.

Camasso, M. J./Jagannathan, R. (1994) 'The Detection of AFDC Payments Errors through MIS and Quality Control Data Integration: An Application in the State of New Jersey', *Administration in Social Work* 18 (2): 45-68.

Deming, W. E. (1994) *Out of Crisis. Quality, Productivity and Competitive Position.* Cambridge University Press.

Ezell, M./Menefee, D./Patti, R. (1989) 'Managerial Leadership and Service Quality: Towards a Model of Social Work Administration', *Administration in Social Work* 13 (3): 473-498.

Feigenbaum, A. (1961) *Total Quality Control. Engineering and Management.* New York: McGraw-Hill.

Gitlow, H./Gitlow, S./Oppenheim, A./Oppenheim, R. (1989) *Tools and Methods for the Improvement of Quality.* Homewood, Ill./Boston, Ma: Irwin.

Grönroos, C. (1989) *Miten palvelu markkinoidaan* (4-5 painos ed.). Number 82 in Ekonomia. Espoo: Weilin & Göös.

Grosser, G. (1995) 'Qualitätsanforderung an und Qualitätssicherung in der Sozialen Arbeit', *Soziale Arbeit* (5): 168-170.

Ilmonen, K. (1995) 'Agentti, yksilöllistyminen ja moraali', *Sosiologia* 32 (1): 26-37.

Kelly, A. (1991) 'The "New" Managerialism in the Social Services', pp. 178-193 in Carter, P./Jeffs, T./Smith, M. K. (Eds.), *Social Work and Social Welfare Yearbook* 3.

Lindqvist, M./Sihvo, T. (1994) *Muutossuunnat kunnissa: tietoja sosiaali- ja terveydenhuollon menoista, säästöistä, rationalisoinnista, priorisoinnista ja karsinnasta 1992 ja 1993.* Helsinki: STAKES.

Makela, M. (1994) *The Effectiviness of Quality Assurance in Primary Care.* Master's Thesis, McMaster University.

Mäntysaari, M. (1991) *Sosiaalibyrokratia asiakkaiden valvojana. Byrokratiatyö, sosiaalinen kontrolli ja tarpeitten sääntely sosiaalitoimistoissa.* Number 51 in Sosiaalipoliittisen yhdistyksen tutkimuksia. Tampere: vastapaino.

Mäntysaari, M. (1993) 'Toimeentulotukipäätösten laadunohjauksen ongelmia', *Sosiaalinen aikakauskirja* (3): 39-42.

Mäntysaari, M./Aalto, A.-R./Maaniittu, M. (1996) ... *ja täytyy olla hirveän vahva. Asiakaspalautetta sosiaalihuollosta.* Aiheita. Helsinki: STAKES.

Martin, L. L. (1993a) *Total Quality Management in Human Service Organisations.* Number 67 in Sage Human Services Guide. Newbury Park/London/New Delhi: Sage.

Martin, L. L. (1993b) 'Total Quality Management: The New Managerial Wave', *Administration in Social Work* 17 (2): 1-16.

Nüssle, W. (1994) 'Qualitätssicherung in der Sozialarbeit. Tabu oder Notwendigkeit?', *Neue Praxis* (5): 434-442.

Perälä, M.-L./Räikkönen, O. (1994) *Parempaan laatuun hoitotyössä. Kartoitus sosiaali- ja terveydenhuollon organisaatioissa.* Number 158 in Raportteja. Helsinki: STAKES.

Pollitt, C./Bouckaert, G. (1995) 'Defining Quality', pp. 3-19 in Pollitt, C./Bouckaert, G. (Eds.), *Quality Improvement in European Public Services. Concepts, Cases and Commentary.* London/Thousand Oaks/New Delhi: Sage.

Priestley, M. (1995) 'Dropping "E's": The Missing Link in Quality Assurance for Disabled People', *Critical Social Policy* 15 (2/3): 7-21.

Schiff, G. D./Goldfield, N. I. (1994) 'Deming Meets Braverman: Toward a Progressive Analysis of the Continuous Quality Improvement Paradigm', *International Journal of Health Services* 24 (4): 655-673.

Tegethoff, H. G./Wilkesman, U. (1995) 'Lean Administration. Lernt die öffentliche Verwaltung bei der Schlankheitskur?', *Soziale Welt* 46 (1): 27-50.

Voutilainen, P./Soveri, P./Sairanen, S. (1994) 'Terveydenhuollon laadun kehittämisen nykytila Suomessa', *Dialogi* (4): 17-19.

CHAPTER 4

Quality in Personal Social Services: The Developing Role of User Involvement in the UK

Peter Beresford
Suzy Croft
Clare Evans
Tessa Harding

1 Introduction

Experience in the UK indicates that user involvement, undertaken seriously and on a basis of equality, can be both a route to quality and a measure of it.

But the definitions of quality that service users emphasize are substantially different from those that professionals or service agencies would be likely to select. Service users are interested not in the efficiency or effectiveness of service systems but in what services can help them achieve, in the purposes and outcomes of such services, in the effect on their lives. They also emphasize that the way in which services are delivered – the extent to which behaviour from workers is or is not empowering – is a crucial and necessary component of quality.

The fundamentally different value bases and priorities of service users and service providers make dialogue challenging. Two different paradigms are at stake – and the professional/managerial paradigm has a much longer history, stronger powerbases and greater access to resources than that of service users. There are also powerful competing pressures vying for attention.

However, with the growing strength of the disability and service user movements in the UK, and genuine efforts and support from allies both inside and outside the service system, experience and confidence about engaging in such a dialogue is growing on both sides. If the experience of successful user involvement is brought to bear on the debate about defining and measuring quality in personal social services, it seems likely that a new paradigm will emerge, based neither on a business nor on a professional model, but on a new model more suited to the purpose.

2 Defining Quality

The question of quality, and the development of quality standards to improve services, have largely been pursued by service agencies in the UK in a development parallel to, but separate from, new efforts towards user involvement. Requirements for monitoring, inspection and evaluation in community care have provided the impetus for such work. The White Paper, "Caring For People", which underpinned the National Health Service and Community Care Act 1990, set out the objectives early on:

> It will be essential that whenever they purchase or provide services, Social Services Authorities should take steps to ensure that the quality to be delivered is clearly specified and properly monitored. (Section 3.4.9)

There are of course a number of ways in which one might go about defining and measuring the quality of personal services; the approach in social services so far has leaned heavily on ideas developed in business organizations and in health services. Consequently, the two dominant approaches to "quality" that have been developed in personal social services are industrial or business approaches and professional approaches.

These two dominant approaches to quality definition and measurement have some serious limitations for the personal social services. They include:

- reliance on traditional paradigms of "quality", despite the fact that the community care reforms particularly, with their emphasis on the centrality of the service user, highlight the need to develop fresh approaches;
- a strong tendency to "bureaucratize quality" – that is to say to develop voluminous and detailed formalized criteria, which inhibit the very innovation and responsiveness which the reforms were designed to enhance and which rarely reflect the priorities and concerns of service users;
- the fact that views about what constitutes quality are based very largely on the cultural and professional assumptions of those who either purchase or provide the service, not on the perspectives of those who use it.

This last constitutes a severe limitation and is perhaps not surprising, given that the whole quality debate has been conducted very largely by service purchasers and providers, with service users involved at best peripherally. Given community care's commitment to the consumer as an active partner in both policy and practice, the quality debate, in failing to include this perspective, inevitably loses credibility, particularly amongst service users themselves.

A number of commentators have pointed to the inadequacies of business models and the limits of their transferability to social services (Priestley, 1995: 15). In his paper, Pollitt looks critically at both business and professional approaches to quality improvement in personal social services and community care, asking the question "What would be required to ensure that they actually led to behavioural change?". He finds that business approaches tend to pay more attention to the "end user" than professional approaches. And he concludes that personal social services are particularly suitable for "constructivist" approaches to quality definition, that is to say "where service users play a major role in defining and valuing the dimensions along which quality will be sought, measured and assessed".

Pollitt is led to the conclusion that we need to involve service users in quality developments, and he raises some important questions about how to do this. He points out firstly that, so far, there is only modest understanding of how to "construct fora in which the users can begin to express their wants"; and secondly, that in the UK there has so far been quite limited research into what the users of social services and community care actually do want.

However, there has been significant progress in both areas during the 1990s, particularly the first. Much can be learned from the experience of user involvement to date, and this paper will explore the potential of these recent developments to inform and influence the definition of quality in personal social services. The challenge is to bring the experience of service users fully into the debate about defining and evaluating "quality", making full use of all that has been learned by professionals and service users alike about the necessary preconditions for a productive and equal dialogue.

3 "Consumers" of Social Care?

Cultural values play a deep-seated and often unconscious role in the way personal social services are perceived and provided. The UK approach to personal social services is founded historically not on the right of disadvantaged people to support and equal access to the ordinary things of life, but on a supposedly benign but deeply paternalistic welfare state model – a model which has been much eroded in the last 15 or 20 years.

The political shift to the right in the UK since the late 1970s has resulted in fundamental change in both welfare ideology and the structure of human services.

In the personal social services, two major pieces of legislation have given shape and structure to this ideological shift: the 1989 Children Act and the 1990 National Health Service and Community Care Act. Both have very complex roots; they certainly draw on changing professional values and perceptions of good practice; but both also embody and carry forward the new political Right's thinking about the rights and role of the individual in society and the nature of welfare. It is perfectly possible for commentators to see the NHS and Community Care Act, for example, both as a clear attempt to rein in the costs of social care and reduce the state to a residual role – and as an attempt to make services more flexible and responsive to the differing circumstances and preferences of individuals. The tensions and contradictions resulting from these different motivating sources remain very largely unresolved within the legislation and its associated guidance.

The emphasis in the UK under successive Conservative administrations has been strongly on a market-led approach to welfare, with a changed role for state intervention and a much smaller role for statutory service supply. Local authorities have increasingly been seen not as the main providers of services, but as "enablers" and purchasers of services, and government grants which meet the costs of such services have been hedged around with requirements to spend in the private sector. Consequently there has been a tremendous growth in private providers, first in the residential and nursing home sectors and then increasingly in domiciliary care. Early in 1997 Conservative government proposals seemed to envisage the wholesale privatization of social care, with local authorities responsible only for the planning, purchasing and monitoring of services and retaining only a very limited role as provider for highly specialized functions. However, the election of a Labour government called a halt to these proposals. What remains to be seen is how far New Labour will reverse the shift to market provision and ideology in welfare generally and social care specifically.

One by-product of a market ideology is a more consumerist approach to welfare and a renewed interest in the individual as "welfare consumer". A stated aim of the community care legislation was to provide choice and greater flexibility to the consumer, to move away from the practice of slotting the individual into a service that happened to be available and instead tailor a "package of care" around the particular needs and requirements of that individual, who should be involved in deciding what would best meet his/her own needs. At the same time, consumers and their organizations were to be consulted about community care plans at the collective level; though again real power to determine future plans still lay in the hands of purchasers.

In the market model, therefore, the individual consumer has a role to play in choosing between the products that are available – though not very much real power when it comes to determining which products are available or to deciding what to buy, since someone else is doing the purchasing on their behalf. In practice, the choices open to the consumer, and what he or she eventually gets, are still largely determined by the political, administrative and professional judgements of the local authority, with regard to the range of services deemed suitable and the amount of money that may be spent.

4   The Growth of the User Perspective

The shift towards a market ideology coincides with the emergence of increasingly vocal, well-organized and effective independent service users' organizations and movements. This emergence is a worldwide as well as European development, with growing movements of disabled people, people with learning difficulties, older people, psychiatric system survivors and people living with HIV/AIDS in many different countries.

While progress is sometimes slow and often uneven, the disability and service user movements in the UK have scored some notable achievements. The Disability Discrimination Act is now on the statute book (though a much weaker version than had been hoped for); and legislation to give people the option to receive cash to arrange their own support in lieu of services arranged by the local authority care manager is now in place. This legislation (the Community Care [Direct Payments] Act 1996) has been fought for by disabled people, psychiatric system survivors and people with learning difficulties to enable them to have control over the nature, purpose and quality of the assistance they receive, and it is a notable achievement that it has reached the statute book in a recognizable form, in spite of its (in the UK welfare system) revolutionary nature. If service users are to be seen as consumers, there could not be clearer evidence that existing social service provision was failing to deliver what at least some consumers wanted; they have taken steps to ensure that they themselves will in future do the purchasing, instead of the local authority. They will be true consumers, with real purchasing power. (However, it seems likely at present that only a minority of service users will opt for direct payments, not least because of restrictions on eligibility.)

At the local level, organizations run by service users themselves have in places developed their own Independent Living Schemes and other direct services, and all over the country, disabled people and other service users have formed groups to work together and exert greater influence over the environments and conditions which affect their lives.

Most local authorities and managers responsible for planning and providing services now recognize, at least in principle, that it is important to consult and involve service users in the decisions that affect their lives. The values of social justice and respect for individuals that lie behind that message accord with those of many social service professionals (Morris, 1994), and strong encouragement from the Department of Health in its guidance documents and progress reports has given weight and legitimacy to those principles. It is rare these days for social service professionals not to acknowledge the importance of consulting and involving service users in all aspects of service planning and development.

So a key feature of the community care reforms has been to emphasize the centrality of the service user in policy and practice. This goal, sought by both service user organizations and service agencies, has been concerned to ensure service users a more active role in decisions affecting them and in the organizations responsible for taking those decisions. The 1990s have seen a considerable growth of initiatives for "user involvement" in the planning and development of services, and a plethora of consultations, market research exercises, participative forums, committees and groups, set up by health and welfare agencies, at local, regional and sometimes national level.

However, such involvement has not always been effective. While much has been learned, many initiatives are now being re-evaluated by service users' organizations and independent researchers, both of whom highlight their limited impact and effectiveness and the significant costs, both personal and in terms of resources, to service users (Bewley/Glendinning, 1994).

At the root of the problem, it seems that both the idea of user involvement and schemes for user involvement have frequently become distanced from service users' actual experience of and preferences for services. They have been too removed from reality, too distant from the coal face to have an impact on the day-to-day experience of service users.

User involvement has largely focused on consultation about the drawing up of annual community care plans by local social services departments, which is a requirement of the legislation. Such plans, which are more often descriptive than prescriptive, have only a distant relationship with day-to-day service delivery, and it is hard for those who have been involved and consulted to see the impact of their work. User involvement in this context tends to become "bureaucratized".

Less attention has been paid by service agencies to how service users can play a more central role in influencing the nature and quality of the services and support they receive as individuals. But it is this that is likely to be the priority for most service users and is the underlying rationale behind the idea of user involvement. Service users' organizations themselves are increasingly measuring the value of their involvement in terms of the degree of control individuals can gain as a result, over their own lives and over the interventions of the agencies, services and practitioners which affect them, which entails both individual and collective action. Many attempts at user involvement to date have missed the mark because they have failed to address the issues of purpose and quality most central to users' concerns.

Bringing service users more fully into the debate about what constitutes quality would, then, more closely reflect their concerns and priorities and give greater purpose to their role.

5   Obstacles to User Involvement in the Quality Debate

What then are the obstacles to user involvement in the debate about the quality of services, and how can these be overcome? We suggest that there are three key kinds of obstacle which inhibit full effectiveness: firstly, the communication difficulties to be overcome before service users and providers can engage with each other on a basis of equality; secondly, the nature of the competing discourses; and thirdly, the values which each party brings to the debate.

5.1   Communication Difficulties to Be Overcome

All attempts at user involvement face certain basic difficulties due to the unequal roles and relationships involved.

Firstly, service users themselves are disempowered. It is not easy to participate on a basis of equality with powerful professionals, when people have spent a considerable period – sometimes a lifetime – without control over the decisions which affect their lives and unable to exercise much autonomy. It takes time and resources, as well as determination, for service users to build confidence, decide what they want and make themselves heard. The source of such confidence is usually other service users; the role of independent service user organizations is therefore crucial, and these take time and resources to develop. Until service users have a sense of and confidence in the validity of the contribution they have to make, it will be difficult to establish relationships of trust with professionals and to work together on a basis of mutual respect.

Secondly, the agenda for such involvement is usually set by the professionals involved; not only does that create instant inequality, but the agenda itself and the whole style of working, the way meetings are conducted, the language used, appear obscure and alienating.

Thirdly, amongst both service users and service providers, there are real obstacles to open dialogue, due to fears and anxieties on both sides. The views of service users are often a real challenge to the received wisdom of many professionals. Service users often fear the power professionals have to influence their lives. These fears are deep-seated and genuine and can readily become real obstacles to communication.

Fourthly, it is often difficult for service users to see that their involvement has any effect. It is only by seeing results that service users can have confidence that they are influencing services and creating change. If there is no change, or no feedback about changes that have occurred, then motivation is quickly lost.

Finally there are numerous competing agendas and priorities to that of user involvement; the prevailing culture within local authorities is one in which professional concerns and managerial resource control are the overwhelming priorities. User involvement is set against a background of turbulent organizational change, as social services departments separate their "purchasing" and "providing" roles, local government undergoes a massive redrawing of geographical boundaries, and the interface between health and local authority responsibilities shifts significantly, putting additional pressures on social services. Service agencies are bombarded by challenges on many fronts. Unless user involvement is an integral part of all aspects of service development, it is very easy for it to be relegated to a side issue, where it fails to have a significant impact.

5.2 Competing Discourses

When it comes to the debate about quality, it quickly becomes apparent from the UK experience (and this does not seem to be isolated) that there is not so much one set of discussions going on, as several, including academic, professional, managerial and political debates. While these are overlapping and to some extent interchangeable, a more fundamental distinction can be drawn between personal social services agencies' and service users' discussions or discourses.

The discourses from these two constituencies are fundamentally different in nature, and they do not sit comfortably together. The terms of the debate are significantly and qualitatively different in their objectives, philosophy, concerns, forms and process.

Service agency discourse, not surprisingly, is primarily concerned with policy and services; with service organization, management, efficiency, effectiveness and economy. The involvement of service users in this context is primarily as a source of data to help manage restricted resources, to inform rationing and targeting decisions and to set priorities. The focus has been on refining and adjusting services, not on substantive change. Decision-making has remained with the agencies.

Service users' discourse is concerned much more explicitly and specifically with people's lives; with managing their lives, dealing with difficulties, securing suitable support to live as they want to, maintaining or increasing choices and opportunities and challenging restrictions and obstructions which they face. This discourse is not concerned narrowly with specialist or dedicated health and welfare support and service systems, but also with access to the mainstream: to employment, education, training, public transport and recreation.

The central concern of service users' organizations is to increase people's control over their lives and over the way agencies intervene in them. They place particular priority on ideas and objectives of participation, inclusion, equality, autonomy and rights, stressing the achievement of their civil and human rights, rather than just welfare rights (Croft/Beresford, 1995).

> It is important to us that our involvement is based on our terms and within a background of rights: the rights that we have as citizens like any others – the democratic right to participate in society and to have choice and control over our lives – which must mean that we have as much choice and control as we can over the services we receive. (Evans, 1995)

Service agencies' and service users' discourses therefore reflect totally different starting points, different value bases and different purposes. They have significantly different personal, professional, political and organizational concerns. Under those circumstances, a dialogue is not going to be easy; assumptions have to be questioned and some hard listening done on both sides if people are to understand each other's concerns.

5.3 Different Values

One of the clearest expressions of the different ideologies and value bases of service users organizations on the one hand and of service agencies and professionals on the other, are the models and theories developed by service users. A key example is the social model of disability developed by members of the disabled people's movement.

Thanks to this new thinking, there are now competing models of what disability is and how it is perceived. These have been labelled as the "medical" and "social" models of disability, although Oliver, the disability activist and academic, prefers a slightly different distinction:

> In short for me, there is no such thing as the medical model of disability, there is instead, an individual model of disability of which medicalization is one significant component ... The individual model "locates the problem" of disability within the individual ... it sees the causes of this problem as stemming from the functional limitations or psychological losses which are assumed to arise from disability.

> Disability, according to the social model, is all the things that impose restrictions on disabled people; ranging from individual prejudice to institutional discrimination, from inaccessible public buildings to unusable public transport systems, from segregated education to excluding work arrangements, and so on. Further, the consequences of this failure do not simply and randomly fall on individuals, but systematically upon disabled people as a group who experience this failure as discrimination institutionalized throughout society. (Oliver, 1996: 31-33)

By drawing the distinction between individual impairment and social disablement, the social model of disability enables disabled people to locate the restrictions and problems they experience and make sense of their social relations. Similar developments have taken place among the movements of people with learning difficulties, older people, psychiatric system survivors and people living with AIDS, and these have similarly made it possible for people to reassess the roles and identity attached to them, the oppression they experience and ways in which their rights and needs are or, more often, are not met.

Where the way one sees and interprets the world and its impact on the individual is so fundamentally at variance between two parties to a discussion, it is going to require a great deal of goodwill and a lot of patience to reach understanding.

Furthermore, there is of course an imbalance of power and resources between the two perspectives, which makes such a dialogue even harder to achieve. Disabled people's and other service users' organizations have less funding, less credibility, less support and less access to the mainstream. They cannot assume that their agendas and proposals will be readily accepted either by the service system or by broader society. Instead they see struggling for the acceptance of their goals as an inherent part of what they must do.

Definitions of quality, of course, are based on and emerge from values, whether these are explicit or implicit. Writing about quality assurance for disabled people, Priestley argues that the definition of service quality is value-led and that dominant ideologies have contributed to the continued oppression of disabled people, saying:

> Definitions of quality (used to judge both disabled people's quality of life and the quality of the services available to them) are derived from and determined by a variety of dominant and oppressive social values about the role of disabled people in society ... In this way, the social construction of "quality" is inextricably bound up with the social construction of "disablement". (Priestley, 1995a: 7, 10, 11)

Where service users dispute the dominant values, they are also likely to dispute the quality of services framed within those values. For example, psychiatric system survivors who reject a psychiatric model of "mental illness" are likely to be equally critical of "treatments" based on a medical model, whether or not those meet other criteria for quality. People with learning difficulties who challenge measures of intellectual or "mental" age attached to them, which equate them with children, are similarly likely to be unsympathetic to quality measures built on such (implicit) assumptions about their abilities and emotional development. A segregating institutional service for service users who want to take part in mainstream recreational and occupational activities is likely to fail their quality test, even if it has very high material standards, offers sensitive and appropriate personal support and ensures good accessibility within its premises.

Agencies might develop quality measures for their provision and services based on ideas of ensuring "quality of life", physical conditions and personal rights within them consistent with broader dominant standards; but if such provision and services are not consistent with service users' *own* priorities for their inclusion, participation, autonomy and civil rights, then their movements would be unlikely to accept them as satisfactory.

These three kinds of obstacle to the involvement of service users in defining quality present a somewhat formidable barrier. But there is already a growing body of experience and confidence that such barriers can be overcome, given the will to do so. If quality standards are to reflect the values and choices of service users, service users need to be brought into the centre of the debate about quality.

6   Making User Involvement Work

There is now a significant body of experience, guidance and research from both service users and service agencies about how to involve service users in effective and fully inclusive ways (for example, Hawcroft/Peckford/Thompson, 1996; Harding/Oldman, 1996; Beresford/Croft, 1993; Morris/Lindow, 1993). But it is not simply a question of service users feeding into the fora of service agencies and making themselves heard in that arena. They have also developed their own fora, through their own organizations, groups, initiatives, services, networks, events, newsletters and media, arts and campaigning. The arenas are different, but the messages are clear, loud and lively.

These two areas of development are of course not unconnected. The more that service users develop their own groups and organizations, the more confidence and the sense of common purpose grow, the more ideas are exchanged and developed and the more new ideas for projects and services are generated. The capacity of service users to engage with those who purchase and provide services is enhanced by the vigour, understanding and confidence gained from working together and firming up their views.

The most widespread and concentrated effort to empower and involve service users takes place in Wiltshire, a county in the west of England, where the skills and determination of the local user group, combined with strong backing and financial support from the social services department and its director, have resulted in a lively organization with broad membership amongst disabled people, psychiatric system users and, increasingly, older people. Wiltshire and Swindon Users' Network is now involved in a multiplicity of ways both in running its own projects and in influencing the policies and practice of local service planners and providers. It is democratically controlled by people who have direct personal experience of using social services and most of its workers are service users (Evans, 1995).

The significance of what service users gain from collective action should not be underestimated. Members of Wiltshire and Swindon Users' Network refer to the Network as "one unit" and "a safe environment", somewhere which "draws people in", where they can "feel comfortable and have confidence", and where their needs are recognized – "we get tired, go up and down so much". They receive from other members "not pity, but time", help to "get to know the ropes and learn the jargon", and recognition for the skills they bring with them – experience and skills from the world beyond services which are valued in this new context, but often disregarded by professionals who may see only the "service user" rather than the whole person.

The Network serves as a springboard from which people can go out and engage with service providers, a reference point for discussion of the issues that come up, and a place where growing expertise is shared and developed. People engage with service agencies on the basis of their own experience as individuals, but they have access to the wider experience of the Network and its varied membership as well and can draw in those whose experience is relevant to the service or issue in question. The Network is consciously working to expand involvement:

> We must continue to reach out to try to involve all user groups including those in ethnic minority communities and other marginalized users. We must be sure we do not build structures which exclude less empowered users. (Evans/Hughes, 1993)

The achievement of the Network in creating this environment is very evident: service users are "confident we are making a difference" and point to numerous changes and developments in the services that have resulted from their efforts. A crisis response service is being introduced for psychiatric system survivors. A review is taking place, led by service users, of how occupational therapists organize their work, with suggestions for greater follow-through from hospital to community. There is a proposal afoot for service users to train social services receptionists and help them understand why people need the information they need and how to deal with the anger and abuse front line staff often experience from members of the public.

> User expertise is brought directly to bear on services, making it possible for professionals to learn how to change them, to be more empowering. (Evans, 1995)

Wiltshire Users Network has had the advantage of stable and substantial funding to enable it to develop to this degree and has been able to employ its own workers, themselves for the most part people who use services. It has also gained access to many parts of the service system, with the full support of senior managers. It can now point to its involvement in 71 different undertakings and forms of involvement, some independent projects and some initiatives in collaboration with the social services department and other agencies. These include some powerful and influential roles, such as chairing inspection committees and joint working groups between health and social services providers, and training professionals in assessment and care management (Evans/Hughes, 1993).

> We work on the principle that it is a matter of riddling the system with as many user perspectives as possible and you win some, you lose some, but on the whole, the more opportunities for user involvement you develop, the more impact you can make. (Evans, 1995)

What then are the principles that make possible this level of involvement?

The first is that service users need their own base within which to work together and develop confidence, ideas and accountability, and this base needs to be adequately and securely funded to enable stability and continuity.

Secondly, service users need to be involved from the start and on an equal basis in any initiative to improve and develop the quality of services. Plans, proposals and agendas need to reflect their concerns and priorities as well as those of professionals and service agencies, if the outcomes of such work are to enhance quality as defined by them. Anything less than that and involvement becomes tokenistic and superficial.

Thirdly, steps have to be taken to make it possible for people to participate effectively. Attention has to be paid to the practical details of enabling people to attend accessible venues, suitable meeting times, transport arrangements, facilitation (such as signers or supporters) are prerequisites to involvement. But equally, the process of meetings and events needs to be "enabling". Professionals and managers used to working within agency cultures forget how alien such cultures can be to outsiders: the way decision-making is structured, the language used, the references, even the injokes can be not just unfamiliar but alienating and thoroughly disempowering. Meetings need to be planned in ways which make participation as easy as possible and which ensure that what service users have to say is heard and valued. Explicit groundrules about how people are expected to behave are helpful to set the tone and let people know where they stand.

Fourthly, it is important to recognize that both service users and professionals and managers are often anxious about engaging in discussion on a new and more equal basis. Many service users have a lifetime of experience of not being listened to, and fear renewed rejection. Moreover they are talking from strongly-felt personal experience and talking to people who may have a considerable amount of power over their quality of life. Professionals, on the other hand, may fear criticism or anger, or that they will be unable to meet demands. Many feel a strong sense of personal responsibility for services and can find it difficult not to react defensively when the whole basis of their role and its values may be questioned. These tensions need to be recognized and acknowledged and time made to talk them through, if they are not to inhibit dialogue and act as barriers to change (Harding/Oldman, 1996).

While there is clearly still a long way to go in embedding these approaches to user involvement in the day-to-day working practices of most service agencies, and there are many competing pressures to distract and divert attention, the experience developed over the last six or eight years means that a considerable amount is now known about how to go about effective involvement. There are grounds for confidence that it can have a very significant impact on service development, and therefore on quality.

7 An Alternative Approach to Determining Quality

Whilst the practicalities of effective user involvement may now be known, there is still a very long way to go before service users' different objectives for services are appreciated. It is therefore a matter of considerable concern that quality still tends to be defined in professional terms alone. Any approach to quality definition that fails to take account of the values of the service users themselves is bound to be very limited.

Priestley suggests instead:

> an approach to service quality measurement which takes into account not only the established criteria of outcomes and process but also the service delivery structure, in terms of the degree to which that structure facilitates and empowers disabled people ... to improve their own quality of life. (Priestley, 1995a: 17)

And Evans echoes this point:

> We want to change the culture ... from the concept of us being dependent on them to the concept of our right to independent living and our right to help to achieve that. (Evans, 1995)

Secondly, as Priestley writes, there are not only issues around who defines quality, but who also is involved in the process of improving it. Citing Ackoff, he argues:

> the policy problem should not be how to improve other people's quality of life but "how to enable them to improve their own quality of life ... The key to improved quality of life is not planning for or measurement of others, but enabling them to plan and measure for themselves. (Priestley, 1995a: 17)

There are already a number of initiatives in existence in the UK which are seeking to do exactly this: to enable the quality of a service to be determined by its success or otherwise in achieving what the service users themselves want to get out of it.

One is Choice, a user-led service, offering an independent advocacy and information service, supporting disabled people and other service users to define their own needs and identify the support and services which they want, to live independently. Another is Direct Power, a resource pack for psychiatric system survivors, written by a survivor and developed from the experience of survivors' organizations to help recipients of mental health services regain control over their lives. While the emphasis is practical, it has a clear value base. It rejects:

> ... the notion that people who experience or have experienced mental distress must be "managed" and therefore need a mental health professional to guide them in the art of being human.

Instead it rests on a holistic approach committed to valuing the individual and involving them fully in decisions and activities which affect them:

> We hope that Direct Power will act as a tool which will enable you to have a central role in developing a support and care plan that will be tailored to your individual needs. (Leader, 1995)

Direct Power has sections to help survivors negotiate community care, to define and prioritize their needs, work out how they feel about the services they receive, what support they want and to develop a partnership agreement with intervening agencies. It stresses that it is a resource for survivors to use when and how they want to. Another recent initiative in the UK was based on disabled people developing measures of the quality of user involvement in disability services for service purchasers and providers to apply (Priestley, 1995b).

Some service users, however, preferring the Independent Living approach, have opted out of using traditional services altogether, and appoint, train and monitor their own personal assistants. In doing so, they are making a strong statement that services provided in more traditional ways have failed to deliver the outcome that is sought and therefore fail to live up to their definitions of quality. Their answer has been not greater involvement, but independent action to achieve the outcomes they aspire to.

8 Influencing the Quality of Practice

For many service users who rely on more traditionally provided services, the priority is greater control in their own lives and a more equal relationship with those who deliver the service.

One recent study asked a wide range of service users' organizations what it was they valued in their contacts with social services workers. The consistency of what they said was both significant and remarkable: the single most important factor in a good quality service was the relationship between the individual worker and the service user.

> So often it is the style of the way services are delivered rather than the service itself which produces a quality service. This makes it quite difficult to separate out quality of services from quality of relationships; the home carer who gets you up in the morning can do this in an empowering way which enables you to face the effort of the day positively or in a way which means that you are dressed and ready but not psychologically ready. Beyond the basic skills, this empowering experience comes from the quality of relationships. (*Wiltshire Users' Network*, in Harding/Beresford, 1996)

Service users were quite specific about what made such a relationship:

> These qualities, which are really all commonsensical, are the natural attributes which make most relationships work positively: self-respect, dignity, honesty, confidentiality, trust, reliability, being treated equally, valid and good communication and listening skills, and in particular a sound partnership and an enabling role. (*British Council of Disabled People*, in Harding/Beresford, 1996)

Beyond the quality of relationships, service users mention the quality of skills they believe are needed – listening and communicating, counselling and understanding, and enabling and negotiating are all cited, together with good information and good basic skills and a sense of judgement about risks. They are also explicit about the range and nature of services they would like to see.

The organizations that took part in this study wanted to be involved in defining quality, setting and monitoring standards and evaluating services. They were also clear that they had a role to play in promoting quality through their own involvement in recruiting staff, in designing job specifications, and in all aspects of staff training.

As we observed above, most efforts to date have been directed at involving service users in planning services, on the macro level. But what matters most immediately to most people is the quality of the service they receive personally and on which they may well depend. There is great scope for involving service users to a much greater extent in the day-to-day promotion of quality through direct interaction with staff.

9   Conclusion

Service users therefore are judging the quality of services in two ways: they are concerned that services will help them achieve the outcomes they aspire to; and they are concerned that services are delivered in ways which empower rather than disempower them and their peers as individuals. The motivation for getting involved with service agencies is primarily to achieve these two objectives. User involvement is not an end in itself, but a means of effecting change both in the outcome of services and in the behaviour of workers.

> We are very proactive in seeking opportunities for user involvement ... The aim is not participation for the sake of it ... it is actually to bring about change. Users in the network say "What is the point of me going and being involved, what effect will it have?" and they will not go and participate unless they know that they are going to be able to have an effect by giving their perspective as service users. (Evans, 1995)

It is encouraging that in the UK currently there is a new focus on the outcome of services – not on organizational structure or efficient systems alone, but on the basic purpose of services and what they are there for.

As with the debate about quality, there is an ever-present risk that it is service providers alone who will set the parameters by which outcomes are defined and specified. But a new project, funded by the Department of Health, is setting out to enable service users to develop their own definitions of outcomes: to create the space and the opportunity for people from service user organizations to define desired outcomes from the point of view of their own values, their own priorities and their own form of discourse.

It seems likely that service users will want to avoid coming up with any predetermined set of quality standards. Rather they are more likely to see quality as the extent to which services enable individuals to meet their own aspirations, which will vary from person to person; and as the extent to which they enable people to enhance control over their own lives.

In this context, the participation of service users can be seen as both a route to quality and a measure or criterion of it.

It offers a route to quality in the sense that service users are fully involved in defining, developing, monitoring and evaluating quality according to their own values. Participation is also a criterion of quality since a key objective is that service users have more say and control over their lives and over decision-making about the specific service or arrangements for support.

This approach begins to offer a new paradigm for assessing quality in the personal social services, based neither on a business nor a professional model but rather on a model of personal autonomy and respect for individual choice.

References

Beresford, P./Croft, S. (1993) *Citizen Involvement: A Practical Guide for Change.* Basingstoke: Macmillan.

Croft, S./Beresford, P. (1995) 'Whose Empowerment? Equalising the Competing Discourses in Community Care', pp. 59-76 in Jack, R. (ed.), *Empowerment in Community Care.* London: Chapman and Hall.

Evans, C. (1995) 'Disability, Discrimination and Local Authority Social Services – Users' Perspectives', in Zarb, G., *Removing Disabling Barriers.* Policy Studies Institute.

Evans, C./Hughes, M. (1993) *Tall Oaks from Little Acorns ... The Wiltshire Experience of Involving Users in the Training of Professionals in Care Management.* Wiltshire Users Network and Wiltshire Social Services Department.

Harding, T./Beresford, P. (ed.) (1996) *The Standards We Expect: What Service Users and Carers Want from Social Services Workers.* London: National Institute for Social Work.

Harding, T./Oldman, H. (1996) *Involving Service Users and Carers in Local Services Guidelines for Social Services Departments and Others.* National Institute for Social Work and Surrey Social Services Department.

Hawcroft, L./Peckford, B./Thompson, A. (1996) *Visible Voices: Developing Deaf Service User Involvement in Local Services.* Carlisle: British Deaf Association.

Leader, A. (1995) *Direct Power: A Resource Pack for People Who Want to Develop Their Own Care Plans and Support Networks.* Joint publication by the Community Support Network, Brixton Community Sanctuary. Brighton: Pavilion Publishing Ltd. and MIND.

Morris, J. (1994) *The Shape of Things to Come? User-led Social Services.* London: Social Services Policy Forum, National Institute for Social Work.

Morris, J./Lindow, V. (1993) *User Participation in Community Care Services.* Leeds: Community Care Support Force, Department of Health.

Oliver, M. (1996) *Understanding Disability: From Theory to Practice.* Basingstoke: Macmillan.

Priestley, M. (1995a) 'Dropping "E's": The Missing Link in Quality Assurance for Disabled People', *Critical Social Policy* 44/45: 7-21.

Priestley, M. (1995b) *Improving User Involvement in Disability Services.* Report of the DCIL Living Options Focus Group. Derbyshire: Derbyshire Centre for Integrated Living.

PART II

METHODS

Chapter 5

Professionals and Quality Initiatives in Health and Social Services

Marketta Rajavaara

1   Introduction

In the 1990s, "quality" has become a keyword in the discourse on the evaluation and development of public welfare services, including both health and social services. Because welfare professionals play an important role in the production and supply of health and social services, the implementation of quality reforms is an intrinsic part of their work.

On the one hand, professionals are the main implementors of quality reforms; and the recent "boom" in quality initiatives would not have been possible without their commitment and enthusiasm. The keen participation of welfare professionals in quality initiatives and programmes prompts us to ask whether there might be at least some elements in modern quality management approaches – even those originally developed in the private sector – that resemble the core beliefs and practice ideologies of welfare professionals. Laurence L. Martin (1993: 2) has stressed the similarities between social work's professional epistemology and TQM (Total Quality Management) in arguing that "quality management – unlike most managerial waves – is compatible with traditional human service and social work values".

On the other hand, quality reforms, especially when implemented with a comprehensive, "totalitarian" organizational approach, may create a state of tension *vis-à-vis* professionalism, extending the external control of working practices and restricting the autonomy of professional performance. The commitment of professionals to the implementation of quality reforms might be weak for this reason.

Arguments such as this are frequently put forward in analyses of the role played by welfare professionals in quality management:

> It should be understood that both the TQM process and the implicit higher level of institutional accountability bring a true culture shock to physicians. As members of an ancient and respected profession, they have come to expect autonomy and accountability only to themselves as the norm ... The TQM generation of physicians, however, is the first to be exposed to the microscopic power of modern quality process tools and techniques. It should not be surprising that their reaction to such perceived intrusion and exposure would be initially less than enthusiastic. (Merry, 1990, ref. Morgan/Murgatroyd, 1994: 73)

The aim of this article is to examine the extent to which professionals in Finnish municipal social and health care settings commit themselves to quality reforms, as well as the kind of changes these efforts will bring to professional culture and interprofessional relations. The compatibility of business-oriented quality initiatives with professional culture will be a special focus of analysis. The article is based on a qualitative case study in a social welfare and health office in a relatively large municipality which had taken part in a broader Quality and Community Project organized by the Association of Finnish Local Authorities for the purpose of promoting quality assurance in municipal service provision. The project was based on ISO 9000, but some ideas taken from TQM were put into practice, too.

The pilot project had been completed some months before I carried out the interviews (19), between March and May 1995. The interviews were semi-structured and took between 45 and 90 minutes. The interviewees were managers and professionals[1] (medical practitioners, nurses, day-care managers, social workers, home-help personnel) working in different settings: primary health care, dental health care, child welfare clinics, home-help services, the Social Service department and child day care. All the persons interviewed had taken part in the pilot project as members of quality development teams or as quality coordinators in their units. Some of them had further responsibilities in implementing quality management within their organization.

2 Quality Initiatives and Approaches in Health and Social Services

Markku Temmes (1994: 40-61) has distinguished two "waves" in the modernization of Finnish public administration since the Second World War. During the first wave (1967-1975), that coincided with the expansion of the welfare state, the emphasis was on the development of planning and accounting systems. There were also some efforts to adopt business-oriented management strategies; but these were relatively ineffective and achieved little in terms of dismantling bureaucratic structures and cultures in public administration.

The quality of public services has become an important topic in the second wave of reform ideology. During the second wave (1987 onwards), an increasing emphasis has been placed on the strengthening of market mechanisms and the devolution of power and responsibility. The economic recession that hit Finland exceptionally hard in the 1990s provided further impetus for reform in the supply, allocation, management and financing of public welfare services (Temmes, 1994; Naschold, 1995).

In assessing the compatibility of quality initiatives and professional culture in public health and social-service organizations, one must bear in mind that quality is a very complicated, multidimensional and vague term and that there are many alternative approaches to its measurement and implementation. It may mean different things to politicians, managers, professionals, clients, taxpayers and quality management consultants. Christopher Pollitt (1995) has stressed this kind of constructivist view of quality. Rolland Munro (1995) takes a very interesting constructivist view in analysing quality initiatives from the perspective of understanding quality as a new discursive space for different kinds of interests within an organization.

Furthermore, quality can be understood as a disciplined space (Munro, 1995: 145). This means that quality reforms and programmes can be implemented using various approaches and strategies. Here I distinguish four types of quality initiatives with different origins, approaches and strategies which can be implemented in public welfare organizations. However, in their practical implementation, these quality initiatives may converge to some extent (see Figure 1).

In Finland, as in other Scandinavian countries, the professional model connected with bureaucracy, state and municipal governance has traditionally been the major method of organizing the supply of welfare services. Professionals are used to having some degree of autonomy over the content of their work and some discretionary powers in the supply of services, although these are relative and subordinate to administrative rules and principles.

The professional model is based on the notion that people are capable of controlling themselves by cooperative, collective means and that, in the case of complex work, those who perform it are in the best position to make sure that it gets done well. According to their model, people perceive their work as having interest and intrinsic value, which motivates them to want to do it well (Freidson, 1994: 176). Professionalism implies that professionals have established their own quality-assurance mechanisms in their work practices. Still, there may be some differences between professions and occupations in the institutionalization of professional methods of quality control. Because of the bureaucratic context of professional work, professional quality initiatives and programmes have been developed alongside political-administrative quality reforms and programmes.

Figure 1:   A Typology of Quality Initiatives

Quality initiatives	Origins, context	Approaches, strategies (examples)
Political-administrative quality initiatives	Representative democracy, political control of public service production, citizen rights, equity, legal security, bureaucracy	Legislation, national quality recommendations, national/municipal service standards and quality indicators, patients' representatives
Citizen-based quality initiatives	Participative democracy, citizen society	Social movements' and action groups' concern about quality, campaigns, introduction of alternative service models
Business-oriented quality initiatives	Market mechanisms, productivity, efficiency, consumerism, consumer choice	TQM, ISO 9000, quality awards, benchmarking
Professional quality initiatives	Professional socialization, self-regulation, autonomy	Professional training, conditions of competence, professional ethics, professional audit, peer review, self-evaluation

Citizen-based quality initiatives evolving from social movements and action groups have played a fairly minor role in Finland. According to surveys, there is little impetus to organize collective action for the quality of services or to initiate alternative service models. Despite cost-cutting and "savings" in municipal health and social services, the Finnish population is generally satisfied with the quality of services (Sihvo/Uusitalo, 1993; Lindqvist/Rastas/Sihvo, 1994).

   To a growing extent, quality reforms have been implemented with approaches imported into social welfare and health services from private industry. This trend may hold certain implications for the utilization of professional and political-administrative approaches. This is not to say that their significance will inevitably decline. The crucial question is what kind of balance or mix will evolve in the utilization of different approaches.

Approaches such as TQM and ISO 9000 influence practitioners' work and the scope of individual autonomy in organizations. They do so in a different way than other approaches, but it has yet to be seen what implications this will hold for welfare professionals. In the following section, I will present some findings on these questions.

3   Professionals and ISO 9000 in a Municipal Social Welfare and Health Office – Some Empirical Findings

3.1   *Professionals' Perceptions of the Need for Business-oriented Quality Management*

As mentioned earlier, the quality of services is to some degree regulated and controlled by institutionalized political-administrative and professional instruments in the social welfare and health sector. Thus, in conducting the interviews, my preliminary hypothesis was that welfare professionals would not be particularly receptive to business-oriented quality programmes or approaches. As a matter of fact, I expected to meet outright resistance to them.

To my surprise, most of the interviewed professionals accepted the need for business-oriented quality initiatives in their organization. Still, there were differences in their degree of commitment to these efforts. While the spokespersons for quality were mainly middle managers, most front-line professionals took a keen interest in quality issues. Some, though few, were more sceptical, but none were altogether against the idea of quality management.

Rolland Munro (1995: 131) argues that it is not relevant to ask whether one is for or against "quality". He believes it is more important to ask in what respect one is in favour of "quality" and what interests one brings to it. I began to realize that the quality programme that had been launched in the organization might serve some professional interests and concerns that had been latent or repressed earlier.

The interviewees pointed out that the quality management project came from the "top", initiated by upper management. The reorganization of services and the integration of social and health care services in the municipality in 1993 was seen as the major motivation for introducing the project.

After reorganization, we had two different work cultures in our organization. Some kind of shared goal and common language between social and health care workers were urgently needed. For instance, we wondered whether we should talk about treatment plans or service plans. We have had high expectations of this new quality language.

The "warming" of interprofessional relations and the development of collaboration between professionals and service units were goals that raised the greatest hopes among the interviewees, both among the managers and those in front-line positions. The development of multiprofessionalism and interprofessional collaboration turned out to be the most widely-accepted target of the quality programme.

Some other motives and needs were mentioned, too. Some interviewees referred to the need for greater efficiency as an important motive for the quality project. The opportunity to give voice to service users and to develop more customer-oriented services was also mentioned. Some professionals remarked on the need to document work and to evaluate the effectiveness of services – these needs were seen as being associated with the pressures to legitimize the role of municipal services and to raise their profile in the eyes of citizens and politicians.

3.2   Practical Issues and Constraints Related to Implementation

One of the biggest difficulties that arose in the discussions concerning the implementation of the programme was participants' uncertainty about the goals and objectives of the quality-management project:

> We were taking a leap into the unknown. We had no idea where we were going and where the project would take us.

Most of the participants regarded their training as inadequate. Although most of them had taken part in various development initiatives before the project was launched, they considered the approach in this one to be different from their earlier work experience.

The problem was partly caused by the unclear concepts and demands of ISO 9000 which had to be translated to meet the needs of the municipal service organization. The huge and burdensome job of implementing it, notwithstanding its technical complexity, was a target of criticism. Nevertheless, most of the participants believed, though not with great enthusiasm, that the ISO approach could be utilized in social and health care services. Since the project had been added to their existing workload without any extra resources allocated for this purpose (except for consultation), this caused burn-out and motivation problems among some participants.

Some of the problems related to the implementation of the programme could perhaps be characterized as expressions of the tension between the exceptional, pioneering and stimulating "project culture" and the ordinary, everyday "system culture" of the organization (Fisker, 1994: 37). This tension was manifest in various ways. Firstly, there was considerable confusion among participants as to how they should allocate their time; whether to use it for completing project tasks and meetings (totalling about 150 meetings per year) or for interaction with clients.

Secondly, the meetings of the Quality Development teams caused irritation among colleagues who sometimes had to complete their unfinished work.

But most interestingly, conflicts between project culture and system culture arose when the interviewees evaluated the future of quality efforts in their organization. Even those who were most enthusiastic about the quality project were rather sceptical about its continued success. The problem of commitment to development work was seen as the most difficult barrier to extending quality within the organization. For these pioneering participants, quality had been a motivating concept, though even they noticed some resistance among their ranks, too. Nevertheless, they were especially worried about resistance among others whose job it was to begin quality development work after the pilot phase. The responsibilies for quality development which the participants had taken on more or less voluntarily, were seen as obligatory requirements for the future.

3.3 Professionals' Perceptions of the Results

Most of the interviewees said that they were still rather uncertain about the results of the quality-management project and its consequences for their work:

> When we began this project, we had no idea what the results would be. Now it has become part of our organization and is here to stay. We'll have to wait and see what it brings.

The participants' shared view was that most of the issues raised by the quality-management project were not fundamentally new, but something they had been pursuing for years, at least in their own profession or service unit:

> In my mind, there was nothing all that revolutionary about it. For example feedback from clients is nothing new to us. I suppose that most of the issues we dealt with were things we had reflected on earlier, too.

> One of the aims of this project was to increase client-centredness. But in social work, this has always been our core aim. So why make so much fuss about it?

Nevertheless, there were some differences of opinion in the professionals' evaluations of the learning processes during the project. Especially those involved in social work and child welfare clinics felt that they had little to gain from the project in terms of their professional thinking, emphasizing the point that client-centred responsiveness is a core feature of their work. They felt that in primary health care or in dental care, things might be different, since the core aim of their work is the management of illness, not interaction with clients.

Interestingly enough, professionals in these service units partly shared the same views:

> I think that the most useful element in the approach was that we paid attention to service processes, since our professional culture has hitherto concentrated solely on operations and the individual action of each professional.

By contrast, when the interviewees reflected on the results of the project in their respective units, scepticism regarding social work's client-centredness was also expressed.

Colin Morgan and Stephen Murgatroyd (1994: 139) associate the underuse of TQM strategies in social work with its strong tradition of advocacy on behalf of the client in view of which TQM brings nothing new. Another reason for the different learning processes in the various service units might be the way in which services are organized. In health care settings, there is a multiplicity of occupations and professions whose collaboration is the basic condition for client processing; whereas in social work, interaction concentrates on individual client-professional relations. In a team-working unit, the analysis of service processes and negotiations concerning service requirements is more useful, as they actually can reveal new perspectives and motivate reforms.

Although the participants' evaluations of the results of the project were moderate, some interesting results were reported. Firstly, the interviewees judged it to be a positive result that they now had a fuller understanding of what quality is about and how it can be measured and improved. In this respect, the project had increased their personal skills and the overall expertise of the organization. Quality had also meant opportunities to advance one's own career, give lectures or even to take more rewarding management jobs. What was actually happening was that "quality" was creating managers and experts out of professionals.

Secondly, the interviewees reported changes in their conceptions of their own organization. Especially for quality coordinators, participation in quality development teams was an opportunity to gain a more comprehensive picture of the organization. The similarities and differences in the work cultures of individual service units became more apparent, and progress towards a united vision and common goals was reported. These changes were believed to facilitate collaboration between units and professionals.

Thirdly, the interviewees perceived encouraging progress in the trend towards standardization and systematization of work and the development of contract culture among professionals:

> I was pleased to discover that quality is a contract-based concept. Because we have resource problems and we have to do the same amount of work despite our diminishing resources. I no longer worry so much or feel guilty if we don't succeed in getting everything done!

Though the evolving contract culture was believed to be beneficial both for clients and professionals, the interviewees' accounts and justifications stressed its importance for workers. Some reported that they became more resistant to the pressure of heavy workloads and that they no longer worried or even thought so much about practical performance-related details, since these things had been negotiated and were documented in the process briefs and quality manuals. However, most interviewees were unsure whether anyone actually used the manuals.

Fourthly, some interviewees, chiefly those in managerial positions, reported a tendency towards neutralization of interaction between professionals. They noticed that the systematization of feedback systems had the positive consequence that quality problems were not seen as caused by "difficult personalities". This meant that giving feedback to peers and other professionals had become a less emotional event.

Fifthly, those working in middle management, but also some front-line professionals in health services, indicated some changes in professional accountability and in its nature. In dental care, the importance of teamwork between dentist and nurse, and their shared responsibilities, became more evident. These minor signs of change could be interpreted as shifts from hierarchical accountability to lateral accountability (Munro, 1995), and from medicine domination to shared responsibilities between health professionals.

Sixthly, increased sensitivity to quality issues and client demands were reported:

I would say that I now give more thought to what the patient wants and expects when he comes here, not what I judge to be important in his situation.

Several examples of increased sensitivity to quality issues were described: for instance, colleagues' disturbances during client meetings caused more irritation among professionals than they had done before.

The interviewees expressed disappointment concerning results, too. Some of them had expected more radical innovations and new concepts in the way services are supplied. There had been no reduction in workloads, either. Some participants also observed that the quality management project did not touch the core of their professional work or have any innovative impact on its content (see Morgan/ Murgatroyd, 1994: 76-77). Professionals noted that in client interactions and professional discretion, they had essentially the same degree of autonomy as before.

4   Discussion

If one reflects on these accounts of the results, one can conclude that there are at least some elements in the professional cultures of health and social care organizations that make it feasible to implement business approaches to quality, such as

ISO 9000 and TQM. Firstly, since self-regulation mechanisms in most welfare professions are perhaps rather weakly institutionalized and subordinate to bureaucratic governance, professionals are already used to rules and detailed regulations, in which case ISO 9000 brings nothing fundamentally new to their work.

Secondly, professional epistemologies and business approaches to quality may have some elements in common, such as an emphasis on client or customer needs. Tuckman (1995: 75) notes that the rhetoric of TQM actually appears to draw it closer to the labour process of the professional than of the mass-production worker, as there appears to be a move towards autonomy and discretion.

Thirdly, there might be some elements of modern welfare professionalism that are unsatisfactory to workers (see Davies, 1995: 135-137). These repressed needs of professionals might be met at least to some degree by business approaches to quality:

a) Professionalism is divisive; it fragments welfare work into different service units, professions and occupations and into different professional languages. This condition seemed to distress the professionals interviewed, who strongly advocated increased interprofessional collaboration and the development of a common service language.

b) Professionalism emphasizes individual responsibility for the quality of services in circumstances where staff have little control over the resources available for supplying these services. This perspective helps us to understand the professionals' positive comments on the evolution of a contract culture which enables them to regulate the quality of services in a way that takes into account the available resources.

c) The traditional professional doctrine and training of welfare professionals does not touch on management issues. However, many practitioners will sooner or later advance to organizational positions where management skills and expertise are vitally important. The implementation of quality thus provides an opportunity to improve one's management skills and advance one's career.

Fourthly, since the labour force in social and health services is predominantly female, the question of gender might also be a relevant issue when considering the compatibility of business-oriented quality management and professional cultures in health and social services. Janet Newman (1995: 207) has made the point that men tend to dominate the technocratic and bureaucratic quality-assurance approaches linked to BS 5750, but female involvement in quality has brought "softer" approaches based on customer care and user involvement. Yet the final test comes in the practical implementation of quality-management approaches; women may perhaps have the ability to soften even the most technocratic approaches.

The application of these approaches might potentially bring changes to social and health services. On the other hand, it is questionable whether these changes are those most urgently needed, given the present state of welfare services. By creating a contract culture among professionals, business approaches to quality might have some effect on producer quality, i.e. the intrinsic features of the service as seen by those producing it (Pollitt/Bouckaert, 1995: 16). But considering the development of user quality (the quality of the service as seen by the user), their potential for change is less evident.

As emphasized earlier, when professionals utilize these approaches, they bring their professional interests and concerns to the implementation processes; and this will be visible in the results of the programmes, too. The crucial question is how welfare professionals as implementors orientate themselves; depending on their goals and preferences, quality reforms can advance both the status quo and change in health and social services.

Note

1   There is some conflict between professionalism and managerialism. Still, I have not made a clear distinction between managers and professionals in social and health services for several reasons. Firstly, in Finnish social welfare and health organizations, many of the middle managers also see clients, while front-line workers may also have managerial duties. Secondly, when I coded my data, I noticed an ambivalence in both managers' and professionals' perceptions of themselves. Nowadays, it is not fashionable to represent oneself as a professional, though not as a manager, either. It also seemed that the interviewees sometimes talked as managers, sometimes as professionals. Therefore, I prefer using the term "professional" or sometimes "welfare professional" in quite a broad sense to refer to highly-educated experts in welfare organizations.

References

Davies, C. (1995) *Gender and the Professional Predicament in Nursing.* Buckingham and Philadelphia: Open University Press.
Fisker, J. (1994) 'Kokeilustrategia muutosvoimana', in: Lindqvist, T./Rajavaara, M. (eds.), *Kehittämistyö itseanalyysiin.* University of Helsinki, Research and Training Centre of Lahti, Publications 8; STAKES (National Research and Development Centre for Welfare and Health), Reports 147, Helsinki.
Freidson, E. (1994) *Professionalism Reborn. Theory, Prophecy and Policy.* Cambridge: Polity Press.
Lindqvist, M./Rastas, M./Sihvo, T. (1994) *Väestö, asiakkaat ja sosiaalihuolto. Väestön ja asiakkaiden mielipiteitä sosiaalihuollosta.* STAKES (National Research and Development Centre for Welfare and Health), Reports 167. Helsinki.
Martin, L.L. (1993) *Total Quality Management in Human Service Organizations.* Sage Human Services Guide 67. Newbury Park, London and New Delhi: Sage Publications.

Merry, M.D. (1990) 'Total Quality Management for Physicians: Translating the New Paradigm', *Quality Review Bulletin* 4 (5).

Morgan, C./Murgatroyd, S. (1994) *Total Quality Management in the Public Sector.* Buckingham and Philadelphia: Open University Press.

Munro, R. (1995) 'Governing the New Province of Quality: Autonomy, Accounting and the Dissemination of Accountability', in: Wilkinson, A./Wilmott, H. (eds.), *Making Quality Critical: New Perspectives on Organizational Change.* London and New York: Routledge.

Naschold, F. (1995) *The Modernization of the Public Sector in Europe. A Comparative Perspective on the Scandinavian Experience.* Labour Policy Studies 93. Helsinki: Ministry of Labour.

Newman, J. (1994) 'The Limits to Management: Gender and the Politics of Change', in: Clarke, J./Cochrane, A./McLaughlin, E. (eds.), *Managing Social Policy.* London, Thousand Oaks and New Delhi: Sage Publications.

Pollitt, C. (1995) 'Improving Quality in Public Services: New Opportunities for Democracy?'. Paper presented at the 12th International Symposium "Towards More Democracy in Social Services: Models and Culture of Welfare". 11-13 October, University of Bielefeld.

Pollitt, C./Bouckaert, G. (1990) 'Defining Quality', in: Pollitt, C./Bouckaert, G. (eds.), *Quality Improvement in European Public Services. Concepts, Cases and Commentary.* London, Thousand Oaks and New Delhi: Sage Publications.

Sihvo, T./Uusitalo, H. (1993) *Mielipiteiden uudet ulottuvuudet. Suomalaisten hyvinvointivaltiota, sosiaaliturvaa sekä sosiaali – ja terveyspalveluja koskevat asenteet vuonna 1992.* STAKES (National Research and Development Centre for Welfare and Health), Research Reports 33. Helsinki.

Temmes, M. (1994) *Hallinto puntarissa. Hallintouudistusten arvioinnin mahdollisuudet ja edellytykset.* Ministry of Finance. University of Helsinki, Department of Political Science.

CHAPTER 6

Measuring Quality in Personal Social Services?

Monica Dowling

1   Introduction

> Quality ... you know what it is, yet you don't know what it is. But that's self-contradictory. But some things *are* better than others that is they have more quality. But when you try to say what the quality is, apart from the things that have it, it all goes *poof!* There's nothing to talk about. But if you can't say what Quality is, how do you know what it is or how do you know it even exists? If no one knows what it is then for all practical purposes it doesn't exist at all. But for all practical purposes it really *does* exist. What else are grades based on? Why else would people pay fortunes for some things and throw others in the trash pile? Obviously some things are better than others but what's the "betterness"? So round and round you go, spinning mental wheels and nowhere finding anyplace to get traction. What the hell is Quality? What is it? (Pirsig, 1974)

This chapter intends to get some traction on the concept of quality by investigating ways in which it can be measured in relation to community care policies and practice. Spinning mental wheels around the idea of quality will also include considering a wider framework within which user and carer research is sited in relation to community care. The three crucial issues which are to be considered are: How can quality be measured? How can social service users and carers contribute to a quality service? How can the quality of services be improved within a community care framework? Fieldwork findings from research in progress with Surrey social service users and carers will be integrated into the discussion where appropriate.

For the purposes of this study, but bearing in mind the debate surrounding who are users and carers as far as social services care is concerned (Barnes et al., 1996), "Users" are defined as individuals requiring social services help. "Carers" are defined as individuals who have, are or will provide family and community care for individual users. These definitions are necessarily broad because social service users and carers are not a static population. Birth, accidents, illness and the ageing process will mean that family members may suddenly or gradually require care in the community. Death, recovery from illness or accidents and teenagers growing older may mean that such services are no longer needed. Targeting policies of many social services departments may mean that potential users and carers are denied services unless they are in high need due to financial constraints. However the geography of where the individual lives and the timing of when they ask for help will determine whether they are defined as a social service user or carer by their social services department. "In and Out of Care" is as relevant for users of community care services as it is for children and young people using residential care.

2   How Can Quality Be Measured?

The dictionary definition of quality relates to degree of goodness or worth – a subjective description which reinforces Pirsig's (1974) discussion. The first diagram presented here suggests two models for assessing the quality of social services care. The models differ from management models and those related to TQM and the health services (Pollitt, 1996) in that they are grounded in qualitative research methods that are generally if not wholeheartedly accepted by the academic community.

The first measurement of quality on the right of the diagram is concerned with a methodology that understands process and interaction rather than merely outcomes. If we are concerned with means as well as ends in providing community care, it will be important to evaluate the ongoing attributes of day care or a night-sitting service as well as outcomes such as whether social services recipients have a Care Plan or have been satisfied with the promptness of response to telephone enquiries.

Participant and non-participant observation are ethnographic methods which are particularly useful for understanding the interactions between professional workers, the management hierarchy and social service users and carers. Such methods can explain why particular processes are unsatisfactory for users and carers, professionals and management by analysing prevailing attitudes and actions, the culture of the organization and the wider social policy environment (Satyamurti, 1981; Dowling, 1994). Participant observation offers a surprising, realistic and valuable method with which to understand for example how poverty impacts on social service users, and what role social workers play in this process. It may be equally useful for similar studies which seek to discover how individuals translate attitudes into

Figure 1:   Quality by Evaluation. Two Measurements of Quality in Social Services

Both of these measurements of quality of social work practice can lead to an improvement in services from an empowerment, managerial and consumerist perspective

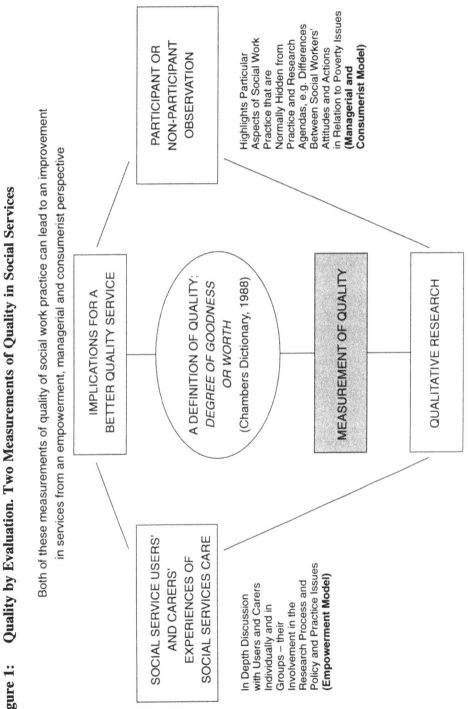

actions and it appears relatively unacknowledged as a research methodology that can lead to action research and the development of policy initiatives (Burgess, 1982; 1988). As a method of evaluating quality in social services, it is useful from a managerial and consumerist perspective because it allows purchasers and providers of services to understand how the organization operates at different hierarchical levels (Foot Whyte, 1984).

In-depth interviews and group discussions with users and carers as an evaluative method on the left of the diagram are part of a larger tradition of emancipatory qualitative research (Dowling, 1992; Rogers/Pilgrim, 1996), which aims to give individuals power to define their own research agendas and to have a say in the research process. Such research is now commonly connected with the idea of empowerment. Whether such research is ever really empowering for users and carers is a difficult question to answer. Some users and carers in this research who had a poor experience of community care or child protection policies did thank the interviewers for their help and in talking through the experience appeared to regain some personal power.

> *Mrs. Q.*: I am quite pleased that you came to see me because I feel I know a little bit more of what I should be asking for and I feel that you have reinforced me to say. Because I think I don't know how much I should really be saying because I feel helpless.
> *Int.*: Please be assured that you have every right to express your ongoing concern as K's parent and to be critical of the services and demanding of them to ensure that he comes out of this sorted out. You don't want to lose your son in care for years and find that at the end of it he is no better, or worse than when he went in.

Each user and carer interviewed in the research programme in Surrey has also been provided with a copy of the initial report for their client group which may stimulate more discussion in the follow-up interviews 12 months later.

User and carer monitoring groups have discussed whether the community care issues demonstrated in individual interviews is illustrative of the wider concerns of users and carers in each social service designated client group. A networking process has meant that individuals who are interested in the research in each client group are brought together to discuss the research issues that have been identified. In the ten research monitoring groups – one for users and one for carers in each of the five client groups – the process of discussing issues concerned with community care and feeding back comments on drafts of each report appears to be empowering in that users and carers are sometimes stimulated to further action. For example users on the mental health service monitoring group have formed themselves into a consortium to offer training on user issues to social services departments and intend to develop research as user academics. In the carer research monitoring group for children and families a parent of a disabled child commented on the draft qualitative report – *"I found the whole exercise very interesting as I am always happy to get involved in anything like this, in the hope that one day special needs children will get the services they deserve."* One of the users on the older people's research monitoring group who is a resident in a home applied to be an assessor of Surrey residential homes after his participation in the group, and asked me for a reference for the part-time post. He succeeded in his application.

3   How Can Social Service Users and Carers Contribute to a Quality Service?

The strengths and weaknesses of community care policies in relation to three different perspectives are illustrated in the following two diagrams. They demonstrate how user and carer perspectives fit with service models that until comparatively recently have been wholly concerned with professional and managerial issues. User and carer opinions are sought from both a consumerist and empowerment perspective. The difference between them being that the former benefits the organization with little regard for feedback or involvement with users and carers while the latter has a fundamental aim of ensuring that users and carers have more say in the policy-making process. Any research that is funded by a local authority can be accused of only being concerned with quality indicators, and satisfactions and dissatisfactions with current services with no requirement on the authority to implement recommendations. However the current research for Surrey although only 20 months into a 36-month programme is already creating a climate for change with elected officials and professional officers.

More than 200 social service users and carers in Surrey have been involved in discussing community care provision. They have included older people, individuals with mental health difficulties, learning disabilities or physical disabilities, parents of children with special needs and young people defined as "beyond care and control" or in need of protection. Most social service users and carers interviewed and involved in group discussion were clear and forthright in voicing their satisfactions, dissatisfactions and suggestions regarding how care in the community could be improved. From their perspective they understood the concept of quality and what could be defined as a quality service.

> *Mr E.:* I would like to see the Social Services more obvious at school level and information facts available to parents. There is an annual review of the child's Statement. I don't think it's beyond anyone's ability as part of the Statement for there to be Social Services involvement a little box on the Statement to the effect that this child is now or may be moving on to higher education. Parents feel that there will be a housing issue and Social Services should get a copy of that and pick up on these bits, then to contact the parents, make their own assessments using their own skills as to how able the parents are to look after the child over the next few years and then

Figure 2:   **Strengths of Current Policies and Practice Regarding Community Care**

SCIENTIFIC/MEDICAL PERSPECTIVE	CONSUMERIST/MANAGERIAL PERSPECTIVE	EMPOWERMENT PERSPECTIVE
"FITNESS FOR PURPOSE" HAS BEEN DEVELOPED FROM THIS PERSPECTIVE. MEDICATION, AIDS AND ADAPTATIONS ALLOW THE USER TO LIVE AS COMFORTABLY AS POSSIBLE IN THE COMMUNITY. EPIDEMIOLOGICAL, STATISTICAL AND FINANCIAL INFORMATION REGARDING THE NEEDS OF PEOPLE LIVING IN THE COMMUNITY AND IMPLEMENTATION OF POLICIES IS ORGANIZED THROUGH QUANTITATIVE DATA COLLECTION.	RESPONSIVENESS – DERIVED FROM THE "EXCELLENCE" APPROACH TO QUALITY IN COMMUNITY CARE, → THE DESIRE OF PROVIDERS TO SATISFY CUSTOMERS, → FLEXIBLE AND INFORMAL SYSTEM. PROVIDERS AT ALL LEVELS ARE RESPONSIBLE FOR SERVICE (HORIZONTALLY RATHER THAN VERTICALLY ORGANIZED STRUCTURES). A SERIES OF POLICIES AND PRACTICES THAT ENABLES WELFARE WORKERS TO GET CLOSE TO THE PUBLIC AND RESPOND QUICKLY (PFEFFER/COOTE, 1991).	THE PUBLIC HAVE ACTIVE INFLUENCE IN PLANNING AND DELIVERY OF SERVICES, → INDIVIDUALS ARE EMPOWERED AS CUSTOMERS AND CITIZENS. THERE IS A CHOICE BETWEEN ALTERNATIVE SERVICES AND/OR SUPPLIERS. PUBLIC PARTICIPATION, RIGHTS FOR CUSTOMERS AND CITIZENS (FINKELSTEIN/STUART, 1996) AND AN OPEN SYSTEM (PFEFFER/COOTE, 1991).

Figure 3: Weaknesses of Current Policies and Practice Regarding Community Care Services

SCIENTIFIC/MEDICAL PERSPECTIVE	CONSUMERIST/MANAGERIAL PERSPECTIVE	EMPOWERMENT PERSPECTIVE
WHAT *CAN'T* YOU DO? E.G. CRITERIA FOR ASSESSMENT OR ATTENDANCE ALLOWANCE. THIS PERSPECTIVE MAY CONCENTRATE ON IMPAIRMENT NOT DISABILITY OR WHOLE SITUATION OF USER AND CARER.	RESPONDS TO CONSUMERS' VIEWS BUT IS CRITICIZED FOR A SUPERFICIAL APPROACH WHICH DOES NOT LEAD TO CHANGE IN COMMUNITY CARE POLICIES OR PRACTICE.	CAN BE SEEN AS TOO RADICAL AND IDEALISTIC AND NOT PART OF CURRENT POLICIES AND PRACTICE.
INDIVIDUAL PROBLEMS, E.G. NOT BEING ABLE TO GO TO THE CINEMA IN A WHEELCHAIR → CAN LEAD TO "BLAMING THE VICTIM" AND LOW SELF-ESTEEM.	SERVICE PROVIDERS WANT TO MAXIMIZE THE THREE E's, *ECONOMY, EFFICIENCY* AND *EFFECTIVENESS*. THIS CAN LEAD TO TARGETING AND RATIONING CONTROLLED BY SERVICE PROVIDERS.	STIGMA IN RELATION TO INDIVIDUAL SITUATIONS AND/OR SOCIAL SERVICES CARE MAY PREVENT INDIVIDUALS FROM WISHING TO PARTICIPATE IN USER/CARER MOVEMENTS.
QUANTITATIVE DATA CONCERNING COMMUNITY CARE CAN DESCRIBE PROVISION OF SERVICES AND FINANCIAL EXPENDITURE BUT MAY NOT EXPLAIN INDIVIDUAL USER AND CARER NEEDS.	SERVICE USER ORGANIZATIONS ARE CONCERNED THAT CONSUMERISM IS TOKENISTIC AND ACTS AS A PUBLIC RELATIONS EXERCISE.	THIS PERSPECTIVE TENDS NOT TO RECOGNIZE PROFESSIONAL EXPERTISE AND THE ULTIMATE AIM MAY BE TO ABOLISH PROFESSIONAL CARE IN FAVOUR OF USERS AND CARERS HAVING RESOURCES TO ORGANIZE THEIR OWN SERVICES – WHO WANTS CARE IN THE COMMUNITY?
		EVEN A LESS RADICAL VERSION MAY EXPECT TOO MUCH CHANGE FROM SOME PROFESSIONALS IN TERMS OF GIVING AWAY THEIR POWER AND SALARIES AND DOWN-SIZING THEIR OPERATIONS.

look at long-term decisions. To educate the parents, to give sufficient facts for them to then be able to start asking sensible questions about the child's options, the parent's options, what is part of the infrastructure. If there are charitable trusts which you should get in touch with now who may provide a house which can transfer to the local authority, who they are, what they are. Things like that. Have you made a will? You have a child with problems, may we respectfully suggest you look in our direction. So you cover two things, your child and possible extra funding for Social Services. OK this will be directed at your child but so what? If it means buying a house and your child is one of four in that house, well ... We want E to have as fuller life as possible, and we want him to get out there and start doing it as quickly as possible. We don't want the situation of him living at home with us when he is still 30 as he won't have any social life, – he'll be lost in this house.

A quality service in relation to social services care needs to be worthy of recipients' approval. They need to be satisfied with the services they are receiving within the constraints of social services expenditure. If users and carers are not satisfied, another aspect of a good quality service may be their ability to complain and have the situation "put right" or for their recommendations regarding how a better quality service could be achieved taken seriously (Wilson, 1996).

Mr RG.: When you first found about the difficulties with your child did social services actually come and see you – or was it you phoning them? (To other Research Monitoring Group members). My opinion is that the Health Service should have a requirement to contact Social Services when anybody is diagnosed with whatever. Our experience was that our daughter was diagnosed as autistic at two-years-old, we went away, my wife was suicidal, it's one of the worst things that can happen to you. We wrote to Social Services they didn't even bother to reply to the letter. The reason was they didn't have a case manager in F. That is totally inexcusable, if there is not a case manager in F, those letters should be sent somewhere else for a reply. They are understaffed, these Managers keep changing from one office to another there is no continuity – nobody is taking responsibility. We were very upset with social services. We had no help at all.

Mrs D. was fostering a child with severe learning and physical disabilities. M. was initially diagnosed as having a limited life span but was now a teenager.

Mrs D.: Because of her bed wetting we go through an awful lot of bed linen and we have been through two mattresses in four years. Y. authority was always aware of these sort of things. Surrey have never said to us once "Do we need anything?". There were things that were standard with Y. M. has allergies, she is allergic to anything just about except for meat and two veg. She can start vomiting and get diarrhoea. It can go on for three or four days at a time. We have had it where she cannot control it, projectile vomit. Y used to say to us, "every four months we will have your carpets cleaned for you". They would clean her bedroom, the bathroom and the living room and that was done automatically. I never asked Surrey, it wasn't worth it – I knew I would never get it.

However, Mrs D. after much discussion with Surrey, admitted that she was finding care for M., that had gone on far longer than she was expecting, extremely difficult and Surrey arranged for long-term residential care for M. Mrs D was mostly satisfied with the way that this move was being handled.

4 How Can the Quality of Services Be Improved within a Community Care Framework?

Defining a quality service and then improving it from a user and carer perspective will have different flavours depending on the service required and the type of care provided. For example young people in residential or foster care had different perspectives regarding a quality service to those receiving mental health services.

T. is 14 and has absconded from school regularly for the last two years. She had been staying with foster parents because she was sleeping rough and her parents were concerned about her whereabouts in relation to possible criminal activities and her sexual behaviour. At the time of this interview, she had returned home to live. Quality of care for her was being settled in a school she liked, while an improvement in care would have been for the whole process to have been speeded up.

> T.: ... in Year 10 and 11 we are all put in the same class, and there are two teachers for seven pupils – so we get a lot of attention – all the teachers are like social workers – you can talk to them – they don't have favourites we are all treated the same which is good not like at a larger school, where they have favourites – I was never a favourite of any teacher ... Social Services sent me there so that was one good thing they did for me, it took me three months to get into that school.

A user member of the research monitoring group for mental health service users and carers felt that the quality of community care services for mental health service users is about providing a safety net for those discharged from hospital.

> Mr C: I think still largely with mental health the problem is loneliness and isolation. They're in their bedsits, they don't see anybody, they've got no money to go anywhere and in some ways it's quite nice for them, usually it's the social worker, then they lowered the salary and called it Community Support Worker. They would come along and knock on their door and say "Put the kettle on" or "I'll put the kettle on, you sit down and we'll have a chat for a minute". To some extent that's what a lot of them wanted. It's almost buying company, the government paying for their company. There probably is a better way of doing it than that but that's what they see the social worker as I think.

Improvement in the service would have meant employing a larger number of community support workers – preferably ex-users – to support individuals with mental health difficulties in the community.

Figure 4:   Quality by Evaluation

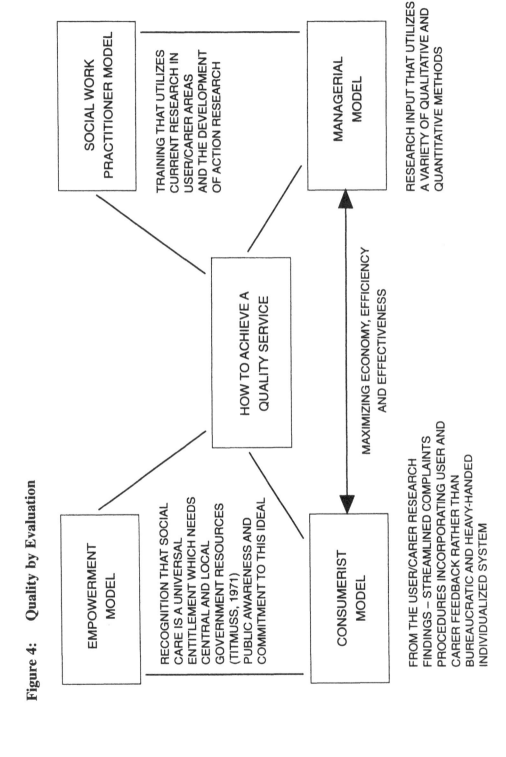

The medical perspective (see Figure 3) can pathologize mental health service users and "blame the victim" so that research that investigates the quality of after-care services, particularly from user and carer perspectives, is not recognized at all. Clinical research tends to exclude the views of patients or portray them as passive objects of study. For example the Medical Research Council's priorities for the funding of schizophrenia research ranks evaluation of services to patients as eighth out of ten priorities and user evaluation of services and treatment is not ranked at all (Rogers/Pilgrim 1996).

Using in-depth qualitative research can illustrate individuals' experiences and give indications of what they would consider a quality service. Although users and carers in different social care groups had varied satisfactions, dissatisfactions and recommendations for a better quality service, there were some strongly held opinions which transcended all user and carer groups. These were mainly concerned with the value and necessity of clear and accessible information in order that users and carers can make informed choices about the care provided. Although quality cannot be ensured by enabling customers to choose what they buy in an open market, people can make choices that are meaningful to them, if they have information regarding the alternatives open to them (Pfeffer/Coote, 1991).

Even if people were generally satisfied with actual services provided by social services in terms of home care, there was a significant level of dissatisfaction about such matters as lack of information about care options and the right of access to care plans, review notes and procedures, case records and complaints' procedures. Some people expressed this concern in general phrases such as *"we don't know much about it"*, or when asked about their expectations of Social or Health Services replied, *"we didn't have any information about what they do"*.

The final diagram (Figure 4) illustrates ways in which a better quality service can be achieved within social services departments. The perspectives included here do not rely on research inputs from users and carers alone but suggest that such research should be an integral part of a research and training input that can achieve a better quality service.

5 Conclusion

> Users of welfare services are not isolated individuals engaged in a series of one-off exchanges with welfare providers. Each individual's needs are interrelated, as well as being linked with those of others. This implies that it is necessary, if our interests are to be served, to have integrated planning for the system as a whole (Pfeffer/Coote, 1991: 25).

The principle of universal entitlement to social care is illustrated with a reference to Titmus's (1970) article on the gift of blood – blood donoring is still an active act of citizenship in the 1990s. Recognizing that the common bond of giving and receiving when and where it is appropriate to the individual may seem impossibly altruistic but a start could be made by the elimination of judgements about who is more deserving in community care - user or carer. This paper is mainly concerned with the establishment of a "voice" (Hirschman cited in Pfeffer/Coote, 1991) for social service users and carers. The market option of "exit" in relation to community care services is only available to those with resources or who are so dissatisfied they would rather do without any social care services.

Although it needs to be re-emphasized that this study of users and carers is exploratory in terms of its methodology and tentative in terms of its recommendations and conclusions, there have been a significant number of interesting findings that need to be backed up by further in-depth qualitative research. Perhaps the most important as it is a key principle in the Community Care White Paper (1990), is that social service users and carers are keen to have more of a say in the way community care services are provided for them.

It appears that the user and carer contributions are not always sufficiently appreciated or expected when planning community care services. However with a growing consultation process between user and carer groups and social services departments, it should be possible for all potential users and carers as well as those already receiving a service from social services to be provided with information regarding such groups. Not all users or carers will wish to be involved, but the networking approach that we have organized as part of the research process, indicates that users and carers may well feel less isolated in the community if they have user and carer group contact telephone numbers and the numbers of telephone information/support lines.

Walker (1993: 221-222) suggests an empowerment approach to community care planning. These series of qualitative studies for Surrey Social Services Department are aiming to emulate this approach in terms of giving social service users and carers a more powerful voice in establishing their views on the direction of community care services for the future.

> ... the user-centred or empowerment approach would aim to involve users in the development, management and operation of services as well as in the assessment of need. The intention would be to provide users and potential users with a range of realizable opportunities to define their own needs and the sorts of services they require to meet them. Both carers and cared for would be regarded as potential service users. Services would be organized to respect users' right to self-determination, and dignity ... Thus user involvement must be built into the structure and operation of SSDs and not bolted on.

References

Barnes, M./Harrison, S./Mort, M./Shardlow, P./Wistow, G. (1996) 'Users, Officials and Citizens in Health and Social Care', *Local Government Policy Making*, forthcoming.

Burgess, R. (1982) *Field Research: A Sourcebook and Field Manual.* London: Allen and Unwin.

Burgess, R. (1988) *Studies in Qualitative Methodology.* London: JAI Press.

Dowling, M. (1992) *Poverty and Social Work.* Unpublished Phd Thesis, University of Sheffield.

Dowling, M. (1994) 'The Restructuring of Welfare – What's in It for Social Service Users?', in: Page, R./Deakin, N. (eds.), *The Costs of Welfare.* Aldershot (England): Avebury.

Foot Whyte, W. (1984) *Learning from the Field: A Guide from Experience.* London: Sage.

Pfeffer, N./Coote, A. (1991) *Is Quality Good for You?* London: Institute for Public Policy Research.

Pirsig, R. (1974) *Zen and the Art of Motorcycle Maintenance.* London: Bodley Head.

Pollitt, C. (1996) *Business and Professional Approaches to Quality Improvement: A Comparison of their Suitability for the Personal Social Services.* Paper at International Seminar, Helsinki, 12-14 April.

Rogers, A./Pilgrim, D. (1996) 'Experiencing Psychiatry: An Example of Emancipatory Research', in: Wilson, G. (ed.), *Community Care – Asking the Users.* London: Chapman and Hall.

Satyamurti, C. (1981) *Occupational Survival, The Case of the Local Authority Social Worker.* Blachaell.

Titmuss, R. (1970) *The Gift Relationship: From Human Blood to Social Policy.* London: Allen and Unwin.

Walker, A. (1993) 'Community Care Policy; From Consensus to Conflict', pp. 204-226 in: *Community Care, A Reader.* Hampshire/London: MacMillan.

CHAPTER 7

Towards a New Client Orientation through Continuous Improvement

Maria Oppen

1 Introduction

In the wake of major restructuring in the public services along quasi-commercial lines, managerial concepts and methods that originated in the private sector are being transferred to public and welfare organizations in practically all OECD countries. Total Quality Management (TQM) is one of these approaches, and it is increasingly seen as the most promising and comprehensive strategy for the public sector to build quality right into the "production" process and delivery system of social services and to continuously improve them according to changing demands. Moreover, TQM is rapidly becoming an explicit managerial philosophy and toolbox for a structural and cultural transformation of bureaucratic organizations. TQM initiatives are reported at hospitals, day care institutions, schools, and municipal service departments for the elderly, usually connected with a variety of measures for improving productivity and efficiency.

The aim of this contribution is to explore the adaptability of the TQM-based strategies to public service organizations in the broader context of fundamental changes in the politics and the organization of the welfare state. On the basis of research into the modernization of health insurance organizations in Germany, it can be shown that a variety of these ideas and instruments are well suited for the successful implementation of client-centred structures of work and service provision. Nevertheless, business-oriented TQM requires modifications if it is to be installed in a public sector environment in such a way as to overcome a number of problems.

Changing Concepts of Quality in Changing Environments

Debates on deficiencies in the quality of social services and in the client orientation of welfare organizations in Germany, as in most other countries, have been
running for many years. Earlier, the concern with quality was generally implicit
rather than explicit: quality seemed to be mainly "the missing feature in services"
in all sorts of respect. However, in the scientific and public discourse over the
shortcomings of public services, the understanding of quality and client orientation has become more and more differentiated and comprehensive. Five stages can
be discerned where different quality dimensions were being highlighted; each stage
is connected with some form of political, institutional and organizational change:

MODERNIZATION BY AMALGAMATION: In the late 1960s and early 1970s, with the
mergers of smaller local authorities into larger local entities, bigger, more hierarchical and anonymous bureaucracies emerged. The concentration of functions and
the centralization of responsibilities, combined with the increasing regulation of
social and personal relations in an extending welfare state, were regarded as the
central causes of the growing gap between service organizations and the public
(*"Bürgerferne"*). The accessibility of services, transparency of responsibilities and
procedures, as well as the responsiveness of civil servants and service systems,
were critically illuminated.

MODERNIZATION BY PROFESSIONALIZATION: Associated with the reorientation of social politics from a compensatory to a preventive model, the range of personal social
services widened decisively in the early 1970s. Scientific expertise and such professional groups as education specialists, social workers, doctors and psychologists expanded enormously throughout the public sphere. In this respect, a dominance of experts with regard to the needs and standards of professional practice,
a bureaucratization and rule orientation in the handling of sensitive social problems and cases, and a further shift in the balance of power towards the professionals were all observed. In accordance with the ideas brought up by the "new social
movements" and in line with changing social values, there has been pressure for
a move towards both a restriction on intervention in the private sphere and a more
active role of clients concerning participation in decision processes or control over
measures taken and over procedures, as well as an activation of self-help and support
of self-help groups.

MODERNIZATION BY COMPUTERIZATION: Since the beginning of the 1980s, new risks
of deteriorating service quality have been discovered. Following the introduction
of information technologies in parts of the public sector, dangers of an increasing
standardization, formalization and uniformity of already-routinized service provision, as well as a growing "transparency" of the clients instead of the public agen-

cies involved have increasingly been identified as problems. It has been argued that the externalization of preparatory work to the clients and the growing demands for dealing with computer-based service production fosters the inequality of access to and distribution of services in a way that reinforces social stratification. Such dimensions of service quality as the equity and adequacy of welfare provision, limitation of interaction costs from the client's perspective, data protection and privacy, have all been stressed in this context.

MODERNIZATION BY CONSOLIDATION: Financial cut-back policies during the 1980s were another reason for quality being widely discussed in public. The political limitations of public expenditure led to decreasing standards in some welfare sectors; other services were not adjusted in order to meet new demands in a more flexible and pluralistic way; and under the headline of subsidiarity, some welfare functions were left or devolved to the lay system (families, self-help groups, non-profit organizations). These developments increased the need for new forms of service planning, coordination and integration. Above all, the quality of client orientation became dependent on the effective networking of different suppliers as well as on the provision of comprehensive advice and guidance to clients in the context of an increasingly complex public-private mix.

MODERNIZATION BY ECONOMIZATION: In the early 1990s, Germany entered – later than in many other countries – a fifth stage in which quality was invoked in relation to an entrepreneurial system of welfare service production. Widely termed as "New Public Management", a transformation process from a bureaucratic to a more market-like model was initiated in most OECD countries. By means of privatization and contracting-out, the state was to be reduced to its so-called "core functions". Large hierarchies in public organizations began to be broken down to a variety of more or less autonomous agencies. Responsibilities for tasks and budgets started being decentralized, and hierarchical and regulatory modes of control are currently being replaced by agreements or contracts. According to the underlying market philosophy, competition and consumer choice are now seen as central driving forces in an attempt to raise the efficiency and flexibility of service production.

With this commercialization of the public sector and its vision of creating modern, customer-oriented service organizations, the concepts and meanings of service quality are now being challenged. In contrast to the past, these now have to be debated in a much broader sense. Quality is increasingly becoming a central issue both in the market philosophy of state functions and in public spending as a parameter for directing, controlling, assessing and evaluating, both politically and managerially, the agreed-upon new production standards and service levels.

Thus, the interest in quality in the public sector is not new: what is new is the obvious acceptance of the view that quality is inherently an objective issue; that it can be "analysed, assessed and made the object of a concerted campaign of action" (Bovaird, 1996: 61). And in contrast to earlier concerns with quality, in the era of New Public Management (NPM) it has taken on various meanings for different stakeholders. Quality has thus become a controversially-debated and highly-politicized feature both of social services and of the welfare state as a whole, between different actors – politicians, public managers, competitors, employees, service users and citizens – against a background of tight fiscal restrictions.

A number of public organizations have already been competing for high scores in expert ratings and benchmarking processes in quality dimensions and best practices on both a national and international scale. Public contractors or purchasers have had to define quality into agreements and have started to impose conformance to some kind of quality assurance standards on external providers, or even to apply for their own accreditation for certain standards (e.g. ISO 9000). Competing providers operating under recently installed market-like conditions have tried to win bids or attract customers by guaranteeing high-quality services. Contract management is now based upon defined results and performance standards which have to be assessed in quantitative as well as qualitative terms. Market research has been initiated to find out about actual or expected standards of quality as perceived by users or citizens. Last but not least, the measurement of employee performance in service delivery is a prerequisite for developing new systems of performance-related pay.

What sometimes is referred to as the "quality revolution" in a period of public-sector transformation, is clearly linked to the neo-liberal (New Right) critique of the state and the bureaucracy, of the costs of public services and of a "civil-service mentality" (Tuckman 1995). By implementing market-like structures and cultures into the public sector, it is argued, it will be possible to meet customers' demands better and at distinctly lower costs. Part of the increasing appeal of Total Quality Management to public managers is that it promises considerable savings if the slogan "doing it right the first time" is fulfilled.

2   Philosophy and Principles of TQM

TQM was initially an outgrowth of concerns with Quality Assurance, where "fitness for use" and "conformance to standards" were associated with component manufacturing by sub-contractors and with just-in-time production methods. Whereas Quality Assurance broadly aims at preventing problems with quality by establishing a high-quality management system and assessing its adequacy, TQM is a more comprehensive approach to "improving competitiveness, effectiveness and flexibility through planning, organising and understanding each activity, and involving each individual at each level" (Oakland, 1993: 40).

To achieve Total Quality, a management system is required which seeks continuous improvement of structures, processes and outcomes, one which is to become the shared responsibility or, in the rhetoric of quality gurus, "obsession" of everybody involved in the design, production and delivery of services. Included are not only all sections of the organization (acting as internal customers according to the Japanese principle of "the next process is your customer" – see Lillrank/Kano, 1989) but also the supplier network, on the one hand, and the final service users and indirect beneficiaries (the citizens or the society as a whole) on the other.

In practice, a wide range of methods are being introduced in the public sector under the label of TQM, with little consensus on the scope of the term. Rather narrowly-limited projects – such as training in "customer awareness", surveys of perception of and satisfaction with services, and new forms of information policy – are just some examples (Pfeffer/Koote, 1991). Indeed, in some cases so-called TQM initiatives and the measures being invoked in its name are directed exclusively towards cost-cutting or service reductions in certain segments.

Although there seems to be some variation in interpreting the concept of TQM, many authors agree on a number of basic principles (Swiss, 1992; Oess, 1989; Hoffjan, 1994; Keehley, 1992):

The customers are the ultimate determiners of service quality, and not the people who serve them. The customer is anyone who receives the service (or information), regardless of his or her position inside or outside the organization. Customer expectations and solutions to quality problems have to be explored by surveys, discussions, joint improvement teams or through other feedback channels. Identifying and describing the users and their demands and perceptions is just a starting point for balancing the different requirements of citizens, employees, politicians, unions or external groups, as well as for specifying service features.

Quality has to be built into the service early in the design and production process, rather than "inspecting it out" of the process. The service has to be designed to be easily produced and if the personnel has the proper working conditions, training, resources and incentives to maintain high quality, to recognize defects and to avoid them, quality control and rework or users' complaints can be avoided. The results will be lower costs and higher consumer satisfaction.

Quality is the result of effective cooperation and coordination across departmental boundaries, and not of individual efforts. "When quality slips, it is almost always the system that is wrong, not the people" (Swiss, 1992: 357). In this respect, an individually-oriented appraisal and reward system is thought to mislead the employees. An effective system should encourage and enable all of them to perform well. This is not only a matter of training ("TQM starts with training and ends with training" – Oess, 1989), but of working structures that promote learning. Demming (1982) emphasizes the necessity of breaking down departmental barriers because horizontal communication and information (instead of rivalry) are essential for the quality of processes and output.

Quality requires continuous improvement. "Quality is considered a journey, not a destination" (Keehley, 1992: 12), because consumers' attitudes and expectations are changing. And this means constantly adaptating input, structures and processes. Quality Management organizes the critique, examination and improvement of "doing things better" through the use of certain procedures and tools.

Quality improvement requires everybody's participation. A core principle of TQM states that, with regard to re-training and management guidance, the employees are the experts for solving problems and improving processes. Organization-wide participation is crucial because employees are the ones who have to execute the principle "doing it right the first time". In quality teams or circles, it is necessary to break down hierarchical barriers and to discuss mistakes and defects and their prevention "without fear" between managers and staff.

TQM is therefore based on participatory leadership. Quality requires a total organizational commitment that focuses on all activities and on consistently producing and improving quality. The empowerment of employees for such a demanding quality approach is a vital task for management. Self-managed teams have to be built up, which, after some training (in job skills and improvement methods) and performance feedback, can take over responsibilities for decision-making and improving service delivery right at the level where customer satisfaction is constituted (Bovaird, 1996). An atmosphere of openness and trust – a prerequisite for delegating responsibilities – has to be established, one which again fosters initiative, autonomy and the ability to solve conflicts and problems.

Most of these management principles are not new. What is new is the holistic framework for concerted action: all members, structures and processes of an organization constantly have to change in order to improve quality. Some authors especially point to the initiation of cultural change as a factor distinguishing TQM from its origins in quality assurance (Tuckman, 1994). Where TQM is introduced in association with new working methods and work organization – such as team concepts or internal markets – and with a distinct customer orientation, cultural change will occur as a transformation of the employees' attitudes to working roles and styles, supplanting hierarchy with self-management and individual responsibility. In this way, TQM contributes to the ongoing development of NPM, as it creates a way of seeing organizational relations as market relations (ibid.: 731).

3 Continuous Improvement in a Health Insurance Fund

In general, German local health funds (*Ortskrankenkassen*) as well as some other public funds operating on national, industry or enterprise level, are non-governmental organizations subject to public law. They are self-governing bodies with elected board members (representatives from unions and employers' associations). Formally, the funds have been locally decentralized; after some changes in federal law, there has been a decisive development towards a "holding-like model" at the federal level. Historically, some competition has always existed between the different public and private funds regarding those groups of clients who were eligible (especially white-collar). Presently, eligibility is being extended to a nearly universal "freedom of choice".

The main function of any health insurance fund is certainly processing the insurance itself; but it also includes settling (collective) contracts with such service providers as doctors, hospitals or care centres. For the majority of the insured, the system works quite noiselessly, without any direct personal interaction – especially since benefits, services and entitlements are highly regulated by state law. There has, however, been a growing demand for personal information and advice by certain groups of clients – mostly the elderly, unemployed or low-income members who suffer from complex health problems and who are in need of benefits and services from a variety of welfare branches and service producers. In many such cases, the performance of service delivery by health insurance funds has actually grown into a dimension of interactive risk management, mediating between the different providing and financing parties and advocating clients' interests and demands in view of very complicated and constantly-revised regulations and domineering experts.

Though discretion in allocating benefits and services is rather limited, health insurance funds have quite some autonomy in fixing contribution rates, organizing the delivery process and – for the time being – in offering voluntary services in the field of health promotion and prevention. Building up a more client-oriented organization for service production and delivery has increasingly been emphasized in the insurance sector as a competitive edge. Meanwhile, such additional health promotion activities as fitness programmes or courses on nutrition or drug abuse have undergone quite some criticism as being inefficient and costly publicity measures.

The local health insurance fund examined below illustrates the implementation process of continuous improvement and how the culture of the organization underwent a change from a bureaucratic control-oriented to a client-oriented mode of service production.

3.1 A Brief History

The insurance agency in question[1] is a rather small one for its type, with slightly over 100 employees and roughly 50,000 insured (plus their family members). The starting point was the assignment of a new director – an economist – to the top of the administrative management. The director was immediately confronted with a number of serious problems:

- a decreasing market share (a loss of members) over a longer time period due to tough competition;
- shrinking revenue from contributions due to a changed structural composition in the membership (lower income, higher unemployment);
- rising expenditure due to scientific and technological developments in the medical sector;
- high staff turnover due to rather unattractive working conditions and career prospects; and
- relatively underdeveloped preventive measures and a rather erratic variety of health promotion activities.

The top manager, supported by the head of the self-governing body, started a process of change through continuous improvement. The strategy had its roots in various management approaches, not explicitly in TQM – at that time a foreign word in Germany, even for the private sector. But the principals being followed were mainly the same.

The *initial step* of the change process was clearly implemented top-down. A kind of mission statement was released that indicated the continuous loss of contributing members in the past and the corresponding reductions in the workforce. In order to avoid a further loss of jobs and, in the long run, to survive as an autonomous organization – it was argued – a major transformation into a modern service business with a distinct customer orientation had become necessary. To be able to compete successfully for additional members, the bureaucratic image (of a fund largely for blue-collar workers and the poor) was to be replaced by a culture and outward appearance of a flexible, efficient, innovative and business-like organization where customers could not only rely upon the high-quality provision of all mandatory services but also receive additional benefits from so-called "voluntary services". A clearly-stated goal was that higher priority should be given to preventive action, not only through additional service offers but also in administrative case-handling with the prospect of savings in curative expenditure over the long run. Three main paths towards a new client orientation were emphasized:

- product innovation (the readjustment of existing services and the introduction of new ones);
- process innovations (the simplification of procedures and organizations, new technology and working methods);

- social innovations (new management styles and tools, as well as new forms of cooperation, communication and training).

A *next step* was to set the initial agenda for change at the management level. For this purpose, the "organization's readiness for transformational change" (Reid 1995: 193) was assessed; this required the identification of the initial units, followed by possible savings and additional costs as well as expected barriers and opponents.

It was concluded that restructuring should start in the service department, the largest of the four departments, because of its specific closeness to the customer and the costs of a wholesale change process. Four main goals for restructuring were formulated and transmitted to all staff members:

- to build flatter structures by delegating responsibilities to the "front line";
- to introduce self-managed teams with equal qualification and pay levels;
- to integrate formerly horizontally-fragmented tasks as well as paperwork and direct services; and
- to make the client the centre of all the organization's activities.

The *third step* was a rather radical top-down intervention by stipulating an exchange process across departmental borders to place the formally most qualified and personally-motivated staff into the new client-oriented team structures on a voluntary basis. The reallocation of personnel was supported by a range of training facilities. After a major overhaul of the whole building, a new and larger reception area was established which enabled teams to cooperate in fulfilling their administrative tasks and, at the same time, be available for encounters with clients.

As a *fourth step*, after the teams had organized themselves, the actual participative improvement process itself was then initiated. Cross-functional and cross-sectoral groups and projects were successively built up with short-term defined tasks. At the beginning, these were centred around innovating work processes according to customer demands with the aim of more or less all-around service provision:

- identifying the main customer groups with their different demands, as experienced by the employees (contact analysis), and reflecting on customer-oriented segmentations;
- identifying the main processes according to the core priorities of the organization, tracing inefficient rules and routines as well as sources of defects and delays, and making proposals for simpler structures and processes;
- clarifying the new profiles of hierarchical positions, of responsibilities and of the various competences of service providers; and

- exploring demands and possible benefits for employees (greater discretion, better qualifications, less stress) and of possible losers in flatter structures, and then suggesting new tasks, responsibilities and training requirements for the latter.

The *fifth step* followed after the new organization of service production and delivery had been implemented. The staff began to accept their new functions and responsibilities and incorporated client orientation into their decision-making and interaction. The improvement groups then started to make suggestions for the involvement of users in the search for such innovations as

- encouraging clients to make complaints and suggestions, and then systematically evaluating them;
- making surveys on demands and perceptions of both the service profile and delivery; and
- using other feedback channels, such as involving user groups in the improvement process.

Organizational structures and processes were then adapted according to customer expectations.

A further step envisaged was the investigation of relationships, cooperation and contracts with external organizations (doctors, hospitals, schools and enterprises), with the aim of transorganizational improvement of the overall "process chain"; special emphasis was put on the development of corporate and community-based prevention strategies.

3.2 Major Effects

Approximately three years after restructuring activities had been initiated, an improving organization emerged as opposed to the traditional model (see Table 1). Furthermore, a variety of positive results with respect to client needs and expectations could be observed. Here, I concentrate on the central group, the insured users.

ACCESSIBILITY: Opening hours had been extended immensely and ran from 7:30 a.m. to 6:00 p.m.; two additional local advice offices had been opened, and more employees had been assigned for face-to-face work. There were virtually no queues. And quite some improvements were made concerning the clearness and simplicity of basic information on services, standards and application procedures.

SPEED OF DELIVERY AND RESPONSIVENESS: Resulting from the "lean" organization, a decisive gain in efficiency could be observed; the reduction of multiple processing and rework in general led to quick decision processes and a shortening of response time. Indirect service work concerning acute demands (such as distribution of monetary benefits, vouchers and other allowances) were processed and posted immediately ("the same day", according to set standards); due to the delegation of competence to the "front line", most decisions (with clearly stated exceptions) were made directly in the presence of the client by the employee with no need to consult superiors or other units.

COMPETENCE AND RELIABILITY: In contrast to the earlier bureaucratic procedure, the problem of finding the person in charge vanished. Employees "all-around" responsible for direct personal services became highly skilled (highest level of vocational training and additional courses in inquiry and problem-solving methods) and highly motivated through an evolving service culture and positive client feedback. Clients themselves felt that their needs and expectations, especially in situations of severe and complex health problems, were being handled comprehensively. They appreciated the provision of more comprehensive information and the fact that they were being supported professionally and even with empathy. The feeling of coming face to face with authority had widely been replaced by one of cooperation.

QUALITY "IN FACT": New working procedures of integrated case-handling, decision-making and mutual control by small teams aware of the whole case history and who often knew the client personally were not only more efficient: the number of errors or incorrect decisions was reduced (to those mainly due to data-input mistakes) thanks to better skills and team cooperation and a kind of monitoring system implemented across work teams discussing complicated or unclear cases. And, in accordance with client orientation, claimants were being instructed on alternative services or additional provisions, thus enabling them to play an active role in the decision process and to exert choice.

ADDITIONAL SERVICES: The former in-house provision of a number of direct services in the health-promotion and -prevention field (such as courses and counselling on the special health risks of various drugs or on nutrition, sports, or the environment) were outsourced to more professionalized providers. The fund reduced its operations in these fields to information and advice about who is providing what kind of service to what quality standard. Coordination, networking and the financial support of external service provision and self-help activities were systematically extended. And quite a few innovations were introduced in the rehabilitation sector, where direct assistance was offered for arranging benefits, medical treatment and occupational settlements.

Table 1: Traditional and Improving Organization of Service Production According to TQM Principles

	Traditional Organization	Improving Organization
Planning	Short-term, based on legal obligations and curative intervention	Long-term, based on improvement mission, preventive orientation
Clients	Needs and services defined by experts and law. As a central obstacle to an efficient bureaucracy. Must adapt to administrative structures and procedures	Needs and services defined additionally by clients' expectations and suggestions. As a centre of all activities. Structures, processes and interaction organized according to the clients' conditions
Products and services	According to separate legal obligations by the respective departments	According to user groups' expectations and by cross-functional teams
Work organization	Hierarchical structure and centralization of decisions and control. Horizontal and vertical fragmentation of tasks and processes	Decentralization of responsibilities, flatter structures. Vertical integration (teamwork, "all-around" competences), user-group specific segmentation
Qualification	High standard at entrance, erosion of skills and knowledge by specialization	High priority on further training and on working structures that promote learning (rotation)
Errors and problems	Do not exist or are tolerated to a certain degree, "inspected out" and sanctioned above that standard	Are a valuable starting point for improvement activities aimed at "doing it better the next time"
Improvement	Focused on "one-time breakthroughs" in a special area by individual managers and inspection specialists	Is a continuous and holistic approach. Teamwork across boarders of organization, internal and external
Contracts	Based on costs	Based on costs, quality according to end users' requirements

4 Suitability of TQM to Welfare Services

4.1 Barriers

TQM is an approach developed in the business world most especially for the production of industrial goods. In public service organizations, one is confronted with a number of implementation problems specific to the public sector that do not have a major impact on private industry. Two of these seem to be especially important: the political arena to which the improvement strategy has to be adapted differs in many aspects from the managerial regime; and the quantity/quality dilemma that public organizations face is unknown to the market sphere.

TQM must start at the top of the organization and have its full support with an "almost single-minded commitment to quality" (Swiss, 1992: 359). Empirical results so far indicate that successful basic restructuring processes in the public sphere are built on a strong coalition of top managers and leading politicians from the respective governing bodies. But rapid turn-over at the top, combined with a political culture and structure open to outside forces, constitutes an organizational regime that is necessarily weaker than those in private enterprises. Therefore, in a political arena, it is more difficult to "maintain the constancy of purpose required by TQM" (Rago, 1994: 63).

The strategy of continuous improvement is clearly not a "quick and cheap solution" to organizational problems; on the contrary, it is rather demanding in terms of resources. Gains in efficiency and quality may not be observable for five to seven years after the start of continuous improvement processes (see Kamiske/Malorny, 1994). Yet politicians usually do not think and act in the long term; they need quick results dictated by election periods. This is especially true during times of fiscal austerity, where cost reduction is the main, if not the only, goal. The initial organizational consensus in our health insurance fund that is said to be vital for long-term success eroded with a changed composition of board members and the subsequent designation of a new chief executive who was obviously not convinced of the organizational model and participation principle; this development clearly placed a question mark over the scope for the ongoing routinization of continuous improvement.

Some features of service quality standards are set politically by federal programmes, laws and regulations. Social policy is one of the fields that is constantly subject to state intervention, especially during times of high unemployment and rising social needs. What constitutes a poor standard that should be improved in the eyes of customers and the service provider today, may thus be sufficient quality tomorrow following political redefinitions. Under such circumstances, it is sometimes difficult to keep staff motivated to participate in the endeavour for improvement at ever-lower service levels. And it is even more difficult to convince clients whose cooperation was asked yesterday in the "search for excellence", of the necessity of reduced service standards today in line with new governmental regulations, especially as users tend not to differentiate between political programmes and their implementation by public service organizations.

Two such examples of state interventions aiming at cost containment may call into question the change-management approach of health insurance funds: the retrenchment of local organizational autonomy in favour of a centralization policy at the federal level has already gone into effect; and the change for a preventive orientation of the overall business strategy presently seems to be counter-acted by a government seeking to cut off the use of funds in the health-promotion field. Under these circumstances, it seems to be a rather difficult task to constantly re-enforce and support the necessary commitment of all members of the organization.

The last problem mentioned strongly relates to the quantity/quality dilemma in the adaptation of continuous improvement to the public sphere. The appeal of TQM in the private sector is tied to the idea of a "chain reaction" (Deming, 1982) of cost reductions in quality inspection, a higher-quality product, a higher market share, more satisfied employees and rising employment. In most social service organizations, the opposite is true. Any definition of quality is always constrained by cost. In the public sector, however, the expansion of services and/or customers is typically not correlated with an expansion of revenue. As the service provider's funding is usually limited, an increase in services provided often goes along with the decrease in the budget share per member or per potential customer entitled to a service. Social service agencies operate in a "market" where demand nearly always exceeds production capacities (see also Rago, 1994): either people actually in need and entitled do not receive a service because of their lack of information and ability to enforce their claims, or clients do not get the full service they require. Thus in the past, inferior services often have been a means of limiting public spending.

The rise of the quality of advice and support given in our health insurance fund raised in many cases the amount of monetary benefits or direct services being claimed. The according rise of expenditures would have had to be counterbalanced in the long run by hindering inadequate or unneccessary claims so as to keep contribution rates stable – a task that actually was not undertaken because of possible negative effects on the image of client orientation. Furthermore, improved quality in labour-intensive direct services is often dependent on the assignment of additional and better-qualified staff. Empirical findings point especially to the resources that can be mobilized by implementing flatter structures, the re-engineering of work processes and the efficient use of information technology. But certainly, the re-allocation of staff from routinized administrative tasks to direct work with clients tends to become distinctly confined once a transformation from a bureaucratic to a business-like service model is established.

To the extent that better service provision attracts more clients without increasing returns, the management of any public service organization frequently has to solve the dilemma of whether to expand services in quantitative terms, or to further improve quality. In contrast to the private sector, where profitability and market expansion are clear targets, the ultimate goal for TQM initiatives in the social service system is far more ambiguous. Hence, integrating the demanding TQM approach to any organization in the welfare sector will inevitably imply debates between politicians, managers, employees, and different groups of customers and citizens over conflicting interests and changing social values.

4.2 Chances

Empirical research suggests that, for a number of reasons, some TQM principles are especially well suited for transforming welfare bureaucracies into client-oriented service providers and especially for continuously improving their quality.

Client dedication has long since been the character lacking in public-service production and delivery. In many welfare organizations, the client was either ignored or regarded as a nuisance disturbing the daily working process. Experts usually defined quality standards according to legal rules and procedures, and face-to-face work was subordinated to internal bureaucratic requirements and traditions. The central importance accorded to clients or customers in the TQM approach is perhaps its most valuable feature. In stressing the need for explicit, public (not necessarily quantified) service standards which reflect (in the public sphere, not exclusively) users' judgement on the effectiveness, adequacy and quality of services, it limits the traditional predominance of "experts" and the power of officials over those "processed" (Walsh, 1990). And the involvement of the client in the production process of services makes it almost impossible to manage quality internally. Feedback systems, from surveys to regular meetings with the user groups or with mixed evaluation panels, can be useful instruments to learn about the users' perceptions, complaints and suggestions, and to take them as a point of departure for the continuous improvement of processes, procedures, staff and the organization of service provision as a whole. Empirical findings have illustrated that actual improvements had been achieved in a number of quality dimensions by putting the client at the centre of all activities, instead of fitting him or her into bureaucratic routines and procedures.

Continuous improvement, if internalized by workers and consistently facilitated by management, is another valuable contribution to building client-oriented and flexible service systems in the public sector. Not only are the client/citizen demands consistently changing due to individual and societal changes: the legal conditions of service provision and the resources available are – as mentioned above – usually unstable. The establishment of this principle will reduce the danger of the innovation process stagnating after the initial positive results, and it will enhance the openness and ability of both an organization and its members to flexibly adapt to changing environments ("learning organization").

There is little doubt that the work-process orientation of TQM, by taking into account the overall "service chain" in connection with a holistic understanding of quality (of work, of results, of management and of the organization as a whole) is especially well suited to service organizations. The first reason is that the major aspect of the interaction between the organization and its customers is the service itself: a process of co-production. The quality of working conditions, work routines, skills and employee motivation are to this extent components of service quality as experienced or perceived by the client. Secondly, the quality of a service naturally cannot be reduced to the interaction process itself. It usually relies to a significant extent on a variety of activities from the back office or some other department which cannot be judged by the client, but where the quality of their work is equally important for the overall quality of the result. One-sided consumerist approaches to quality often fall short of this perspective, concentrating instead on the redesign of the interface between service provider and end-user. A third reason is that this perspective directs management's attention to improvement towards the overall process chain. The treatment or help needed in many social situations is spread over quite a number of different providers. The quality of the service may thus be dependent not only on the sum of the single activities or measures taken, but also on their interplay and harmonization. In the case presented above, a comprehensive management of quality directed towards the "service chain" as a whole – by not only breaking down internal, sectoral and functional demarcations but also the borders towards other organizations in the provision of welfare services – only emerged during the ongoing improvement process.

Worker participation has long been seen as an important prerequisite for successful innovation processes, but one difficult to realize in practice. The TQM concept presents – with such quality infrastructures as quality circles, steering committees or quality managers – not just concrete organizational steps in this direction; it also emphasizes the need for special training programmes to enable participants to communicate, to solve problems and to evaluate goal achievements. The continuous inclusion of all parties involved in improvement processes provides the opportunity to balance differing norms, requirements, expectations and judgements of quality.

Note

1   The case presented here is one of several case-studies that had been prepared during a research project concerning developments in work organization and service quality in the wake of computerization. The database was established in the middle of the 1980s, and a follow-up study was undertaken in 1992 (see Oppen, 1995).

References

Bovaird, T. (1996) 'Performance Assessment of Service Quality: Lessons from UK National Initiatives to Influence Local Government', in: Hill, H./Klages, H./Löffler, E. (eds.), *Quality, Innovation and Measurement in the Public Sector.* Frankfurt.

Deming, W.E. (1982) *Out of the Crisis. Quality, Productivity and Competitive Position.* Cambridge: Cambridge University Press.

Hoffjan, A. (1994) 'Qualitätsmanagement in der öffentlichen Verwaltung', *Verwaltungsrundschau* 1.

Kamiske, G.F./Malorny, C (1994) 'TQM – ein bestechendes Führungsmodell mit hohen Anforderungen und großen Chancen', in: Kamiske, G.F. (ed.), *Die Hohe Schule des Total Quality Management.* Berlin/Heidelberg: Springer Verlag

Keehley, P. (1992) 'TQM for Local Governments', *Public Management* 8.

Lillrank, P./Kano, N. (1989) *Continuous Improvement. Quality Control Circles in Japanese Industry.* Ann Arbor: Center for Japanese Studies, The University of Michigan.

Oakland, J. (1993) *Total Quality Management: the Route to Improving Performance* (2nd ed.). Oxford.

Oess, A. (1989) *Total Quality Management. Die Praxis des Qualitätsmanagements.* Wiesbaden: Gabler.

Oppen, M. (1995) *Qualitätsmanagement. Grundverständnisse, Umsetzungsstrategien und ein Erfolgsbericht: die Krankenkassen.* Berlin: Edition Sigma.

Pfeffer, N./Coote, A. (1991) *Is Quality Good for You?* London: Institute for Public Policy Research.

Rago, W.V. (1994) 'Adapting Total Quality Management (TQM) to Government: Another Point of View', *Public Administration Review* 54 (1): 61.

Reid, M.F. (1996) 'Organizing for Innovation: Triumph of Orthodoxy?', in: Hill, H./Klages, H./Löffler, E. (eds.), *Quality, Innovation and Measurement in the Public Sector.* Frankfurt.

Swiss, J.E. (1992) 'Adapting Total Quality Management (TQM) to Government', *Public Administration Review* 4.

Tuckman (1994) 'The Yellow Brick Road: Total Quality Management and the Restructuring of Organizational Culture', *Organization Studies* 15/5.

Walsh, K. (1991) 'Quality and Public Services', *Public Administration* 69: 503.

CHAPTER 8

Combining Client Interests with Professionalism in the Organization

Gabriëlle Verbeek

1 Introduction

Since the early 1980s, the quality of care and welfare provision has become an important "issue" in the Netherlands, mostly for reasons similar to those in other countries. On the one hand, good care is regarded as very important in Dutch society. It is highly valued. On the other hand, health care provision constitutes a major category of expenditure in the gross national income. One of the reasons behind quality control and quality improvement pertains to the "value-for-money" argument. Another reason has to do with increasing competition in the health-care field, which gives incentives to lower prices and ensures higher levels of quality. Those receiving care set their own requirements as to provision. They want care and assistance to be client-oriented and tailor-made.

From the mid-1980s, quality control and quality improvement have increasingly been the object of policy attention. Care providers, client-interest groups, health insurance companies and governmental agencies have aimed at national agreements on the development of quality-control systems. Since 1990, these national agreements have had to be evaluated and adjusted every five years. Some results of this policy are visible in the service organizations.

2 The Development of Quality Control and Quality Improvement

Numerous methods and systems have been developed to ensure quality care. Table 1 offers an overview of the types of activities undertaken in the Netherlands with a view to providing quality care. The term "internal", as used here, means that the activities were developed by and for the care providers (i.e. care workers and managers) for the purpose of improving their professional performance.

Institutions outside the care-provision sector have also developed various methods and instruments to test and improve the quality of care from an external perspective. These institutions include the Dutch Government's monitoring body on public health, user organizations and insurance companies, etc.

There is a distinction between activities that create the conditions important to the successful provision of quality care and those that involve the actual provision of quality care by means of methods and instruments geared towards quality improvement. The term "quality system" (system of monitoring quality) is used as an umbrella term in the Netherlands. A quality system is a system of established managerial regulations and procedures aimed at ensuring that a product or service satisfies the set requirements.

Table 1:   Overview of Methods and Systems of Quality Improvement from Internal Care Providers and External Institutions

	Internal	External
Conditions of quality care	 • In-service training programmes • Information system • Personal policy • Job description • Views on care	 • Training • Legislation on quality • Description of occupation
Methods and instruments	*Management* • Detection of problems • Market research • Consultation of users • Comparison of organization • Visitation/testing • Quality plan *Professional care workers* • Registration • Accreditation • Visitation • Behavioural code • Supervision • Shared vision • Colleague evaluation • Quality circles • Quality plans • Protocols • Consensus meetings	 • Inspection • Test for users • Insurance policy • Professional codes • Professional standards • Disciplinary rules
Quality system	• Internal quality system	• Certificates • ISO standards

In 1995, a random survey of 1,100 organizations was carried out from all sectors of the care system. The survey indicated that 13% of all organizations have implemented a system of quality monitoring. Here, measures and methods for quality improvement were applied in the entire organization, in all departments and professional disciplines. Additionally, in 59% of the organizations, systems of quality monitoring were in a stage of development, yet no overall management was established; measures were introduced only in some departments of the organization. Another 26% of the institutions were in a stage of initiation, making a plan without any visible actions at the moment. Finally, only 2% of the organizations in this survey did not take any initiative at all.

Such figures suggest that quality improvement finds itself in a rather well-developed stage in the Netherlands. Nevertheless, from a more detailed perspective, major bottlenecks can be recognized. One of them concerns the problem of quality improvement at the operational level in service organizations. When we focus on the interactions between clients and professionals, one of the issues is how to combine a client-oriented approach with professionalism.

Firstly, some general lines of the dilemma involved will be briefly sketched. Secondly, two projects set out to meet the aforementioned challenge will be presented.

3 Clients' Preferences and Professional Practice

An important part of quality management is ensuring a demand-oriented, client-oriented organization. This is so self-evident that it is hardly a matter of discussion. Increasingly, organizations are preparing for user needs with positive outcomes. For example, the quality of hospital food has improved considerably over the past few decades. Some 10 to 15 years ago, hospital food had a bad reputation: tasteless, lacking variety and overcooked. A substantial improvement in quality was achieved by paying more attention to consumer choice, using better ingredients and in particular applying better methods when preparing meals. Nowadays it is fairly normal to have an *"à la carte"* menu in hospitals. Modern techniques have supported this achievement. Hospital cooks have begun to work in a way that is at the same time more professional and more client-oriented. There is no problem in combining these elements.

However, sometimes the issue of combining client orientation and professionalism is more complex. Professional standards and clients' preferences are not always identical. A client seeking professional help may find that a professional will not automatically perform the activities which the client prefers. This can be illustrated with an example in the practice of dieticians, namely the giving of nutritional advice in case of overweight. Obese people experiencing overweight by 20 or 30 kilos want to get rid of their extra weight as quickly as possible. Once they have decided to visit a dietician for nutritional advice, their prevailing orientation is to lose weight fast – and a great many kilos at that. From the medical point of view, however, this might not be the most sensible approach. Rapid weight loss seems to cause metabolic changes which brings people to regain additional weight very quickly.

The dietician encountering the problem of obese persons will generally advise a gradual decline in weight and a careful adaptation of the composition of one's diet. But the client is not looking for this sensible advice: the client wishes to lose weight quickly. This opens the possibility of argument. Many clients tend to reject the dietician's advice because they are dissatisfied with the professional approach.

4   Professional Dilemmas

This example indicates a clear dilemma between professional norms and clients' preferences. So is good care the care which the client is asking for, then? Or is it the care that the professional finds best? The dietician can try to convince the client to stick to a diet which is in his/her best interest in the long run; but this may be unacceptable to the client. Of course, it is up to the client to consent to whichever treatment he/she chooses.

The situation grows even more complex when professional norms or client preferences do not coincide with standards or working routines on the part of the organization by which the professional is employed: for example, the organization's policy to reduce the percentage of client "drop-out".

How must professionals act when their quality standards or those of their clients are incompatible with the "rules" of the care-providing organization? Everybody who has delivered professional care can tell that organizational rules sometimes neglect or even violate the interests of individual clients. Sometimes professionals deliberately and cleverly avoid the organizational rules in order to help their clients adequately. A home-care professional once told me that she would often visit a particular client on her day off, to do a little extra shopping for instance, together with her own shopping. This was against the organization's rule not to get involved with clients outside of working hours. The organization's argument was, "We want to protect our employees' leisure time". And also, "There must be a clear distinction between professional work and private activities". But in this case, the professional chose to follow her own standards and the client's wishes.

The type of problem with which we are dealing here cannot be solved easily. Developing formalized standards and criteria for service delivery is only a partial solution. It will produce a general framework. The standards and values of users, professionals and organizations can be combined to a certain extent. But everyday practice shows that this framework is not sufficient in itself. Professionals experience bottlenecks or conflicts in views and interests on a daily basis.

Vitally important in this context is to make their kind of problems the subject of discussion, training and action. Professionals have to recognize the differences in interests and viewpoints and to make them more explicit. Additionally, they should be equipped with methods that are helpful in dealing with these situations.

5 Equipment on Behalf of Professionals

In the Netherlands, several experimental projects have set out to support professionals with methods to enable them to solve problems and to realize quality improvement. Two of them were carried out by the Netherlands' Institute of Care and Welfare (NIZW) in the sector of home care. We will describe them briefly.

In the Netherlands, there are approximately 150 home care organizations, and more than one million inhabitants a year have dealings with them in one way or another. Assistance and care provision varies from support in domestic tasks to very specialized forms of care, from preventive care for babies and toddlers to care for the chronically-ill and for people with disabilities.

The first project described here is based on the idea of "quality groups"; the second is focused on the concept of "user feedback".

5.1 Quality Groups

The NIZW has initiated this project for quality improvement in home help services. In the Netherlands, about 300,000 households utilize home help services. The majority of clients consists of elderly people who wish to continue an independent way of life in their own home on the basis of additional formal help and care. The professionals working in this area are home helpers. A large part of them are semi-skilled and unskilled women working part-time. They often possess a great deal of practical experience with domestic chores and personal care tasks directed at households with both children and elderly people. The work of home helpers is carried out in a relatively autonomous way. Each home helper has her own group of clients. Each client is visited at least once a week. Problems experienced in the concrete delivery of services are often related to a lack of clarity on the relevant task requirements, rights and duties. Due to the lack of professional standards, considerable differences exist in the mode of job performance of these home helpers.

In the project, we have developed a plan to enhance quality improvement for the practical day-to-day work in home help services. The general objective of the project was monitoring and improving the care provided by home helpers. Additional objectives were stimulating professional development in the group of home helpers, raising the levels of quality consciousness, and reinforcing the learning abilities of home helpers.

Points of departure were initially defined as follows:

1) home helpers are able to improve the quality of their own work;
2) they must be given the opportunity to tackle problems in their work and to solve them as a team and in a methodical manner;
3) they themselves are responsible for the introduction of improvements in their work, supervised by their team managers; and
4) they have to make use of a method that is easy to handle.

The method cannot be too abstract and has to be based both on creativity and the experiences of those who carry out the tasks. The method is carried out by so-called "quality groups". In some respects, the concept of quality groups resembles the Japanese idea of quality circles, although there are major differences.

Quality groups are teams of six to ten home helpers who interact with each other in the normal course of their work. The group chooses a work-related problem which refers to the working situation with the client. The participants have to solve problems within their own range. These are everyday difficulties that are very important to home helpers and clients. Examples listed by the quality groups in our project include inadequate consultations with clients, insufficient knowledge of chronic diseases, incomplete information on cleaning products, problems in planning work activities, managing the keys of clients' homes, and the question of the client-oriented approach to regulations within the organization.

The participants of quality groups must take three viewpoints into account: that of the client, that of the organization and their own, the professional one. For this purpose we introduced the symbol of a "quality triangle". By working with a triangle of norms and interests, we wanted to achieve the goal of home helpers developing their own professional way of thinking while at the same time carrying out their work in a client-oriented way. In addition, they were challenged to gain a better insight into the organizational consequences of their work.

Figure 1:   Triangle of Interests

Table 2:   Quality Groups – Steps in Problem-solving

1 Selecting a subject
2 Deciding on the improvement objective
3 Drawing up a plan of action
4 Implementing and testing the plan of action
5 Monitoring execution and evaluating results

The quality groups were supervised by their natural team managers. We provided these managers with training so that they could apply the method within their teams.

Step by step, a quality group had to go about solving the problem. On the average, the quality groups needed four to five meetings to tackle a problem and introduce a planned change into work activities.

In going through the steps, all sorts of procedures were followed. These included discussion methods, creativity techniques and role simulations. These kinds of procedures were intended to generate and compile ideas for improvements, thereby encouraging each home helper to use her own creativity. But there were also procedures for decision-making, establishing connections, and seeking solutions on a rational basis.

It was the task of the team manager to ensure that all group members participate. Indeed, it was important that all home helpers be involved in finding solutions and putting them into practice.

For example, when studying the subject of "knowledge of chronic diseases", a team felt the need for up-to-date and accessible information on a number of chronic disorders. All team members cooperated in drawing up a list of chronic diseases and disabilities pertaining to the clients with whom they came into contact. Additionally, they established a database on the subject of chronic diseases. It was placed in a location accessible to everyone in the team.

5.2 User Feedback

Another quality improvement project in home care which we directed was the development of "user feedback" for professionals. The objective of the project was to improve professional work in a client-oriented way by means of gathering information on clients' experiences and by using this information in a process of quality improvement. In this project, we set up experiments in teams of home helpers and home nurses. Our point of departure was the idea that professionals can explore, both on a small scale and among their own client groups, the opinions and experiences which clients have had with the care provided. The outcome of such an exploration had to be used for quality improvement. To this aim, we employed a series of steps similar to the aforementioned project.

In consulting their clients, professionals can make use of simple or complex types of exploratory "research". Examples of simple types are collecting user signals, having open talks with one's own clients, and filling in multiple-choice lists on all sorts of aspects of care evaluation. More complex types are conducting interviews, presenting questionnaires or organizing user panels.

Of course, a key problem is how information from clients can be used for quality improvements in professional practice. For one example, the clients of a home care team appeared to be dissatisfied with the way in which temporary replacement of personnel was arranged. The team conducted some small-scale research by gathering information from clients with the aid of a short questionnaire. Clients indicated that they considered it important that the same substitute helper be provided every time a replacement is called for. They also wanted the hours of service delivery to remain the same and preferred to be informed of a professional's non-appearance by telephone as soon as possible.

The team decided to come up with a new replacement regulation in accordance with these statements. The team set a new standard, part of which can be measured. For example, in cases of sudden absenteeism of the professional helper or nurse, the client is to be informed within the hour.

The method of "user feedback" is a way for professionals to arrive at discussion with clients about the service delivered. If professionals seek this feedback to improve their own work, they will rely less often on a defensive attitude when clients respond with criticism. Rather, they are willing to look upon this criticism as an opportunity for improvement.

Not all preferences of clients can be met. The team has to look at their own possibilities and, in some situations, at the possibilities on the clients' part when planning an improvement action.

In general, experiences with user feedback from the project suggest that it contributed to a more client-oriented attitude on the part of participants; in the teams, group cohesion was enhanced.

The method of "user feedback" can be combined with the "quality groups" in the first project. Although this is no easy task, it offers a more ideal approach. A quality group is a stimulus for professionals to improve the work setting, together with colleagues. It reinforces one's professional attitude, group cohesion and group-sustained quality standards within a team. When at the same time users' feedback is taking place, the professional gains insight into the weaknesses of care provision from the clients' point of view. Professionalism and client orientation can be developed simultaneously.

6 Research on Quality Groups

Some research has been done on the implementation of quality care in practice. Once a set of methods for "quality groups" had been developed and trial-tested, a study was set up to evaluate it, focusing on the following questions:

(1) How valuable are quality groups to home helpers in terms of "quality service"?
(2) How valuable are quality groups to clients in terms of "quality care"?
(3) How valuable are quality groups to home care organizations (costs vs. benefits)?

The study was conducted in three home care organizations. In each organization, three teams were followed during the process of introducing quality groups. Using such research tools as systematic observation, written surveys, and user panels, information was compiled both on professional care workers and on users. To carry out a preliminary evaluation, home helpers and managers were given a survey before the quality groups were introduced. After the quality groups had dealt with at least one item, they received a second survey for post-evaluative purposes. Both surveys contained questions concerning team performance (team spirit, attitude towards fellow team members and cooperation), rapport with managers, approach to clients, and personal experience at work (workload, commitment and independence).

The improvement plans (plans of action) developed by the quality groups were examined in the course of the study with regard to their positive and negative effects. In addition, a user panel made up of eight home care users was set up to evaluate whether the items selected by the quality groups as important corresponded to those chosen by the users.

7 The Most Significant Findings

The quality groups proved beneficial to the participants with respect to a number of items. Home helpers appeared to receive better support from colleagues, to intensify their cooperation and to enjoy better relations with their clients. They felt more supported in their work. Managers functioning as supervisors of quality groups also proved to benefit from them in such areas as their effectiveness in supervising teams and individual team members as well as their job satisfaction.

Many of the priority items selected by the quality groups corresponded to those of the users. The numerous changes in the deployment of home care staff due to illness or holiday leaves of permanent staff members proved to be a major problem in daily performance. The quality groups appeared to have focused more attention on this item than any other. The users' panel also indicated this item as the greatest problem area. Given the needs of home care users, we can conclude that all of the attention devoted by the quality groups to this item was indeed justified.

The plans of action developed by the quality groups to tackle the problem of "substitutions/changes in care staff" were examined in comparison to user views. After all, home care users also have their preferences with regard to staff substitution. The users appeared to set great store on consistent deployment of the same care workers, especially for personal physical care (such as assistance with bathing, etc.). Deployment of the same care workers for domestic help (cleaning, etc.) was considered less of a priority, although the users did feel it important that cleaning and other household chores be done thoroughly. The quality groups' plans of action reveal a real effort to meet the needs of users. The plans provide for maximum consistency in the deployment of the same care workers for physical care but allow comparatively more changes in the deployment of household help. These findings reveal that the quality groups have their limitations in areas where they have no say, such as in determining staff numbers or in the overall deployment of resources.

Some research has been conducted on the costs and benefits of employing quality groups in home care organizations. Time accounts for most of the costs of using quality groups (i.e. the time that the group supervisors invest in training and preparations for meetings). The care workers themselves invest little additional time, as quality groups do not require a new system of consultation but can be incorporated into existing consultation structures.

In a few cases, there were financial benefits. One organization, for example, avoided taking on extra temporary staff during holiday periods by coordinating substitution more efficiently. In general, however, the respondents felt that the benefits of the method extended beyond the financial sphere. The method was seen as intensifying cooperation between team members, catering better to clients' needs and enabling the improvement of individual performance, all of which contribute to more effective care provision.

8   Discussion

A major aim of quality improvement in the area of health care and social welfare concerns the continuous attunement of the services provided to the needs and preferences of clients. In the Netherlands, the legislation on clients' rights and the introduction of personal budgets are seen as necessary means towards the achievement of this objective. Clients may become less dependent on care providers and, as a result, can make their own decisions with respect to the care supplied to them.

In this contribution, we have focused on the importance of the interaction between clients and professionals as a core issue in quality improvement. Professionals have to anticipate clients' preferences and to combine this orientation with a development of concrete norms and "good practices".

In this perspective, the professionals themselves have to take responsibility for integrating client interests with professional standards for service delivery. Instead of applying standard prescriptions for handling problems, they can find themselves new solutions and tailor their services. Professionals have to look for the best solution to a problem, given the users' needs, their own possibilities and those of their organization. Interprofessional consultation, as well as communication between professional and client, have to be stimulated.

Although not all differences can be completely bridged at all times, it is a major step forward when client interests, professional orientation and organizational guidelines can be made the subject of discussion. It is a challenge for professionals: combining client interests with professionalism in the organization.

References

Barnes, M./Wistow, G. (1994) 'Achieving a Strategy for User Involvement in Community Care', *Health & Social Care.*

Duijnstee, M.S.H. (1994) 'What Professionals Need to Know', pp. 313-319 in: Stopp, G.H. (ed), *International Perspectives on Health Care for the Elderly.* New York: Lang.

Van Gorp, K./van de Bergh, R. (1996) *Op de weegschaal. Een onderzoek naar de waarde van kwaliteitsgroepen in de thuiszorg.* Utrecht: NIZW.

Harding, T./Beresford, P. (eds.) (1996) *The Standards We Expect: What Service Users and Carers Want from Social Services Workers.* London: National Institute for Social Work.

Kanters, T./Verbeek, G. (1995) *Kwaliteit in werking.* Utrecht: NIZW.

Kanters, T./Verbeek, G./Buenting, M. (1995) *Naar kwaliteit op de werkvloer.* Utrecht: NIZW.

Van de Siepkamp, D./Verbeek, G. (1996) *In gesprek met gebruikers.* Utrecht: NIZW.

Verbeek, G. (1993) *Wat zeggen onze cliënten?* Utrecht: NIZW.

Verbeek, G. (1996) *Het spel van kwaliteit en zorg.* Utrecht: Lemma.

Chapter 9

Quality Management and Quality Assurance in Residential and Nursing Home Care in Britain and Germany

Barbara Klein

1 Introduction

For quite a while, the quality discussion found its way into the area of elderly care. Quality, quality assurance, quality control ... all these terms can be read in nearly every article or heard in many conferences and seminars. Most of the quality approaches discussed can be classified into two main approaches: professional and business (Pollitt, 1996). The professional approach includes peer review by colleagues, as well as standards and ethics given by and controlled within a professional association. This model is closely linked with welfare state development, being supportive of professionalizing Personal Social Services (PSS) (Evers, 1996). The "inspectorate approach" is seen as a model flourishing alongside the welfare state as a provider of universalistic services. Hence, "the inspectorate approach is very much about processes of laying down what is seen as a general standard and about guidance concerning quality control" (Evers, 1996). Pollitt includes in his discussion of business approaches such concepts as Total Quality Management (TQM), ISO 9000, Business Re-engineering and Benchmarking. These approaches or concepts, all derived from a special view on PSS, differ from the professional and inspectorate approach to the degree in which they address the whole firm or organization. They create a high level of collective readiness and commitment to question inherited structures and routines, as well as the otherwise prevailing individual perspectives (Evers, 1996).

Whereas the theoretical make-up of these approaches is similiar in Britain and in Germany (Pollitt, 1996; Evers, 1996), their implementation seems to be quite different. Business approaches in PSS started to be discussed at the beginning of the 1990s. However, in residential and nursing home care, initial implementation followed only in the mid-1990s. The inspectorate approach has a longer history and different outcomes in both Britain and Germany. In the following, a comparison of the inspectorate approach in residential and nursing home care will be undertaken.

Residential care in Britain is an issue discussed in society with an awareness of the problems inherent to ensuring quality care. The discussion started in the 1980s, when an independent review of residential care resulted in the Wagner Report, whose recommendations were widely adopted by both policy-makers and society. In contrast to Britain, residential care in Germany is mainly discussed in terms of expenses and cost-effectiveness. Scandals, and even Klie's research (1994) on constraints, did not result in a public outcry or an increased awareness of the problem.

The improvement of living conditions in residential homes has long been a part of social policy in Britain. In 1991, Quality Assurance Units were set up to ensure the quality of life in residential homes. "Homes are for living in" is not only a leitmotif, but also a model for evaluating the quality of care provided and the quality of life experienced by residents. It provides a basic methodology for the inspection of residential homes in Britain, as well as insight into how the newly-established inspection units in Britain should operate.

The situation in Germany is somewhat different. Although inspection authorities have comparable legal functions with respect to residential homes, their work – which mainly focuses on architectural and structural issues – is neither noticed by the public, nor has it led to the development of comparable concepts or tools.

This contribution attempts to answer the following questions:

- What are the underlying principles adopted by inspection units in Britain and Germany?
- How do inspection units work, and how effective are they?
- What are the future issues to be resolved?

2 Methods

The results of this contribution are based on a survey of all inspection units from Social Services and Social Work Departments[1] in Britain, and all inspection units in the Federal State of Baden-Württemberg in Germany. The survey was undertaken as part of the project "Residential and Nursing Home Care: Quality Assurance Perspectives" funded by the Human Capital and Mobility Programme of the European Community. The response rate of the survey is shown in Table 1:

Table 1: **Response Rate of Inspection Units**

	Sent to	Replies	%
Scotland	12	5	42%
England outside London	85	28	33%
Local Government of London	33	8	24%
Great Britain: Total	130	41	32%
State of Baden-Württemberg, Germany	44	22	50%

Information received from the different inspection units comprised a broad variety of

- annual reports;
- information on residential care;
- inspection reports;
- pre-inspection questionnaires; and
- inspection and registration guidelines.

The information was supplemented with

- interviews with four senior inspectors respectively the heads of inspection units from the Social Work/Services Department in Britain;
- interviews with three senior inspection officers from the Health Board or Health Authority[2] in Britain;
- an interview with one senior inspection officer in Germany;
- observations made during one inspection in Scotland;
- document analysis of inspection reports in Britain and Germany; and
- six case-studies from residential and nursing homes in Germany, and ten case-studies from residential (7) and nursing homes (3) in Britain.

3   What Are the Underlying Principles of Inspection Units in Britain and Germany?

The work of inspection units in Britain and Germany is regulated by a variety of laws, governmental regulations and recommendations. Common areas of responsibility in Britain and Germany comprise registration, inspection and consultancy in homes. They also have in common that their work covers epidemic control inspection, food, food preparation, health and hygiene, and building and fire precautions. A main difference between the two countries lies in the area of responsibility/jurisdiction.

In Germany, inspection units were set up following the introduction of the Law on Homes (*Heimgesetz*). They are responsible for residential *and* for nursing homes in all sectors. Their assignment depends on which Federal State (*Bundesland*) they belong to. For example, in the smaller Federal States like Saarland, Berlin and Bremen, the responsibility for inspection units lies in the central Federal State Authority (*zentrale Landesbehörden*). In some of the larger Federal States – such as Baden-Württemberg, Niedersachsen, Nordrhein-Westfalen, etc. – the District Councils are responsible. However, inspection units can be assigned to the town clerk's office, the social work department, or even the environmental authority. The status of inspection officers is usually low; their inspection task just one from among a range of other tasks (Klie, 1988: 183; 1994: 19).

In Britain, the jurisdiction of inspection units is different for residential and nursing homes, as it also is for England and Scotland. In England, inspection units were set up in 1984 with the Registered Homes Act, which applies to residential and nursing homes. In Scotland, residential care homes have been subject to inspections under the National Assistance Act since 1948; and nursing care homes, under the Nursing Homes Registration Act since 1938.

In England and Scotland inspection units for residential homes are somewhat loosely assigned to the Social Work/Social Services department and are accountable to the Director of Social Work/Social Services. From 1984 to 1991, they were only responsible for the registration and inspection of private and voluntary homes; since 1991, they also inspect Local Authority homes. Inspection units for nursing homes are assigned to Health Boards in Scotland and to Health Authorities in England. Each type of inspection unit operates under different laws and regulations (Klein, 1995).

Looking at the work of inspection units, three core principles characterize their work:

- a "custodian" (*ordnungspolitisches*) model is the basis of the German inspection units for residential and nursing care homes;
- a medical model is the basis for inspections by the Health Board/Health Authority in British nursing homes; and
- inspection units from the Social Work/Services Departments in residential care homes in Britain base their work on a value-based model.

3.1 The "Custodian" (ordnungspolitische) Model in Germany

In Germany, the "custodian" model for the inspection of homes concentrates on building/technical aspects, storage of medication, hygiene and kitchen arrangements. Issues important to residents, such as care aspects and social care, do not receive the same attention as these others (Klie, 1994: 37). In comparison with the British inspectors, German answers to the survey showed that the work of inspection units relied even more heavily on laws and regulations. They seem to be the only means to achieve change, though they usually take up a very long time because of a variety of factors: reluctance and low interest on the part of superiors, a work-intensive proof procedure, and a backlog in the courts. Thus, inspections seem to be a formal check and an administrative procedure to determine whether homes work according to the law or not.

3.2 The "Medical Model" Approach in Nursing Homes in Britain

Inspections units from the Social Work/Services Department view themselves as different from inspection units belonging to the Health Board/Health Authority responsible for nursing homes and vice versa. The main cause of the difference is their view of the underlying model which forms the basis of their inspections.

Inspections carried out by inspection units from the Health Board/Health Authority focus on such medical factors as care plans and records and health and safety issues. Prime standards for good care depend very much on medical care records; social issues central to the value-based model are not considered in the same detail as in inspections by the Social Work/Services Department. However, some Health Boards/Health Authorities try to overcome these shortcomings by conducting joint inspections; but these do not have the same power to impose requirements to improve the quality of care in nursing homes as do the inspection authorities for residential homes.

3.3 The "Value-based" Model in Residential Homes in Britain

Only the inspection units of the Social Work/Services Departments consider the quality of the residents' life. They rely on a value-based model established in "Home Life" (1984) and "Homes Are for Living In" (1989), as the results of the survey showed.

"Home Life" was developed as a code of practice for inspection units, proprietors and managers of homes. It underlines principles of care based on dignity, the right to self-determination and individuality. "Home Life" already formulated the basic rights which were later taken up in "Homes Are for Living In". Here, a model was developed providing qualitative performance criteria for residential care. The model is based on six basic values, which are defined as

- *privacy:* the right of individuals to be left alone or undisturbed and free from intrusion or public attention into their affairs;
- *dignity:* recognition of the intrinsic value of people, regardless of their circumstances, by respecting their uniqueness and their personal needs and treating them with respect;
- *independence:* opportunities to act and think without reference to another person, including a willingness to incur a degree of calculated risk;
- *choice:* opportunity to select independently from a range of options;

- *rights:* the maintenance of all entitlements associated with citizenship; and
- *fulfilments:* the realization of personal aspirations and abilities in all aspects of daily life (*Homes Are for Living In*, 1989).

These basic values are measured and laid out in areas referred to as the "traditional model": physical enviroment, care practices, staff, staff training and development, procedures, case records, documents and meals and mealtimes.

"Homes Are for Living In" developed a matrix that shows the relationship of the "traditional model", on the one hand, and the value-based model on the other. This matrix can be used as a checklist/questionnaire for performing inspections. The basic values are operationalized in such a way that inspection officers can obtain indicators for the extent to which the basic values are realized (*Homes Are for Living In*, 1989: 17). Characteristics of the value-based model are

- a focus on explicit values;
- operationalization in such a way that the desired values can be measured;
- closeness to everyday life; and
- process orientation by showing how to achieve these basic values, and thus establishing a good standard for quality care.

The underlying assumption is that establishing these basic values in residential care homes, and inspecting them according to these standards, will influence the quality of care provided for residents in these homes.

4   How Do Inspection Units Work, and How Effective Are They?

4.1 The Inspection Process

Inspections in the UK are carried out at least twice a year in each home, usually one announced and one unannounced. In Germany, however, inspections are rare occurrences in both residential and nursing homes. On the average, they are carried out less than once each second year but can also happen less than once in five years (Klie, 1994: 22). Inspections are usually announced, unless there is undeniable evidence that the life of residents is threatened or mandatory major improvements need to be checked on. The following figure gives an overview.

An announced inspection in Britain usually takes an entire day but can take up to two days. In Germany, they last on average half a day (Klie, 1994).

Looking at the time budgeted for inspections, German inspectors spend 35 hours per year per home and are thus 10 to 15 hours above the time budget of their British colleagues (Klie et al., 1994). Here, a detailed analysis of time budgets (who spends how much time on which activities) would provide helpful insight as well as indicators for organizational improvements.

Figure 1:   Frequency of Inspections

	Britain	Germany	
	residential homes	nursing homes	residential and nursing homes
announced inspection	once a year	dependent on the inspection units: one announced and one unannounced	dependent on the inspection units: the range varies from one per year up to once every 5th year
unannounced inspection	at least one per year	some inspection units carry out only unannounced inspections	only if there are complaints
frequency of inspections	(at least) two inspections per year per home	(at least) two inspections per year per home	not regulated: in average less than one each second year

Besides the frequency of inspections, another major diferrence between the two countries is the customer/client orientation in Britain, where usually all or the majority of residents are questioned about their opinion of the quality of care, as the following figure shows.

Figure 2:   Persons Questioned in an Inspection

	Britain	Germany	
	residential homes	nursing homes	residential and nursing homes
residents	if possible: all	if possible: all	representative of the residents committee; rarely with some of the residents
staff	yes	yes	yes
management/proprietor/ matron	yes	yes	yes
relatives, friends	are written to and asked for comments and their opinion	dependent on the inspection unit	no

The procedure of announced inspections is pretty similar for all inspection types: a few weeks in advance, the inspection is announced by letter and often accompanied by a pre-inspection questionnaire. After the inspection, a report is written and usually some kind of consent has to be obtained. Inspection reports of the Social Work/Social Services Department are open to the public, which is also a way to push quality forward. Differences are in the composition of the inspection team, as shown in Figure 3.

Not all staff involved in inspecting nursing homes are employed by the National Health Authority. Specialists, e.g. estate agents, will be bought in if needed. Standards for inspections are based mainly on a medical model. However, there are attempts to incorporate the value-based model, e.g. by doing joint inspections. In Scotland, staff involved in inspections are employed by the Health Board. However, here as in Germany, for most inspection officers it is only one task among others.

Additional methods applied and mentioned by the British inspection units were

- direct observation of
  - staff interaction with service users,
  - staff interaction with each other, and
  - service users' interaction with each other;
- direct questioning:
  asking service users, relatives, friends and staff to comment on specific issues;
- discussion and exchange of views formally and informally with service providers;

Figure 3:   Composition of Inspection Teams

Residential Homes in Britain	Nursing Homes in Britain	Residential and Nursing Homes in Germany
• inspection officer • lay assessor	• nurse • doctor • pharmacist • estate agents/engineer • environmental health officer	• inspection officer • representative of the social services • medical practitioner from the public health department • representative of the regional association of voluntary welfare work*

* In Germany, most homes belong to voluntary organizations. The involvement of representatives from voluntary organizations in the inspection process contributes to the status quo. In Britain, inspection officers from the Social Work/Authority Department are also responsible for public homes. Although they are held at arm's length, the discussion still goes on as to how to separate responsibilities.

Figure 4:   Focus of Inspections

Residential Homes in Britain	Nursing Homes in Britain	Residential and Nursing Homes in Germany
• quality of life • care plans • staff issues	• medical issues, care plans	• hygiene and safety • medical and care issues (not always considered)

- inviting written or telephone contact from service users and service providers;
- direct testing, sampling and checking; and
- monitoring and reviewing issues arising from inspections.

Because of the variety of topics which arise when basic values are critically looked at, some of the inspection units select a new theme every year to reflect the views of inspectors on current issues. Examples of themes/topics mentioned were "privacy and dignity", "the social life of residents" and "staff training and development". The focus of the inspections is based on underlying principles and values, as shown in Figure 4.

Having looked at the structural differences of inspection units, the following will present the methods used by inspection units for performing an inspection. The following quotation from an English inspection unit shows the importance of the methods applied.

> The quality of an inspection depends on the reliability, detail and accuracy of the information available. It also depends on the way in which information is put together to give it meaning and relate it to good standards. In order to decide whether a home is doing well or not, standards or criteria should be available by which to judge it: for example, ethical standards (or general rules), operational guidelines, performance standards which can be justified, i.e. work in practice and relation to real life.

4.2   How Effective Are Inspection Units?

4.2.1 Comparison of Recommendations Made in Inspection Reports for Residential and Nursing Homes in One Region in Britain

The underlying assumption is that inspecting residential homes according to value-based standards will influence the quality of care provided in these homes. Nursing homes are not included in these regulations. However, a few local authorities perform a joint inspection among them in one investigated region. Here, inspections of residential homes according to the value-based model started in 1991; and joint inspections of nursing homes, in late 1993. An analysis of recommendations made in the inspection reports from 33 residential and 21 nursing homes in the Central Region shows a total of 596 recommendations made in 1994:

Table 2:   Recommendations for Residential and Nursing Homes in One Region for 1994

33 residential homes	293 (49%)	⌀ 8.9 recommendations
21 nursing homes	303 (51%)	⌀ 14.4 recommendations
Total	596	⌀ 11 recommendations

Nursing Homes received slightly more recommendations than residential homes. Looking at the content, it seems that residential homes have already improved their care standards according to quality criteria, while nursing homes are at the starting point in terms of bringing the social quality of care in line with residential homes. Comparing the recommendations of nursing homes with the recommendations made for residential homes, Table 3 shows that there are some striking differences.

The first three issues, which are about three times as high in nursing homes compared to residential homes, have been the subject of discussion and change in residential homes since the inspections started. No wonder nursing homes lag behind in these issues. Here, inspection units are not equipped with the same powers they have in residential homes. They can only recommend but not enforce recommendations. Care planning, risk-taking and staff issues are not really comparable because of the

Table 3 :   Comparison of Recommendations Made in Residential and Nursing Homes

	Nursing Homes	Residential Homes
Locks and keys for own room, bathroom, toilet, etc.	67%	23%
Phasing out of double and multi-occupancy rooms	60%	23%
Choice of dishes	60%	18%
Building	53%	55%
Care planning	47%	68%
Risk-taking	47%	86%
Staff issues	40%	100%

- *process-orientation of inspections –*
  In "risk-taking", the process orientation can be revealed. In nursing homes, risk-taking was mentioned in connection with keys and locks for rooms: that is, with respect to the basic value of privacy. In residential homes, risk-taking was an issue of the basic value of independence: residents should be supported in their activities and staff should enable them;
- *division of inspection issues between the Health Board and Social Work/Services Inspectorate –*
  Care plans and staff ratios in nursing homes are subject to investigation by the Health Board Inspection, and there is no public access to these data because of data protection.

Recommendations on care plans in nursing homes were mainly aimed at improving the social side of care plans; whereas in residential homes, besides the improvement of care plans, such new issues as the involvement of residents and relatives are raised. This seems to be another prime example of the process orientation of the "value-based model". The empowerment of residents is still just beginning, and these attempts seem to be worthwhile in terms of further development.

Staff issues raised in the nursing homes were mainly with respect to the basic value of dignity: staff should reconsider their attitudes towards residents, and stop using endearments, etc.

Staff issues were mentioned in all residential homes. However, once again, differences in recommendations characterize the process orientation. The issues raised can be divided up into the following categories:

- improvement of the staff ratio;
- training of staff;
- enhancement of staff meetings; and
- a staff supervision and appraisal system.

The main impression of these recommendations is that staff are a critical factor in establishing quality of care. Sufficient staff numbers and adequate training, combined with staff supervision and an appraisal system, are ways to achieve this objective.

4.2.2 Analysis of Court Decisions to Close Down Residential and Nursing Homes in Germany

Court decisions are in fact not comparable with recommendations for residential and nursing homes. However, they provide insight into what kind of problems have to be faced with the custodian model in Germany. The court decisions were all met in one district, and they show that legal decisions take a rather long time and involve a huge amount of paperwork. Even the most humiliating and health-threatening circumstances do not result in early closures. All decisions were based on an abundance of abuses and a deplorable state of affairs: lack of staff (qualified and unqualified), endangerment of health, insufficient personal care by staff, bad environmental conditions, overcrowding, lack of care plans and documentation, overall bad hygiene in both the health and medical areas, insufficient food provision, insufficient heating, embezzlement of monies and allowances, and the critical financial state of the home – high debts, irregular payments, etc. They all had a history of fines to pay and conditions to fulfill. The interviews showed that the work focused on the bad homes and on attempts to improve standards in these homes. However, there are a variety of other factors which influence the outcome of the work of inspection units:

• The attitude of superiors plays a major role, as they usually make the decision on whether to take a residential home to court or not. Before going to court, proof has to be collected, witnesses for the prosecution found and convinced, evidence written up and legal counsel obtained.
• Courts also take their time deciding, and decisions very much depend on what district the court is located in.
• The job status of inspectors is rather low. There is a lack of qualification and training, methods and instruments, and professional exchange.

4.3   Outcomes for Residential and Nursing Homes

An obvious difference in residential and nursing home care in Germany and in Britain is the organization of daily routine. The value-based model pursues under the principle of "dignity" (meaning the recognition of the intrinsic value of people, regardless of their circumstances, by respecting their uniqueness and their personal needs and by treating them with respect), for example, the flexibility of such daily routines as mealtimes, or the choice of when to get up or to retire.

Figure 5 shows how the structure of daily routines is realized in residential and nursing homes in Britain and Germany.

It is usually a policy of admission procedures to find out the daily routines of future residents so that they can maintain their habits.

"Dignity" also implies the chance to retire, thus also referring to the value of "privacy": for example, in your own room. Meanwhile, inspection services from the Social Work/Services Departments in Britain when registering new homes demand that all rooms be single. The analysis of inspection reports shows that this demand is based on a prior recommendation and that the situation has improved continuously. In England, 72% are single rooms; in a selected region in Scotland, it is 60%. In West Germany, however, the share of single rooms is 57%; in East Germany, it is only 36%. However, phasing out multi-occupancy rooms is still a

Figure 5: Daily Routines of Residents

	Britain	Germany
Getting up	as resident wishes	from 6.00 a.m. onwards (by breakfast everybody should be washed and dressed)
Breakfast	till 11.00 a.m.	8.00 a.m.
Lunch	12.00 p.m. or later if wanted	12.00 p.m.
Tea	3.30 p.m. (tea/coffee usually always available)	3.00 p.m.
Dinner	5.30 p.m.	5.00 p.m.
Snack	8.00 p.m.	–
Retire	as resident wishes: some retire earlier, others later, wanderers can walk around	7.00 p.m.

problem. Recent developments show that in the future, care insurance will play a major role in establishing the quality of care. The associations of residential care institutions on a national level, together with the head associations for care insurance, developed general principles and standards for quality and quality assurance. Here, in principle, single rooms are demanded (*Gemeinsame Grundsätze und Maßstäbe zur Qualität und Qualitätssicherung einschl. des Verfahrens zur Durchführung von Qualitätsprüfungen nach § 80 SGB XI in vollstationären Pflegeeinrichtungen*). However, the whole paper does not refer to any values, although the desired results and outcomes are described and are in principle similar to the desired outcomes of British inspection units from the Social Work/Services Departments. The approach of defining desired outcomes seems on the whole too static, because of the lack of flexibility and of chances for further development.

The size of the homes also plays a role in establishing a homely, individual atmosphere: the smaller the home, the cozier and more familiar the environment. Thus, not surprisingly, residential homes in Britain are far smaller compared to those in Germany. Residential homes with more than 40 residents are large homes. The maximum number for registering a residential home is usually between 40 and 50 residents. The majority of homes have between 10 and 20 residents. In Germany, an average of 65 residents live together in a residential home; in a nursing home, the figure amounts to 87 residents on average. The situation of nursing homes in Britain is slightly different. Today, the average is 39 residents, which is nearly double the number in residential homes. A new trend is the beginning globalization of the care sector. International companies have started to discover this market niche and have built huge nursing homes with 100 and more residents. Inspection units cannot prevent this, but they can demand higher staff levels according to the size and structure of the building so as to guarantee their standards.

5   Future Issues to Be Tackled

The following points show the main differences between Germany and Britain:

- Inspection units in Germany rely on a "custodian" model of inspections, which has proved over the last 20 years to be too complicated and circumstantial to be successful in practice. Issues from the value-based model of care are not considered. In the past few years, a discussion about the quality of care has started to emerge in conjunction with changes in the law and with budgetary issues. A model developed by the association for residential care institutions and the head associations for care insurance is outcome-oriented and includes a range of desired outcomes, partly also described in "Homes Are for Living In". However, this model seems to be doomed to failure, as it has a static approach comparable to the custodian model.
- In Britain, quality-of-care issues are not necessarily considered by the Health Authority or the Health Board. Although in some areas joint inspections have started, inspection officers from the Social Work/Services Departments do not have the same power to impose quality of care as they have for residential homes.
- In Britain, inspection units from nursing homes are likely to be organized according to the medical model, similar to that used in Germany, with a predominance of health and medical issues rather than of social issues.
- A striking similarity of the inspections of the Health Authority/Health Board and the German inspections is the multi-disciplinary team. Experts in their own field supervise health and safety, building, medical and drug issues. The objective is to achieve a safe and "healthy" environment where accidents are minimized and food, hygiene and epidemic control effective.
- The inspections by the Social Work/Services Departments have quite a different focus: they are very much value-oriented towards the residents who are the customers of the home. Both their judgements and their opinions play a more important role when compared to the other two agencies performing inspections.
- Staff numbers for inspection units in Britain are higher than in Germany.
- Homes in Britain are inspected more than three times as often as in Germany.
- In Britain, the quality of care is seen as an outcome for users, whereas in Germany it is perceived as how strictly homes comply with the law.

The research showed that the value-based model can trigger a process improving quality. What are the implications for inspection units in British Health Authorities/Health Boards or in Germany if the value-based model is adopted?

- The value-based model – and in particular, talking to each resident and, if possible, to friends and relatives – implies a methodical framework discussing values with respect to desired outcomes. It would involve more time for inspections and thus, the need for more staff.
- It would also mean empowering inspection officers to enforce their recommendations. In Britain, inspection officers from the Social Work/Services Departments can carry out joint inspections, but their responsibility is limited to contractual arrangements and they do not have any power with respect to registration, which remains entirely the function of the Health Authority (*Croner's Care Home Management*, June 1995: 1-132). In Germany, the empowerment of inspection units would give them more scope and flexibility to act.
- There could also be the demand for a stronger focus on health and safety issues because of the increasing frailty of residents. Assessment of care plans by nurses or a GP are viewed as necessary in residential homes by both the Health Authorities and the Health Boards. In the end, this implies that all inspections are carried out jointly in Britain.

Whereas the value-based model is a cornerstone for establishing quality of care in Britain, the question that may be asked is in how far it is transferable to Germany. All research in recent years has shown that inspection units in Germany need to improve their style of work if they are to become more effective.

Changes would be needed to cover

- *the structural or policy level,* to encompass such issues as the empowerment of inspection units and the acceptance and diffusion of a value-oriented model or concept;
- *the management level,* by implementing the value-oriented model and by developing quality standards for the work of inspection units;
- *the organizational level,* by building up methods and tools to improve the efficiency of inspection units; and
- *the qualificational level,* by strengthening the consultation aspect of inspection units.

Notes

1　In England and Wales, the local authorities responsible for residential care are the Departments of Social Service; in Scotland, these responsibilities are carried out by Social Work Departments.
2　In England and Wales, the Health Authority is responsible for nursing home care; in Scotland, these responsibilities are carried out by the Health Board.

References

Croner's Care Home Management (June 1995). Pp. 1-132, Croner Publications Ltd.

Home Life. A Code of Practice for Residential Care (1984)

Homes Are for Living In (1989). London: HMSO.

Evers, Adalbert (1996) Quality Development – Part of a Changing Culture of Care in Personal Social Services. Lecture held for the International Seminar "Developing Quality in Personal Social Services", Helsinki, 12-14 April.

Klein, Barbara (1995) 'Ein Heim ist kein Daheim ...?', *Altenheim* 10: 722-728.

Klein, Barbara (1995) Residential and Nursing Home Care: Quality Assurance Perspectives. Documentation. Unpublished report.

Klie, Thomas (1988) *Heimaufsicht. Praxis, Probleme, Perspektiven*. Hannover: Curt R. Vincentz Verlag.

Klie, Thomas/Loercher, Uwe (1994) *Gefährdete Freiheit. Fixierungspraxis in Pflegeheimen und Heimaufsicht*. Freiburg: Jugendwerkstatt e.V.

Pollitt, Christopher (1996) Business and Professional Approaches to Quality Improvement: A Comparison of their Suitability for the Personal Social Services. Lecture held for the International Seminar "Developing Quality in Personal Social Services", Helsinki, 12-14 April.

Vereinigungen der Träger der vollstationären Pflegeeinrichtungen auf Bundesebene und der Spitzenverbände der Pflegekassen (1995) *Gemeinsame Grundsätze und Maßstäbe zur Qualität und Qualitätssicherung einschl. des Verfahrens zur Durchführung von Qualitätsprüfungen nach § 80 SGB XI in vollstationären Pflegeeinrichtungen*. Entwurf 17.10.1995.

CHAPTER 10

User-centred Performance Indicators for Inspection of Community Care in Scotland: Developing a Framework

Rosemary Bland[1]

1   Introduction

This chapter is concerned with the formal external inspection of the quality of social work services. As a case-study, I consider the development of criteria for use by the Social Work Services Inspectorate in Scotland[2]. The purpose of the Inspectorate is to "work with others to continually improve social work services so that they genuinely meet people's needs and the public has confidence in them" (SWSI, 1996). One way in which services can be improved is to see whether and in what ways they meet existing standards. The Secretary of State for Scotland sets national standards for social work services in some areas, for example in the criminal justice system. However, in most areas of social work local authorities are currently responsible for setting their own standards for services. They are expected to monitor and publish these standards, so that users of services know what they can expect and the public can form its own judgements. In the area to be discussed in this chapter, community care, local authorities are obliged to publish information about their intentions in three yearly Community Care Plans. These should be devised jointly with health, housing and other agencies, in consultation with the people who use their services. In April 1996, the local authority structure in Scotland underwent considerable change. The 12 regional authorities which had previously had a statutory responsibility for social work services were reorganized into 32 unitary authorities which had a slowing-down effect on community care development. Some of the new, very small authorities are not able to provide all community care services themselves and some responsibilities, such as local inspection of residential care, are being purchased from larger authorities. The reorganization has also had implications for Scottish Office inspections of a much larger number of authorities.

The discussion is centred on one approach to inspection of community care services in Scotland. I begin by sketching in the historical policy background which has influenced and informed the approach to quality evaluation and measurement in British public services. I show how improving the quality of social work services was a major objective of the community care legislation and I outline the role of the Social Work Services Inspectorate in monitoring these objectives. I then go on to describe the process by which a framework of performance indicators for inspecting a range of different community care services in Scotland was developed, taking account of the national Policy Objectives for community care laid down in the Government White Paper "Caring for People" (Department of Health, 1989). Finally I discuss how this framework was adapted and used by SWSI to carry out an inspection of the home help service and draw a few conclusions.

2   The Measurement of Performance in Public Services: Pressure from Above

The history of performance measurement and the pursuit of quality in British public services began in the 1980s, with the Government's Financial Management Initiative which was initially focused on creating an Economical, Efficient and Effective civil service (thereafter known as the "3 E's") (James in Kelly/Warr, 1992). This initiative was subsequently extended to the activities of local authorities. With the creation of the Audit Commission by central government, local authority services began to be examined in terms of whether they provided value for money. The Commission highlighted another crucial expectation of public services, namely that they will be delivered equitably. It found that a very uneven pattern of local authority services had developed across the country, in that the care people received depended as much on where they lived as it did on what their needs were (Audit Commission, 1986). The Commission's conclusions about the progress of community care produced a trenchant criticism of the financial arrangements for public funding of residential and nursing home care which they saw as militating against the successful development of care in the community (1986). A range of financial, ideological and political imperatives lay behind the emergence of quality as a goal to be pursued in public services (James in Kelly/Warr, 1992) and this may account for its rather mixed reception among authority staff. One study found Quality

Assurance was being pursued by social services authorities primarily to satisfy internal organizational agendas such as meeting objectives, managing change and providing value for money rather than as a means of improving the experience of service users, which could be all too easily overlooked (James, 1992). There are still problems with legitimating the view of users in local authority social work departments; practitioners fear that encouraging users and potential users to be vocal about services could lead to demand which would outstrip resources. Neither are social workers enthusiastic about having their professional views challenged (Pollitt, 1988; White, 1988; Wallace/Rees, 1988; Carter, 1991).

3 Pressure from Below

At the same time, there was a growing interest in the performance of local government services among consumer groups and the community at large. This resulted in The National Consumer Council undertaking a study of six specific public services in two English local authorities (National Consumer Council, 1986). The Council was concerned that in the supposed quest for economy, efficiency and effectiveness in local authority services, effectiveness was virtually ignored (National Consumer Council, 1986; Pollitt, 1988). The aim of the Council's study was to develop ways of looking at the "outputs of local government – the nature, quantity and quality of services, their effect and the extent to which they met consumer and community needs and preferences" using the "3 E's" framework (National Consumer Council, 1986). The Council hoped that this work would achieve two objectives: firstly, that local authorities would be encouraged to set targets, evaluate and report on their services to consumers and secondly, that consumers would be provided with information to enable them to question local authorities' performance in providing services (National Consumer Council, 1986).

Early findings were that local authorities rarely undertook to find out what people wanted or needed and that services "seem to result more from historical accident than any attempt rationally to match resources to needs" (National Consumer Council, 1986). Individual services were unclear about their objectives. The study group found that objectives were rarely specified in a concise, concrete way and voiced suspicions that "for some services many authorities have no clear idea of what they are trying to do at all" (National Consumer Council, 1986). The report of the study urged local authorities to be more explicit about their objectives in providing services and to set standards by which these could be judged. The Council saw the exercise as challenging the "supremacy of professional and political assumptions about consumers' needs and preferences" (National Consumer Council, 1987). The study concluded that performance measurement at the time "too often springs out of a defensive culture" because measures were imposed from the top down by government or top management as a means of cost-cutting or controlling the workforce rather than to ensure the quality of services and their "fitness for purpose" (National Consumer Council, 1987).

4   Consumerism and the New Arrangements for Community Care

Radical changes in the organization and funding of community care followed the Audit Commission Report "Making a Reality of Community Care" (1986) and the recommendations of the subsequent Griffiths enquiry into community care (Griffiths, 1988). These changes were spelt out in the government White Paper "Caring for People" (1989) and the subsequent National Health Service and Community Care Act (1990). The lead responsibility for planning, coordinating and purchasing care for a number of groups including older people was, eventually, given to local authority social work departments. They were expected to work collaboratively with health and housing authorities as well as private and voluntary sector service providers and to move away from being monopoly providers of services themselves. In Scotland, there is a long tradition of public service and local authorities continue to be substantial providers of services. The government was keen to develop a "mixed economy of care" by involving voluntary, "not for profit" and private organizations in the provision of services (Department of Health, 1989). The necessity for these changes was attributed to two factors; dissatisfaction with the hitherto slow development of community care combined with the rapidly escalating cost to the state of funding residential and nursing home care use by a growing population of older people.

The NHS and Community Care Act challenged local authority social work departments to "re-think their approach to arranging and providing care" (SSI/SWSG, 1991) by moving from a service-led perspective to one which puts the needs of people first, with the aim of making the services provided more responsive to those needs. The objective was to create a new organizational culture in order to empower service users and carers. By adjusting the balance of power between users, carers and service providers, it was hoped that users and carers would be enabled to "exercise the same power as consumers of other services" (SSI/SWSG, 1991). However, the relationship between consumers and public services is not the same as a market relation in the following ways:

1) the consumer may not buy the service,
2) the consumer may have a statutory right to the service,
3) the consumer may be compelled to use the service,
4) the consumer may be refused the service despite being willing to pay for it,

on grounds of not meeting criteria of need determined by a mixture of political and professional judgements (Stewart/Clarke, 1987, quoted in Pollitt, 1988) and the consumer may have no alternative source of service available to them. Additionally, local authority community care service users may come predominantly from social groups which are more likely to have experience of poverty, stigma, prejudice and powerlessness. However, service users are often income and local taxpayers as well and the status of "client" does not deny their "common right to be heard" (Fisher, 1983). Beresford, a researcher and social work services user himself, points out (1988), that "social services users are not a separate marginal group. Who they are depends on *what* is provided and *who* provides it". The criteria of eligibility for a service decided on by local authorities also determine who likely service users will (or will not) be.

Changing the consumer/provider power structure in community care services was nevertheless seen as the best way of guaranteeing "a continuing improvement in the quality of service" (SSI/SWSG, 1991). Great emphasis was laid on the need for community care services to respond sensitively and flexibly to the needs of individuals and carers and to widen "consumer choice" by greater use of the private and voluntary sectors as service providers (Department of Health, 1989).

The legislation inaugurating these major changes to the organization of community care services was implemented incrementally. The first requirement was for local authorities to set standards for services and monitor their quality. This was initially introduced in relation to residential care using the mechanism of local inspection. Authorities were required to set up inspection units to monitor the quality of care in all residential homes, whether run by private or voluntary organizations or by the local authorities themselves. These inspection units were to be in place by April 1991 and involved authorities in devising standards documents for regulating and inspecting residential care homes. Procedures and arrangements to enable service users to make complaints or representations to the local authority about services had also to be in place by the same date. The remainder of the legislation which transferred the funding and assessment responsibilities for long-term care from central to local government did not come into force until April 1993.

In April 1993 an additional national inspectorial role was given to Scottish Office professional social work advisers, in keeping with English, Welsh and Northern Ireland colleagues. Since then, the Inspectorate in Scotland has been developing its new role and relationships with local authority social work departments through the Convention of Scottish Local Authorities, their representative organization. One of the Inspectorate's main functions has been to promote the development of high-quality social work services. The Inspectorate further contributes to quality development by playing an active part in examining Community Care Plans, monitoring performance and offering advice and guidance to local authorities as well as to the Secretary of State (Department of Health, 1989).

5   Defining and Measuring Quality in Community Care Services

The main objectives behind the community care reforms were to secure greater efficiency in service provision, the targeting of services to those in greatest need and the enlargement of choice to service users (Department of Health, 1989). Performance indicators for community care services therefore needed to be able to measure whether or not these objectives were being met.

The use of the three "Es" (economy, efficiency and effectiveness) and "value for money" as criteria for judging performance and quality derived originally from business and industrial management strategies but, as has been pointed out, these criteria are not sufficient of themselves for making judgements about public services since they are not subject to the market forces which influence industry and commerce. Moreover, public services are expected to reflect moral values such as equity in the way they are delivered to citizen consumers (Pollitt, 1988).

A research study undertaken in four local authority social services departments examined whether measurable performance indicators could be developed to judge the success of the community care reforms (Hoyes et al., 1992). The authors concluded that three indicators should be used: allocative efficiency, equity and choice. Allocative efficiency was chosen because it explicitly relates the costs of a service to its benefits. An allocatively efficient service is one which maximizes the difference between its benefits and its costs (Hoyes et al., 1992). It is particularly attractive as an indicator for community care because it can incorporate anything of positive value delivered by the service. The range of possible benefits and beneficiaries can be very broad – from the quality and quantity of the service itself, to its responsiveness and appropriateness in meeting users' and carers' needs (Hoyes et al., 1992). If value for money is interpreted as meaning maximum benefit obtained per £'s worth of cost, then allocative efficiency can be equated with the search for value for money – a key objective of the community care reforms (Hoyes et al., 1992).

The second performance indicator for community care services, equity, reflected the value base of public service provision (Pollitt, 1988). The authors of the study interpreted equity as meaning equality of care and equality of access to care for a given level of need (Hoyes et al., 1992). A major objective of the community care reforms was that services should go to those people who were in greatest need of them (Department of Health, 1989). The final indicator was the extent to which choices were made available to consumers of services (Hoyes et al., 1992). From the point of view of the acceptability of such indicators to social work professionals, equity and choice are among the principles of practice set out in the proposed British Association of Social Workers Code of Ethics for Social Work (Watson, 1985) as is the obligation to contribute to the formulation and implementation of policies for human welfare which in community care terms might (just) be seen as contributing to a service which was allocatively efficient.

When devising performance indicators it is necessary to decide which elements of a service can be measured and how this can be done. There are three constituent component parts to a service; the raw materials such as staff, premises, vehicles, etc., which together produce a service are known as inputs; the service which is produced by these components, e.g. the meal-on-wheels, the respite stay in a residential care home, is the output and the effect on the service user, the outcome. Some welfare economists emphasize that the value or quality of a service should be measured by looking at its effect on the user – the outcome – rather than at the service itself (the output) (Hoyes et al., 1992). However, measuring outcomes in human services is difficult and where contact between the user and the service may be prolonged (sometimes up to ten years or more in the case of home help, for example) it is sometimes acceptable to use performance indicators about the *process* of giving or receiving the service, e.g. with respect, courteously, on time, confidentially, etc., as a proxy for outcome (Hoyes et al., 1992). This is particularly relevant for community care where the service user is likely to be in receipt of several services and distinguishing the effect of any one part of the care package from another in terms of enhancing user welfare might be extremely difficult. Process variables were particularly useful in developing the indicators of user and carer satisfaction. I now go on to discuss the framework of indicators developed for a number of community care inspections in Scotland, the first of which was for the home help/home care service.

6   The SWSI Indicators for Community Care

Caring for People (DoH, 1989) emphasizes that one of the main objectives of the community care reforms is to enable people to live as normal a life as possible in their own homes or in a homely environment in the local community (Department of Health, 1989). It seemed appropriate that the overarching standard for the various community care services being inspected should reflect this objective, hence the standard for inspection was that the service being inspected enabled the service user (who had so chosen) to live in their own home or in homely surroundings. The next step was to identify what the key indicators of allocative efficiency, equity and choice should be. What characteristics should performance indicators possess? One researcher (Carter, 1991) has suggested that they should be:

- relevant;
- resistant to manipulation;
- reliable;
- unambiguous;
- comprehensible;
- usable;
- custom-built; and
- few in number.

The National Consumer Council (1986) developed the framework from which it devised its performance indicators for local authority services in consultation with local authority officers, councillors and consumer groups. The Council started its exercise with five core questions that consumers want to ask about services, the first being "What is the service supposed to do?" That being established (difficulty in establishing a service's objectives is itself suggestive of a problem), four further questions were then pursued:

* Does the service do what it is supposed to do?
* Does it do what it is not supposed to do?
* What is it like to use?
* What does it cost?

The process of applying these concepts to the practical problem of devising the home care indicators became an iterative one. For each of the five questions decisions needed to be made about whether and in what form information might be available to provide an answer and finally, what the key indicator or indicators should be.

6.1 Data Sources

The performance literature makes it clear that indicators need to be of two kinds: quantitative, provided figures used are reliable, and qualitative, particularly when eliciting the views of service users (Gaster, 1991). Some quantitative information is held at Scottish Office level and some at local authority level but how much and in what form at local authority level was a matter of speculation at this stage and likely to vary between authorities. Local authorities complete statistical returns for the Scottish Office about their services on an annual basis. Information is provided about the quantity and frequency of service provision and the number of people receiving individual services at a national and individual local authority level. Characteristics of service users reported include their age, disabilities and frequency or length of service use. Seven such bulletins have been published about community care services since April 1993. It is therefore possible to discern broad trends in service provision and use since the legislation was implemented.

More detailed information about services is collected by authorities for their own internal planning and monitoring purposes. Information for some indicators would be likely to be obtainable from such sources as community care plans, policy documents, service user publicity material, case records, personnel department records, formal complaints registers and, in the case of residential service inspection, from the records of the authority's own arm's length inspection unit.

6.2 Informants

The next question to be decided was which stakeholders in the service would be key informants for performance measurement. As other studies have pointed out (see Gaster, 1991), there are many "actors" with a stake in local authority services, not least elected members, local taxpayers and citizens. Whilst it only seemed feasible to contemplate asking current service users for their views, not least because they are the group with experience of the service, Pollitt (1988) asserts that people waiting to get the service, those needing it but not actively asking for it, and those who may need it in the future, are all potential consumers. For inspection purposes it was decided to focus on the following groups:

- Current Users.
- Carers (usually family).
- Front line staff providing the service.
- Senior and middle social work managers.
- Referrers to the service.

6.3 The Key Indicators

Keeping the need for a small number of indicators in mind (Carter, 1991), ten key indicators, each with a number of secondary indicators, were eventually chosen, based on Hoyes et al.'s three criteria of allocative efficiency, equity and choice used in their study (1992). The likely source of data was provided for each indicator. It became clear from performance literature that the views of service users and their carers were central to the whole process of measuring service quality and detecting where improvements or changes were needed (Wallace/Rees, 1984; Martin, 1993). The research literature on internal and external evaluations of the home care service provided authoritative guidance as to what elements of service were considered to be essential, were valued or were sometimes lacking. Not surprisingly, most of the key indicators related to Allocative Efficiency and within that criterion the highest number of secondary indicators related to users' and carers' views. The final draft produced seven key indicators of allocative efficiency, two key indicators of equity and one key indicator of choice, as follows.

6.3.1 Key Indicators of Allocative Efficiency

Three quantitative and four qualitative indicators were chosen.

1) The cost per hour to the service provider per assessed user unit of need (using long, short and critical intervals of need as devised by Isaacs and Neville, 1976).
2) The number of emergency or social admissions of people using or awaiting home care to residential, nursing home or hospital care over 12 months.
3) The percentage of people assessed as needing a defined level (high need) of service who are actually receiving that level of service.
4) User expressed satisfaction with the service (using benefits, information, participation, representation and ease and pleasantness of use as indicators).

5) Carer expressed satisfaction with the service (using benefits, information, participation and representation as indicators).
6) Referrer expressed satisfaction with the service (using information, liaison and quality of service as indicators).
7) Staff expressed satisfaction with the quality of the home care service offered to users and carers (using a number of indicators associated with establishing the service's "fitness for purpose").

6.3.2 Key Indicators of Equity

The aspect of quality being explored here, was how far the home help/care service was made equally available to people with similar needs and whether the charging policy was equitable. Two indicators were chosen; one qualitative, the other quantitative, i.e.

8) The extent to which the service is available to eligible people and their carers with assessed needs in a given area, in accordance with their needs regardless of gender, race, disability, social class, income or location.
9) The extent to which charging inequities for the service to different client groups are minimal or non-existent.

The final key indicator, number 10, was that of *choice*. This sought to explore how flexible the service was in the way it was offered and delivered and the choices which were available to users and carers as a consequence.

Each key indicator had a varying number of secondary indicators, involving a quantitative and qualitative mix. An example may clarify the kind of information being sought. The third key indicator – "User expressed satisfaction with the service" – was investigated under five secondary indicators including "Ease and Pleasantness of Use". Six indicators were chosen as likely to provide evidence of users' views about this aspect of the service. They were a mixture of user judgement and objective evidence, to be obtained from departmental records. There was also the possibility that service managers, front line staff and users and carers would have differing views and experiences of service quality, such as whether cover provided when the usual home help was unavailable was thought by users and carers to be "adequate". In such cases, a final judgement would lie with the Inspectorate.

Ease and Pleasantness of Use would be evidenced by:

1) The extent to which the user's dignity and privacy are safeguarded and how this is monitored (particularly for people with severe learning difficulties or dementia, people from black or ethnic minorities and those with a first language other than English).

2) Whether the service is provided sensitively, courteously, punctually, reliably, confidentially, and in a way that is acceptable to the user.
3) The extent to which adequate cover is provided when staff are absent.
4) The number of written expressions of satisfaction or dissatisfaction (if any) with the service from users and/or carers over 12 months.
5) The results of any surveys of service user views carried out by the local authority and any subsequent effects on policy or practice.
6) How any claims for loss, damage, accident or theft have been handled.

This model for inspection was subsequently used to develop key indicators for a number of other community care services for other client groups, including day services for people with a learning disability and for community-based services for alcohol and substance misusers, using the user and carer focus and drawing on relevant effectiveness research, not least any evidence from consumer studies, where these existed, of service users' and carers' views.

7   From Model Indicators to Inspection Tools

The principle of focusing on users' and carers' views of services as criteria of quality was agreed by the Inspectorate and the work on indicators for performance measurement of home care services was taken forward by them to prepare for an inspection of the service in a number of locations during 1994. When the inspection was eventually undertaken, the ten key indicators had been changed into ten key questions, which addressed the criteria of allocative efficiency and equity, with choice addressed by questions about the flexibility and range of services available. The user and carer focus had also been retained as follows:

The Ten Key Questions

1) What are the views of users and carers about the service?
2) How flexible are services in responding to individual needs of users and carers?
3) Is the range of home help/home care services sufficient for users and carers?
4) How reliable are home help/home care services?
5) What is the quality of assessment of need of people receiving home help/home care services?
6) To what extent are services provided on the basis of assessed need?
7) To what extent are home help/home care services directed at those older people most in need?
8) To what extent are services available to older people with similar assessed needs irrespective of gender, race or income?

9) How well are the home help/home care services coordinated with social work, occupational therapy, community health services and independent providers?

10) How well are the resources for home help/home care managed?

Individual local authorities were sent details of these key questions before the inspection took place, so that they knew on what basis their service would be judged. The avoidance of the managerialist vocabulary of Performance Indicators was probably wise in the context of social work which is sometimes suspicious of approaches which are derived from industrial and commercial management practice rather than public welfare.

The ten key questions were addressed using the secondary indicators that had been developed during the theoretical study. These questions formed the basis of individual items using a range of data collection techniques. The views of users and carers were canvassed in two ways; firstly by commissioning a survey in the six areas of Scotland chosen for the inspection and secondly by more detailed semi-structured interviews with a sample of users and carers chosen on the basis of the extent of their service use and their living situation (whether or not they lived alone). This produced survey responses from more than 500 users and 130 carers and a set of extended, semi-structured interviews was conducted by inspectors with a further 85 users and 33 carers during the course of the inspection. Together, these interviews provided invaluable information about variations in the pattern of service being provided in the six areas and the needs of the older people themselves.

The ten questions formed the basis of focus group discussions with other stakeholders; with home helps, home care managers, social workers and care managers as well as individual interviews with senior managerial staff. Similar focus groups were conducted with referrers; community nurses, occupational therapists and social workers as frequent referrers of people to the home care service and using the same set of questions. Views of General Practitioners who are also key referrers to the service were obtained via a postal questionnaire which produced an unexpectedly high response.

How these indicators were subsequently modified and adapted for use by the Inspectorate provided useful information about the agendas being addressed in inspections. Some indicators had disappeared (for reasons such as the unlikelihood of information being available or the complexity of data sought) while other, organizational agendas, had been inserted such as the quality of inter-agency coordination and the efficiency of resource management, both of which have implications for the services provided to users.

The topics of quality and indicators of performance are not yet part of the culture of local authority social work departments. Purists might find some of the indicators originally devised too modest or vague but data is not yet available for even some of these. If social work department front line staff are to take on ownership of the notion of quality indicators in their work (Carter, 1991; Gaster, 1991) which is essential if they are ever to be anything more than a top-down control mechanism, first attempts at indicators will have to be modest and few. Modest statements of service objectives would be a significant first step. The drawing up of service specifications for potential independent providers can be one way of staff defining what the objectives and expectations of a service should be, with possible positive effects on the quality of their own, internal services. Departments do not, on the whole, survey service users about their satisfaction or views of services on a routine or regular basis so there is little data of this kind available. Inspections will have to be conducted using snapshot rather than longitudinal data for a while until longitudinal planning data becomes available and the use of information technology is developed further. Complaints procedures are not always easy to follow or well explained and since service users are reluctant to be seen to "complain", the value of complaints is, as yet, limited as a contribution to information about service quality. The imbalance of power between service providers and service users is graphically illustrated by the "gratitude" and high level of satisfaction so often expressed when users are asked their opinion of services by providers and which may mask dissatisfactions. The survey of home help users illustrates this point very well. One question asked whether the home help came often enough to be able to do what was needed, to which a respondent replied "yes" but followed it with a spontaneous comment that "she could do with more time".

The home help/home care inspection provided valuable insights into the inspection and data collection process; ten key indicators proved to be too many and we posed too many questions. The inspection collected an enormous amount of data, which took a long time to process. If inspections are to be useful to agencies, feedback needs to be given while it is still relevant. Clearly there is an optimum to be struck in terms of collecting sufficient data to make reasoned and informed judgements about service quality. What this balance is should become clearer with more experience of inspection.

Until recently, local authorities have not had information about unit costs of their services but their commissioning and purchasing role under community care has made this knowledge essential and it should be easier in future to develop some quantitative performance indicators around service costs. It is not a pointless exercise to have indicators or criteria for which there is, as yet, no information, since by asking about it, staff are made aware of aspects of service to which they should be giving some attention. In the home care inspection, none of the staff interviewed in the six areas had considered the possibility of service biases or inequities arising on grounds of gender or ethnicity but acknowledged the importance of this for users of the service. The legitimacy and appropriateness of seeking to make user and carer views of the service the focus of the inspection was not contested openly by staff perhaps because, like users of social work services, they had no clear expectations about what to expect (Gaster, 1991) by way of Scottish Office inspection. User and carer interviews were crucial in revealing the disparity between authorities' changing service priorities and users' preferences and enabled this to be raised in discussion with senior managers and in the subsequent inspection report.

8   Conclusion

Community care in Britain has been operating the new legislation for just four years, so the learning curve about practice and how to inspect it is steep. The home help service has been in existence for far longer than this but it too is expected to change its focus from a service-led response to a needs-focused one and this is taking time. However, this is a service which, on the whole, is much appreciated by users because of individual home helps' flexibility and responsiveness to their needs and wishes – a sign of quality which must be safeguarded. The dilemma for local authorities is how to meet differing levels of need for home help assistance within finite resources. Some are managing demand by changing eligibility criteria and the introduction of charges in what had previously been a free service in many areas. This has resulted in some older people choosing to buy the help they need privately or trying to do without formal assistance at all.

Indicators of service quality must reflect service users' needs and wishes if inspection is to play any part in their empowerment (Pollitt, 1988) since there are signs that the "mixed economy of care" will not necessarily result in increased choice of service providers. For the Inspectorate, the refinement of key questions or indicators must continue if inspections are to be useful in developing service quality. Performance indicators for inspections need to include time to reach accurate, measured and fair judgements about services for reasonable cost.

The inspection revealed that community care implementation has to be a gradual process which will take time to develop but the importance for staff morale of acknowledging and highlighting good practice cannot be exaggerated. At present, there is a dearth of some kinds of information, about overall potential need for services within areas to assist future planning and detailed information about service costs. Systems for these are being developed using information technology. From the service users' and carers' points of view, their empowerment still has some way to go and authorities have a major role to play here, both in developing the information they make available and the extent to which they involve consumer groups in service planning and development. Asking stakeholders' views about services from their unique perspectives enables a rounded picture to be built up which cross-references differing responses and in some cases, illuminates why shortfalls occur in the service and how they might be overcome.

The objective of inspecting community care services is to improve their quality by achieving greater efficiency, targeting those in greatest need and by enlarging choices available to users. This can only be done successfully if the people who use services or benefit from them have their views listened to and acted on. Those who commission, manage and deliver services need to set explicit standards against which their quality can be judged, based on what service users want and need. Decisions about services which have been taken locally can then be subject to the democratic process; citizen consumers can hold elected members accountable for those decisions. Scottish Office inspection is most likely to have a positive effect on the quality of social work services if it is experienced as an enabling rather than a fault-finding process and staff are persuaded that providing high quality services is both feasible and essential.

Notes

1　University of Stirling. The author is currently on secondment to the Social Work Services Inspectorate. Any opinions and views expressed in this paper are personal and do not necessarily reflect Scottish Office or UK Government policy.

2　The administration of social work in the United Kingdom is not uniform. Scotland is covered by different legislative and administrative arrangements.

References

Carter, Neil (1991) 'Learning to Measure Performance: The Use of Indicators in Organizations, *Public Administration* 69 Spring: 85-101.

Davies, Bleddyn/Knapp, Martin (1981) *Old People's Homes and the Production of Welfare*. Routledge and Kegan Paul.

Department of Health (1989) *Caring for People: Community Care in the Next Decade and Beyond*. Cm 849. London: HMSO.

Department of Health, Social Services Inspectorate/Scottish Office, Social Work Services Group (1991) *Care Management and Assessment: Practitioners Guide*. London: HMSO.

Fisher, Mike (1983) 'The Future of Client Studies', in Fisher, Mike (ed.), *Speaking of Clients*. Joint Unit for Social Services Research, University of Sheffield.

Gaster, Lucy (1991) *Quality at the Front-Line*. Bristol: SAUS Publications.

Griffiths, Roy (1988) *Community Care: Agenda for Action*. London: HMSO.

Hoyes, Lesley/Means, Robin/Le Grand, Julian (1992) *Made to Measure? Performance Measurement and Community Care*. Occasional Paper 39. Bristol: University of Bristol, School for Advanced Urban Studies.

Isaacs, B./Neville, Y. (1976) *The Measurement of Need in Old People*. Scottish Health Services Studies 34. Edinburgh: Scottish Home and Health Department.

James, Ann (1992) *Committed to Quality: Quality Assurance in Social Services Departments*. London: HMSO.

James, Ann (1992) 'Quality Counts: Achieving Quality in Social Care Services', in Kelly, Des/Warr, Bridget, op. cit.

Kelly, Des/Warr, Bridget (1992) *Quality Counts: Achieving Quality in Social Care Services.* London: Whiting and Birch Ltd.

Martin, Lawrence L. (1993) *Total Quality Management in Human Service Organizations.* London/New Delhi: Sage Newbury Park.

National Consumer Council (1986) *Measuring Up: Consumer Assessment of Local Authority Services: A Guideline Study.* London: National Consumer Council.

National Consumer Council (1987) *Performance Measurement and the Consumer.* London: National Consumer Council.

National Health and Community Care Act (1990). London: HMSO.

Pollitt, Christopher (1988) 'Bringing Consumers into Performance Measurement: Concepts, Consequences and Constraints', *Policy and Politics* 16 (2): 77-87.

Social Services Inspectorate/Social Work Services Group (1991) *Care Management and Assessment: Practitioners' Guide.* London: HMSO.

Social Work Services Inspectorate (1996) *Purpose and Responsibilities.* The Scottish Office, HMSO Scotland.

Stewart, J./Clarke, M. (1987) 'The Public Service Orientation: Issues and Dilemmas', *Public Administration* 65 (2): 161-178.

Wallace, Alison/Rees, Stuart (1988) 'The Priority of Client Evaluations', in Lishman, Joyce (ed.), *Research Highlights in Social Work 8 – Evaluation*, Second Edition. London: Jessica Kingsley Publishers Ltd.

Watson, David (ed.) (1985) *A Code of Ethics for Social Work: The Second Step.* BASW/ Routledge and Kegan Paul.

White, Ian (1988) 'Consumer Influences: Challenges for the Future', in Allen, Isobel (ed.), *Hearing the Voice of the Consumer.* London: Policy Studies Institute.

PART III

CASES AND COMMENTS

Quality Assured or Quality Compromised? Developing Domiciliary Care Markets in Britain[1]

Brian Hardy
Gerald Wistow

1   Introduction

The promotion of quality was central to the objectives of the major changes in adult personal social services introduced in Britain between 1991 and 1993. The aim was to improve both the quality of services and the quality of life of the most vulnerable people in society. In effect the changes focused on both the process dimension of quality – how care is produced and delivered – and also its outcome dimension, in terms of a government commitment to extend opportunities for choice and independent living (Secretaries of State, 1989). The essence of the reforms is indeed a twofold commitment: to ensuring that people are able to live at home, or in "homely" settings in the community, rather than in residential settings; and to ensuring that care will be based not, as historically, on what services were available but on an assessment of individual needs and the provision of services tailored to meet those needs. The fundamental premise is that living in the community, rather than in residential settings, is what the overwhelming majority of people want. Thus, good quality social care was defined not merely in terms of the inherent characteristics of services and their providers but, more fundamentally, in terms of the extent to which individuals could choose to live in their own homes with the support of appropriate domiciliary care services.

The organizational and funding arrangements designed to secure such improvements, along both dimensions of quality, involved the introduction (or, more properly, the reintroduction) of market forces into the supply of social care. The Government's belief was that a more mixed economy of care would encourage "innovation, diversity, proper attention to quality and the interests of consumers" (ibid.: par. 2.21). Indeed, the previous government came to office with an election manifesto in which the Prime Minister emphasized that "we are leading a drive for quality throughout our public services" (Major, 1992).[2] The introduction of competition was integral to this overall approach since, as Connolly et al. (1994) argue "choice, meaning choice between competing providers, (was) seen as the best spur to improved quality". However, markets are not only characterized by competition but also by contracts and service specifications which provide further incentives for enhancing quality: and, as Flynn and Common (1990) have argued, specifications which focus on outcomes rather than inputs can be important in creating more responsive services and encouraging innovation.

The purpose of this chapter is to review the extent to which, in Britain, the introduction of market forces and contracts in social care thus far constitutes an effective mechanism for enhancing the quality of domiciliary services. Its principal focus is on the implications and consequences of contracting arrangements for the quality of service delivery processes and of their outcomes for users. Before addressing such issues, however, it is important to note two factors: first, that the concern for quality in the personal social services predated the introduction of the current market "reforms" and is best seen as having a number of different origins; and second, that social care in general – and domiciliary care in particular – are perceived by many to be qualitatively different from other services, and thereby less appropriate to delivery via market mechanisms.

2 The Roots of a Growing Concern about Quality

Five key influences can be identified as responsible for a growing interest and concern about quality in social care in the 1980s (Wistow, 1991). First, there was evidence of poor performance: on the one hand, certain deep-seated weaknesses which led, *inter alia*, to user dependence rather than user independence; on the other hand, certain well-publicized scandals involving abuse of some of the most vulnerable members of society – whether children, old people, or people with learning disabilities. The government's acknowledgement of, and concern for, such abuse is manifest in recent policy guidelines and, in the case of abuse in people's own homes, is reflected in a report in 1993 optimistically entitled "No Longer Afraid" (Social Services Inspectorate, 1993). Second, as public expenditure constraints tightened throughout the 1970s and 1980s, it became clear that assumptions of progressive improvements in service standards via increasing levels of expenditure were ill-founded. Instead attention would have to shift to a concern for value for money (for achieving greater efficiency, effectiveness and economy) and, therefore, to a concern for the quality of service outputs and outcomes rather than the quantity of service inputs. Third, and bolstering this increasing concern for the quality of service outcomes, was the rise throughout the 1980s of a powerful consumerist movement. This development reinforced the view that service users should be active consumers rather than passive clients or recipients. This concern was further fuelled by the growing assertiveness of carers – the informal care sector – and the acknowledgement of their enormous contribution as the main providers of social care. Support for carers was one of the cornerstones of *Caring for People* in 1989 and the growing recognition of their contribution – worth an estimated £30 billion a year saving to the Exchequer (Wicks, 1994) – was reflected in last year's Carers (Recognition and Services) Act which gives carers the right to a separate assessment of their needs. Fourth, there was an increasing consensus, amongst both service professionals and groups representing service users, that personal social services should be designed around a clear set of values which express ordinary life ("normalization") principles. "As a result, planning and development activities have become increasingly oriented towards enhancing the quality of individuals' lifestyles and their experience of service delivery" (Wistow, 1991). Fifth, there was the broader shift to a "new public management" with the attendant transfer of many private sector management techniques and the associated disciplines supposedly induced by competitive market forces.

3 Social Care and Domiciliary Care Are "Different"

There has been an implicit concession by the government that welfare services are different from other public sector services and cannot be left wholly to free-market management: Thus "Civic Conservatism" represents an acceptance of the need at the most general level for a public sector role not only in service purchase and regulation but also some provision (Willetts, 1993). Nevertheless, market disciplines, it is argued, can be instilled by the introduction of competition between a diversity of providers and by contractual relationships between purchasers and providers. There was, however, a widespread view amongst the local authorities in our Mixed Economy of Care study that even if such market mechanisms were appropriate for the planning and delivery of some local authority services (such as cleaning) they were inappropriate for the personal social services because, as it was said, "social care is different". It is important to stress that this view transcended party politics and was held by Conservative as well as Labour-controlled authorities.

There is a widely acknowledged difference between public and private services – not just those in the field of social care. As Wilding notes: "In the commercial world, Quality is much more a private issue between buyer and seller. In the world of welfare there are other stakeholders" (1994). In other words, the quality of public services must be judged not just by the traditional standards of "accessibility", "acceptability" and "effectiveness" for service users but also in terms of their equity between service users (actual and potential) and also between service users and citizens as taxpayers.

But in terms of personal social services, as Adalbert Evers also makes clear, the difference lies elsewhere – what he refers to as the "structural difference due to the fact that a personal service is constituted by a personal interaction in contrast to a material good and product" (Evers, 1996) and what Wilding describes as some individual element: "At the heart of education, health and personal social services are personal relationships. The quality of these relationships is crucial to the quality of the service" (1994: 59). As one of the Directors of Social Services in our study said:

> Making contracts for window cleaning is one thing because if the contractor fails to clean 10 per cent of the windows you're all right; but if a domiciliary or residential care provider doesn't feed 10% of your clients you're really in trouble" (Wistow et al., 1996: 28).

We found local authorities identifying differences between the personal social services and other goods and services – even those within the public sector – along five main dimensions (Wistow et al., 1996). First there was vulnerability of the service recipients. This had been illustrated by the tragedy – referred to by a number of local authorities – of a user murdered by a carer working for a private domiciliary care agency. As one officer remarked: "it is a pretty crude example but it does make you realize the potential hazards and the potential risks". To some authorities this case reinforced their misgivings about the appropriateness of contracting with for-profit providers in an unregulated market. To others the concern was less about the "commercialization of care" than about the need for "an awful lot of work on specification, monitoring and quality". There was also concern that the very nature of *personal* social services is such that they do not lend themselves to conventional contract specifications. If it is tailored to the needs of particular individuals, the service, by definition, is non-standardized: unlike "tins of beans flooding out, each person with a stroke is going to have to have a specially designed package".

The second main difference between personal social services and other services was perceived to be the capacity of the users involved to act as consumers in a market place. One interviewee clearly described this difference, by contrasting the decision to choose a bar of chocolate and the decision to choose a social service. The former, he said, was a market with which people were "familiar" and operating in daily. Social care however: "Is something that's very, very special ... it's not something you find out about very quickly. You don't know about the market." Moreover in "inspecting the goods" potential users can judge physical attributes fairly readily but not such intangible but crucial aspects of care as the attitude of staff.

The third main difference was held to be the difficulty of specifying and measuring outcomes such as dignity and quality of life. One interviewee contrasted the complexity of securing, potentially through contracts with a multiplicity of providers, such outcomes with "the sort of tenders which are about how high you want the grass and how often you want it cut". The fourth difference between personal social services and other services was said to revolve around the very personal nature of such care and the imperative that there be not only continuity on the part of the provider but the right personal characteristics. As one interviewee graphically remarked:

> It may not matter who picks up your rubbish bag in the street [but] it does matter who wipes your bum ... And that ought to be the same person day in and day out because it's a very personal service and you have to trust that person.

This element of trust is doubly important in the case of domiciliary care. Most such care "takes place behind closed doors, in individual units" (Leat, 1993) with the person providing care "generally working in isolation on a one-to-one basis with the person needing care. There are no other work colleagues working alongside, to check out the right way to undertake a task nor a line manager to directly supervise the quality of the care provided" (JICC, 1994). Moreover, many of these staff are "not members of any profession, subject to no code of professional standards or ethics [and] often ill-paid and self-employed" (Leat, 1993). In addition, the majority of those receiving such care are old, many are frail and many live in isolation, without good family or community support networks (JICC, 1994; Richardson/Pearson, 1995).

Thus, if social care is in some significant respects qualitatively different from other goods and services, so too is domiciliary care different from other types of social care. Part of this difference is, crucially, the difficulty in assuring quality whether by traditional professional approaches (such as inspection) or by the business approaches adopted from the private sector. As the above analysis indicates, the emphasis on quality in the recent policy and organizational changes to the personal social services is neither wholly professionally nor wholly managerially driven. Rather, it is multi-faceted in its origins. In the same way, approaches to quality assurance also reflect professional and business influences, as Evers and Pollitt demonstrate elsewhere in this volume. In the case of social care, Alaszewski and Manthorpe (1993), identify five types of approaches to quality assurance which include professional peer review systems, external inspection and internal standard setting. What is significant about all of these approaches is that, in principle, they might be developed and applied in a wide range of organizational contexts, whether markets, quasi-markets or traditional hierarchies. Yet none of these sources deals with the extent to which market forces and service specifications, *in them-*

selves, help to promote and sustain high-quality services – a belief which, as we have indicated, is an underlying assumption of current policy for social care in Britain. The remainder of this paper deals with the implications for quality of the introduction of market forces. More particularly, it focuses on the implications of contracts and purchaser/provider relationships for quality in domiciliary care markets. The importance of this perspective is both in the centrality of domiciliary care to current concepts of good quality care and the fact that domiciliary – unlike residential – services are almost wholly unregulated.

4   The Domiciliary Care Industry and Its Regulation

As indicated above, better quality social care is seen in government policy to depend upon extending domiciliary care principally through the independent sector. However, that sector is both small and young. In addition, it is subject to little regulation. In their recent consultation document, *Moving Forward*, government Ministers acknowledge that "regulation and inspection have a key role in safe-guarding the standards of services provided for users of social services" (Department of Health and Welsh Office, 1995: 1). In view of this statement there is an apparently glaring anomaly in the domiciliary care market as compared with residential and nursing home care. Under the terms of the 1984 Registered Homes Act and the 1991 Registered Homes Amendment Act, residential and nursing homes are subject to a national framework of regulation and inspection – a framework that is the principal focus of the *Moving Forward* review. By contrast, domiciliary care (and day care) is subject to no such national framework. Even though the procedures for registering and inspecting residential homes (by local authorities) and nursing homes (by health authorities) are set locally, and even though there are no mandatory national standards, the legislation provides a clear framework for initially screening and subsequently inspecting the quality of care to residents. In two recent circulars – LAC(95)12 and HSG(95)41 – the government has underlined that the primary objectives of this regulatory framework are "to protect residents and maintain standards" (Department of Health, 1995: LAC(95)12, par. 5). Despite this statement, there is no comparable system for protecting residents receiving care in their own homes. Instead, the contracting process and internal quality assurance schemes are said to provide other ways of specifying and monitoring standards. It is, however, worth noting a view from the home care industry that "the content of state regulation and most independent quality assurance schemes overlap so little that it is difficult to see how one could replace the other" (Laing/Buisson, 1994). It is also worth remembering that not all domiciliary care businesses are seeking publicly-funded clients and that there are no public contracting processes through which quality can be assured for private payers.

In resisting a mandatory national system of regulation the government is ignoring the requests of both local authorities and providers within the domiciliary care business. Such calls are based on widespread concern and in some cases a belief that:

> it will only be a matter of time before there is a major scandal in domiciliary care ... because consumers are not afforded the same protection of residential, nursing and care homes. (Laing/Buisson, 1994)

In view of the refusal of the government to enact legislation, a Private Members Bill – the Registration of Domiciliary Care Agencies Bill – has now been drawn up which, if enacted, would make it illegal to carry on a domiciliary care business without a license granted by a local authority. Such licenses, granted for three years, would be denied or revoked if the applicant was found to be "not a fit person", or the business premises were unsuitable, or the agency was being improperly conducted. If enacted there would be subsequent regulations setting out requirements in respect of, for example: records, charging, advertising and the qualifications of those involved. Local authorities would also have powers of inspection – though not in users' own homes. In the absence of such a mandatory framework, the government continues to rely on its own Social Services Inspectorate, on voluntary frameworks agreed between purchasers and providers – nationally and locally – and on the contracting process at local level.

Concern about the absence of a statutory framework has led to the production of voluntary frameworks. The principal ones are the UKHCA's own Code of Practice (adherence to which is a requirement for members) and the *Framework for The Development of Standards for the Provision of Domiciliary Care* produced in 1994 by the Joint Advisory Group of Domiciliary Care Associations. This group represented the interests of service professionals, local authority purchasers and independent sector providers. The aim of the framework is to provide guidance and standards for the provision of "high quality services", the provision of which is said to be "vital for the success of community care policies and for the long-term future of supporting the increasing number of frail and dependent people in their own homes" (Joint Advisory Group, 1994: 1).

5 Quality through Contracting

We can categorize the concerns about quality through contracting being assured or compromised under three main headings:

- Inappropriate contracting arrangements.
- Resource pressures.
- Purchaser/provider relationships.

5.1 Inappropriate Contracting Arrangements

Under this heading we want to deal with five main emerging issues. Before doing so, however, it is important to make two caveats. First, local authority social services departments have only recently taken on a market-management role. Historically they have been weak in precisely those areas that they are now required to quickly develop – namely, needs assessment, service specification and contract design, negotiation and monitoring. There are, in other words, technical skills and competencies to be acquired and developed. There is also, as discussed below, much misunderstanding or mistrust to overcome in relations with some of the providers with whom they are expected to contract. The second main caveat is that the views expressed by providers cannot be wholly disinterested: if they are critical of contracting arrangements, it may well be because they are simply not being given what they regard as the right amount or right type of business. At the same time, however, we have some evidence which suggests that on the basis of their expressed motivations and revealed business behaviour, most providers apparently give a higher priority to service quality than to profit maximization. The principal emerging problems with contracting arrangements can be described under the following headings:

- duplication and laxity of provider accreditation;
- inflexibility of contracts;
- inappropriate contract types;
- multiplicity of providers and carers; and
- inadequate monitoring and review.

5.1.1 Duplication and Laxity of Provider Accreditation

In the absence of a national regulatory framework, many local authorities, and mainly in the last two years, have established their own schemes to accredit domiciliary care providers. They have faced a number of problems. First, they cannot compel providers to seek such accreditation. Second, they have difficulty in simply identifying lists of existing providers. Third, by law they cannot charge providers for such accreditation – either initially or subsequently. By contrast, residential and nursing homes are required to pay annual registration fees to local and health authorities respectively.

The concern of some providers is twofold: first, that such accreditation arrangements, being local, are enormously variable across local authorities. Providers wishing to operate across authority boundaries must seek accreditation in each of the authorities operating such schemes, unless there are reciprocal arrangements between local authorities – or the sort of multi-authority scheme adopted by the London Boroughs – to accept the accreditation given to a provider by another authority. Without such arrangements, the administrative costs to providers can become a significant burden. The second concern amongst providers is that, in some authorities, accreditation procedures are too lax: not only are they insufficiently rigorous at the outset (in, for example, taking up personal and business references, or seeking police vetting) but sanctions are infrequently applied thereafter. There was also a related concern that there was a presumption by purchasers of equality amongst providers once the latter had been accredited – that they were each a quality provider. That being so, the only way the local authority could select from amongst accredited providers was on price.

One provider was severely critical of a local authority which, she said, undertook no checks despite the voluminous paperwork required from potential providers. Her warning of the dangers of such laxity was a stark one: "what we want", she said, "is a few good deaths and then they might work out that sending the cheapest provider into frail elderly people in a remote village isn't a clever thing to do".

Much of the criticism of such laxity, however, was aimed not so much at local authorities but at the government for its refusal to create a mandatory national framework of registration and inspection. There was a widespread acceptance that, in the absence of such a national framework, local authorities were right to establish local systems of regulation. There was also some recognition of the resource pressures which at least affected, even if they should not wholly undermine, local authorities' attempts to vet and police provider standards. There was, however, widespread concern amongst providers about the sheer *"naïveté"* or "immaturity" of some authorities. The worry was not only an understandably self-interested one from providers regarding themselves as penalized for charging a "realistic" price for quality but also a disinterested one on behalf of users. As one provider graphically put it:

> If we allow the cowboys to develop, we [quality providers] are going to end up destroyed and people are going to die and be maltreated.

There was, it was widely argued, a need for much tighter vetting and control by social services departments if there was to be no legislation requiring registration.

Linked to the issue of accreditation is that of quality assurance schemes themselves. Some, but by no means all, local authorities, do require as part of their accreditation schemes that providers have in place – or, at the very least, demonstrate that they are developing – quality assurance schemes. These may either be internally developed or externally validated systems. The most common of the latter schemes, which have been a "burgeoning market" (Laing/Buisson, July 1994) in the care home industry in the 1990s, are BS 5750 (now BS EN ISO 9000) and Investors in People. One of the acknowledged shortcomings of such systems is that they are restricted to the essentially second-order measurement of management processes and human resources functions rather than the first-order measurement of the quality of care delivered. There has also been a recognition of the difficulties of applying BS EN ISO 9000 to services where, unlike, for example, manufacturing production, "it is not so much a question of 'right first time' as 'right only time'" (Freeman-Bell/Grover, 1994). As the "human resource analogue" of BS EN ISO 9000, Investors in People is portrayed as more appropriate to service industries; but like BS EN ISO 9000, Investors in People "says nothing about the quality of care as perceived by residents and their relatives" (Laing/Buisson, July 1994).

Part of the difficulty for local authorities in insisting on such schemes is that they have until recently been rare in local authorities themselves. A survey in 1992 showed that only a minority of local authorities in Great Britain had been awarded quality management certificates – as few as 16% of London Boroughs. Moreover of those with a certificate only 19% had one for more than one service and less than 10% of all certificates were for services other than civil engineering, or those not subject to compulsory competitive tendering (Freeman-Bell/Grover, 1994). The survey authors concluded that "little has yet been achieved by local authorities in introducing quality management" (ibid.: 566). Perhaps unsurprisingly, in view of these figures, only 4% of authorities required service providers with whom they were contracting to have in place quality management systems satisfying the requirements of BS 5750.

A survey of all social services departments in the UK in 1993 similarly showed that only two of the 132 departments had produced draft BS 5750 documents. Moreover, there was little evidence of a commitment to quality amongst senior managers or elected members and little evidence of user involvement in standard setting. The authors concluded that although several departments had "started the quality journey, many have yet to embark on this process" (Isgrove/Patel, 1993). Another problem for social services departments is that of adopting schemes appropriate to personal social services. In its own publication, *Committed to Quality*, the Department of Health acknowledged that BS 5750 "is too narrow and literal a system for use in human service organizations overall": although it might "sometimes be used as part of a wider system" (Department of Health, 1992: 8). A third problem for local authorities is that such quality management schemes are expensive to develop and may, therefore, go beyond the reach of some small-scale providers.

5.1.2 Inflexibility of Contracts

One independent sector interviewee said she had specifically asked for contracts to be drafted so that she had "the flexibility to respond to need". From her point of view this was necessary for two reasons: first, because social services staff were unavailable "out-of-hours"; "at the weekends everybody disappears and I'm left to make decisions". Second was the concern about adhering rigidly to a contract and therefore sometimes doing precisely what the client themselves said they did not want or need. She gave the example of having a contract to give a lady lunch: "you get round there and Mrs. X wants some fish from the shop. Now this is a legal document and if you get some fish and leave it for her to cook for herself later on you're actually breaking the contract". Her general experience was that if she discussed this with the responsible care manager (or social worker) as soon as possible there was usually no problem. But part of the problem was that it did depend upon individual care managers being prepared to relax the terms of the contract – and it did depend upon her being able to contact the care manager at short notice.

This, however, was not always the case with other providers in other authorities. One cited the case – very similar to the above one – of a service user for whom the company had a contract, *inter alia*, to cook lunch between 12.00 pm and 13.00 pm. On one occasion the carer arrived to be told the user did not want lunch cooked that day but would like something from the local shops. Accordingly, the carer went to the shop to buy some lunch. While doing so she was seen by one of the local authority's care managers who was "contract monitoring" in his car nearby. The next day the company's proprietor was telephoned and told that her care worker had broken the terms of the contract – by leaving the user's home between 12.00 and 13.00 and visiting the local shops. When the proprietor tried to explain that the departure from the letter of the contract was directly due to the user's request, she was told that the contract had been breached and it was therefore terminated. Her company received no future business from the local authority for the next six weeks.

We need to stress that such cases were not a commonplace for all providers in all localities. Moreover, where they did occur, providers said that it was often more a reflection of the attitude of an individual care manager than of the authority as a whole. But such cases should not be dismissed as wholly atypical or simply the product of an individual's approach to contract compliance. It is the threat of losing contracts in similar circumstances which constrains some providers from altering contracted care packages and others from extending or altering contracted times. Yet the very essence of the current policy changes – the measure of improved quality – is that services meet individual needs, as chosen by users themselves. This is not to suggest that users are sovereign and can solely determine altered or additional services. However, in the kinds of cases referred to above, quality services might reasonably have been described as those which responded flexibly and sensitively to the users' changing needs. This is what is meant by user choice, by needs-led services, by flexible and appropriate packages of care and by the provision of independent living. In the light of these findings, it is significant that the Audit Commission has also found that inflexibility – the inability to adjust services to fit users' and carers' needs – was a "particularly common complaint" across all services, residential and non-residential (Audit Commission, 1994: 8).

5.1.3 Inappropriate Contract Types

In the purchase of both residential (including nursing) and non-residential care services local authorities are using three basic types of contract: block, cost and volume and spot. Our evidence on the purchase of residential care in the first three years of the current reforms is that local authorities were primarily using spot contracts with individual providers for individual service users. Typically, however, such arrangements were increasingly taking the form of a "pre-purchase" or "call-off" agreement. In so doing, providers were agreeing to the terms of a service specification setting out for example, broad service principles, objectives and pricing arrangements. Individual service contracts negotiated for particular clients would be drafted in terms of the personal requirements of the particular individual within the terms of this broader pre-purchase agreement. Being a signatory to such an agreement constitutes no guarantee of clients but it does offer purchasers a panel of providers with whom they can try to place clients and do so without lengthy contract negotiation. The evidence is that in the domiciliary care market, too, most local authority purchasers are predominantly using spot contracts, commonly on the basis of pre-purchase agreements. In this market even more than in the residential care market – because the workplace is someone's own home – purchasers argue that they cannot consider block contracts with new providers who have yet to prove their ability to deliver high-quality services cost-effectively. However, independent sector providers argue that reliance on spot contracts is having a seriously detrimental effect on their business. The UKHCA argued in 1994 that a "concentration on spot, rather than block, purchasing was inhibiting the expansion of services" (UKHCA, 1994). Providers, it was said, were "unable to commit resources to expanding services, or extending them into new areas, because they had no assurance that they would be able to sell the service in sufficient quantity to cover their investment" (ibid.). Spot purchasing, together with contracts for single hours work "affected the quality of the service provided in that it proved far more difficult to provide continuity of care" (ibid.).

What is clear is that a spot contract for residential care is a significantly different arrangement from a spot contract for domiciliary care. The former will typically comprise a contract of some months or years duration. By contrast a contract for domiciliary care will typically be for hours or even part-hours duration. In addition, domiciliary care is different from residential care as a business in being inherently more discontinuous, fragmentary, and intermittent. It is also geographically dispersed rather than concentrated. A domiciliary care provider will therefore need potentially to negotiate and manage a large number of spot contracts – for different users in different localities – to acquire the same volume of business as that transacted in one residential care spot contract.

The consequences, especially for the smaller domiciliary care providers, are potentially crippling unless there is a sufficient volume of local authority referrals or unless they have relatively stable income streams from private payers. For those many providers encouraged into the market by local authorities on the "promise" of a reliable flow and high volume of referrals, the spasmodic and scant referrals that they eventually received – especially after the local authority funding crisis in Autumn 1994 – has had serious consequences. One of the most immediate is the loss of suitably trained staff. Indeed, without the prospect of a continuous stream of work, it is difficult both to recruit and to retain suitable skilled staff, in what in most localities is a highly competitive labour market. According to one provider, it was not possible to assess the quality of staff until they had been in employment for six to eight weeks. But they could only be kept in employment "on a fixed number of hours basis". While local authorities "held rigidly to spot contracts", it was argued, "the opportunity for consistency and reliability is very suspect". The relevance of such concerns is indicated by a survey of independent sector providers which showed only 2% had block contracts with local authorities and only 5% had cost and volume contracts. By contrast 65% had only spot contracts (Young/Wistow, 1995).

Some small providers said that they had set up in business, post 1993, because they had been encouraged, in rural areas especially, to provide a highly localized community service. There is here – in terms of perceived quality – a direct parallel with small independent-sector residential homes. We have found a preference amongst many local authorities for such small homes precisely because they are deemed to give a personal, homely and therefore high-quality service (Wistow et al., 1996). Equally, we found purchasers – and residential home owners too – fearful of the threat of such homes either being bought up or priced out of the market by the large national companies. There is a similar threat in the domiciliary care market where small-scale providers giving an equally valued personal and community service (often in rural areas) risk being squeezed out of the market. In this case, pressure arises not just from the competitive pricing of larger companies but from their reliance on an anticipated volume of local authority referrals – a volume sufficient to negate some of the problems of spot contracts. Indeed we have seen examples of such providers already having left the domiciliary care market: providers, in one case, offering a service based explicitly on the continuity of care to users by "familiar local faces". Many local authorities which accept their responsibility for actively shaping the domiciliary and residential care markets nevertheless acknowledge that they do not have sufficient monitoring mechanisms to alert them to the vulnerability of such preferred "quality" providers. Moreover even if they could identify such business vulnerability many profess a powerlessness to sustain the businesses.

There are, however, two principal mechanisms available to purchasers to provide such support: the payment of quality premiums (as, for example, by the former Humberside County Council to residential and nursing homes) and the negotiation of block contracts. The latter, it was frequently argued by providers, would stabilize businesses by allowing good staff to be retained: in effect, such an approach has been conceded by the local authority purchasers and recommended by the Audit Commission. According to the Association of Metropolitan Authorities' Under-Secretary in 1995 "cost and volume contracts have much to recommend them because of their combination of certainty and feasibility" (AMA, 1995). The Audit Commission has similarly suggested that local authorities "may wish to provide greater stability and security to some non-local authority services by providing more block contracts for at least some parts of the service" (Audit Commission, 1995).

5.1.4 Multiplicity of Providers and Carers

Speaking on behalf of her clients, one provider said that it was a common complaint that "they're looking after me but I've had 27 different people this week". Even allowing for hyperbole, this statement highlights the often-repeated criticism of local authority contracting procedures, that they lead to a multiplicity of providers and carers. As we indicated previously, it is the essence of personal care services that they are personal and a large part of the quality of such care is that it is provided on a continuous basis by a trusted carer. As Leat has argued:

> genuine continuing competition is likely to lead to regular changes in suppliers. This in turn will affect continuity of care ... [which] ... is not an administrative convenience nor a desirable addition but is central to the definition of quality care. (Leat, 1993)

According to many providers interviewed in our study, such continuity of care is frequently broken as local authorities tend to use the independent sector as "stop gaps" to provide the sort of "out-of-hours" work, at night, at weekend and over bank holidays which many local authorities' in-house services find it difficult or costly to provide. The complaint from providers is not just that they are given this intermittent and difficult work but that too often it is the majority of their contracted work. Also, in the view of providers, local authorities frequently contract with one independent-sector provider for one item of care – for example, house cleaning or shopping; with another provider for "out-of-hours" personal care or night-sitting; and retain some core services (i.e. from 9.00 to 17.00 o'clock and comprising basic personal care such as provision of meals and bathing) for in-house provision. Other research demonstrates the increasing differentiation of domiciliary care services by which individuals:

> may receive care from community nurses, a social services "shopper", a social services "cleaner", a social services "personal care assistant" or private agency cleaners and care assistants. (Richardson/Pearson, 1995)

As these authors conclude, "in domiciliary care, several different workers performing different elements of care, under increasing cost and time pressures may preclude the establishment of a caring relationship" (ibid.). Thus, whilst such contracting behaviour gives apparent flexibility to local authority purchasers it does not aid the stability of small providers and is detrimental to the quality of care for users.

5.1.5 Inadequate Monitoring and Review

Given the special nature of care delivered in someone's own home and the problems associated with provider registration and accreditation and the vetting of individual carers it is of paramount importance that once awarded contracts are properly monitored and reviewed – and where necessary terminated. The Department of Health's practice guidance to local authorities (Department of Health, 1995) states quite simply that: "The contract manager will monitor the quality of services offered as part of the contract management function" (par. 5.6.1). The guidance is couched in terms of a straightforward collation of views from inspection units, care managers and users themselves via formal complaints procedures or satisfaction surveys (though there is no mention in this section of the views of providers).

The other source for obtaining users' views is, of course, the review of individual care plans. It has been claimed by providers, however, that typically care reviews are not taking place as planned on a regular and formal basis. Part of the problem for providers is that they are often not invited to review meetings; or, if invited, they are expected to attend without being paid to do so. For local authority purchasers the problems of contract compliance are threefold: first, the inherent problem of being present to monitor the care received in someone's own home; second, the well-known problem of most clients being unwilling to complain – either out of gratitude for any service or for fear of the withdrawal of services; and third, the problems of cost associated with rigorous monitoring procedures involving, *inter alia*, the employment of contract compliance staff.

5.2 Resource Pressures

It is self-evident that inadequate resources represent some threat to service quality irrespective of whether services are being delivered through market mechanisms or by traditional bureaucracies. The worry for many independent sector providers is that resource pressures are leading local authorities to behave in ways detrimental to the quality of services delivered and the stability of their business. As we have argued elsewhere:

> Resource constraints which lead to "stop-go" purchasing policies constrict and limit business confidence and the expansion of existing independent sector organizations. Perhaps even more importantly, they are also likely to inhibit the growth of new providers. (Young/Wistow, 1995)

There was a widespread view amongst providers in our study that whatever the aspirations and intentions expressed in *Caring for People*, services increasingly are resource-led not needs-led. In many authorities, as the most recent Audit Commission report (March 1996) confirms, care managers or other budget holders are being required to operate within budget ceilings and tight eligibility criteria. As one provider remarked, initially: "It was the client and the care package first, now it's the other way round; they give us a price and we work a care package into that price, which mightn't be the best care package for that person".

The clear consequence of tightening eligibility criteria is that the threshold for receipt of any care is raised and increasingly those deemed to be at minimum risk may receive no service at all or merely "minimal physical maintenance" (Richardson/Pearson, 1995). The latter, the authors argue, is to be distinguished from social care which is emotional and affective in character. It is also crucially dependent upon social relationships – upon the ways in which the care task is undertaken. However, resource constraints, these authors claim, lead to purchasers concentrating upon minimum physical maintenance. Moreover the pressure is to seek the most competitive provider not in terms of quality but of cost. Many providers in our study argued that in yielding to this pressure, purchasers were penalizing quality providers – those who invested in staff training and quality assurance and who paid decent wages – and favouring less reputable providers capable of quoting much lower prices because they invested little or nothing in training or quality assurance and paid low wages.

5.3   Purchaser/Provider Relationships

The principal focus of this paper, as with that in much of the literature, is on the means by which purchasing authorities can ensure service quality through the initial selection of quality providers and through the subsequent process of contract specification, negotiation and monitoring. It is clear, however, that quality services require not just quality providers but quality purchasers: a crucial determinant of quality being precisely the relationship between local authority purchasers and service providers no less than it is between providers and their employees or between the latter, carers and service users.

The evidence of our research is that many local authorities have a clear preference for dealing with voluntary and non-profit providers rather than private providers. This preference was based on three factors: trust, track record and transactions costs. Voluntary agencies were seen to be more trustworthy because they generally shared the same service values as local authorities with whom they had worked closely for many years. Moreover, and partly because of such inherent trust, the transaction costs of dealing with voluntary agencies – both in terms of contract specification and contract monitoring – were considered lower than those involved in dealing with private providers. The latter, in 1991, were widely seen as inappropriate providers of social care – a perception based on the assumption that they were by definition motivated by the pursuit of maximum profit. In the last two years research has revealed a lessening of this suspicion of private providers. It has also indicated that many small private providers of residential care – many of whom have a background in the caring professions – are not principally motivated by profit maximization.

We have argued elsewhere (Wistow/Hardy, 1996) that local authorities must increasingly act as "mature" purchasers: by recognizing the diversity of motivations, by acknowledging the vulnerability of many small providers and therefore by setting their relationship with providers not in the adversarial terms that have characterized much recent practice but in terms of partnership. One model here is the sort of relational contracting (Dore, 1986) long found in Japanese industry where, rather than being straightforwardly competitive, contractual relations are frequently based on long-term partnerships. As Colling argues, relational contracting recognizes "that quality service is contingent upon mutual dependence, goodwill and long-term commitment and investment" (Colling, 1995).

6   Conclusion

This paper poses the question whether the quality of personal social services to people living at home – and thereafter their quality of life – is being assured or compromised by the development of markets for domiciliary care. There is as yet no clear answer to that question, not least because most of those in the best position to judge – service users – have yet to be asked. What we have tried to indicate, however, is that the initial frameworks for developing these markets seem unable to guarantee such quality. Some local authorities will argue that they lack the resources; others will argue that they lack the appropriate regulatory framework; others will argue that there are insufficient independent-sector providers. Some providers, on the other hand, will argue that local authorities lack either the will to develop independent sector provision or the competence to do so. What is certain, however, is that whilst securing quality may be the underlying aim of the current changes, it is also the overriding problem.

Notes

1   The paper draws on a number of pieces of work undertaken by the authors, especially a long-term study commissioned by the Department of Health – The Mixed Economy of Care research programme – which is being undertaken in conjunction with our colleague Ruth Young at the Nuffield Institute and with Professor Martin Knapp, Jules Forder and Jeremy Kendall at the PSSRU (L.S.E.). We draw also on work undertaken

over the last two years by Gerald Wistow and Ruth Young on behalf of the United Kingdom Home Care Association (UKHCA) – the national representative organization for domiciliary care organizations (in all parts of the independent sector), a core aim of which is to promote and ensure the highest-quality service provision.

2   This paper was written before the election of the Labour government in May 1997. All subsequent references in this paper to the government are in respect of the previous Conservative government.

References

Alaszewski, A./Manthorpe, J. (1993) 'Quality and the Welfare Services: A Literature Review', *British Journal of Social Work* 23 (6): 653-665.

Audit Commission (1994) *Taking Stock: Progress with Community Care*. London: H.M.S.O.

Audit Commission (1996) *Balancing the Care Equation: Progress with Community Care*. London: H.M.S.O.

Colling, T. (1995) 'Competing for Quality: Competitive Contracting and the Management of Quality in Local Management', *Local Government Policy Making* (21) 4: 33-42.

Connolly, M./McKeown, P./Milligan-Byrne, G. (1994) 'Making the Public Sector More User Friendly? A Critical Examination of the Citizen's Charter', *Parliamentary Affairs* (47) 1: 23-36.

Department of Health (1992) *Committed to Quality*. London: H.M.S.O.

Department of Health and Welsh Office (1995) *Moving Forward: A Consultation Document on the Regulation and Inspection of Social Services*. London: Department of Health.

Department of Health (1995a) *Regulation of Residential Care Homes*, LAC(95)12. London: Department of Health.

Dore, R. (1986) *Flexible Rigidities: Industrial Policy and Structural Adjustments in the Japanese Economy 1970-80*. London: Athlone Ross.

Evers, A. (1997) 'Quality Development – Part of a Changing Culture of Care in Personal Social Services', in: Evers, A./Haverinen, R./Leichsenring, K./ Wistow, G. (eds.), *Developing Quality in Personal Social Services – Concepts, Cases and Comments*. Aldershot: Ashgate.

Flynn, N./Common, R. (1990) *Contracts for Community Care*. Caring for People Implementation Document. London: Department of Health.

Freeman-Bell, G./Grover, R. (1994) 'The Use of Quality Management in Local Authorities', *Local Government Studies* (20) 4: 554-569.

Isgrove, R./Patel, A. (1993) 'Quality Progress in U.K. Social Services Departments', *International Journal of Public Sector Management* 6 (6) 55-66.

Joint Advisory Group of Domiciliary Care Associations (1994) *A Framework for the Development of Standards for the Provision of Domiciliary Care*. Milton Keynes: JICC.

Joint Initiative for Community Care (1994) *The Provision of Care Services to People in their Own Home: A Disaster Waiting to Happen*. Luton: LGMB/ADSS.

Laing/Buisson (1995) *Community Care Market News* 1 (4). London: Laing and Buisson.

Leat, D. (1993) *The Development of Community Care by the Independent Sector*. London: Policy Studies Institute.

Major, J. (1992) *Conservative Party Manifesto, 1992*. London: Conservative Party.

Richardson, S./Pearson, M. (1995) 'Dignity and Aspirations Denied: Unmet Health and Social Care Needs in an Inner-city Area', *Health and Social Care in the Community* 3 (5): 279-287.

Platt, D. (1995) *Contracting – The Purchaser Perspective.* Presentation to the UKHCA Spring Convention, Manchester 9 March.

Secretaries of State (1989) *Caring for People: Community Care in the Next Decade and Beyond.* Cm. 849. London: H.M.S.O.

Social Services Inspectorate (1993) *No Longer Afraid: The Safeguard of Older People in Domestic Settings.* London: H.M.S.O.

Social Services Inspectorate (1993a) *Raising the Standard: the 2nd Annual Report of the Chief Inspector, 1992/93.* London: H.M.S.O.

United Kingdom Home Care Association (1994) *Progress and Problems with Contracting: Views from the Independent Domiciliary Care Sector.* London: UKHCA.

Wicks, M. (1994) 'Community Care Costs. The Mixed Economy of Care', *Bulletin* 3, December. Leeds: Nuffield Institute for Health and P.S.S.R.U./L.S.E..

Wilding, P. (1994) 'Maintaining Quality in Human Services', *Social Policy and Administration* 28 (1): 57-72.

Willetts, D. (1993) 'Why Tories Ought to Care', *The Independent* 1 October.

Wistow, G. (1991) 'Quality and Research: The Policy and Legislative Context', *Research Policy and Planning* 9 (1): 9-12.

Wistow, G./Hardy, B. (in press) 'Competition, Collaboration and Markets', *Journal of Interprofessional Care* 10 (1).

Wistow, G./Knapp, M./Hardy, B./Allen, C. (1994) *Social Care in a Mixed Economy.* Buckingham: Open University Press.

Wistow, G./Knapp, M./Hardy, B./Forder, J./Kendall, J./Manning, R. (1996) *Social Care Markets: Progress and Prospects.* Buckingham: Open University Press.

Young, R./Wistow, G. (1995) 'Provider Power', *Community Care* 17-23 August 1995.

CHAPTER 12

Rationality and Management in Public Care Services[1]

Sturle Næss
Kari Wærness

In this paper, we shall present the results of an evaluation study on the public care services for the elderly in a middle-sized Norwegian municipality (Næss/Wærness, 1995). This municipality has to a very great extent implemented new methods for organization and management which are nowadays recommended by the Ministry of Social Affairs. Our study can therefore be seen as a "case-study" on the implementation of new organizational models in public care services in Norway; it can be used to illustrate why the "managerial approach" is not the right one for bettering the quality of public care services for elderly people.

1   Principles for Developing Quality by New Methods for Organization and Management

Governmental authorities in Norway have in recent years made an effort to *de-institutionalize* long-term care for the elderly, and to substitute it with open care services at the municipal level (NOU, 1992: 1). Three major principles for organizing these services have been suggested to reach this goal. First and foremost is that the responsibility for housing and care services should be separated. This means that, independent of how much care and help the individual elderly person might need in everyday life, organized services connected to housing, as in nursing homes, should *not* be offered as a permanent service. Second, institutional care and home-based services should have a joint budget, joint management and a joint pool of care workers. This organizational change is called "the great integration". And third, municipalities should be divided into smaller geographical service areas to keep service organizations from becoming too large and complex. The major argument behind the government recommendations is the following: independent of the individual elderly's need for care and help, home-based care services are *qualitatively* a better alternative than residential care. In addition, home-based care services are economically more efficient than institutional care. Government authorities have underlined that the quality argument is the most important. And quality is defined in the following way: public care services should primarily be oriented towards the goal of fulfilling individual needs for help.

Here we want to question the possibility of this reform leading to both more *effective* and more *efficient* public care services.

Different Views on Quality

Government authorities define "quality" in public care services as fulfilling clients' individual needs.[2] In this discussion, the need for "autonomy" has been the central one. Lack of autonomy has been defined as the most negative aspect of institutional care and has been an important argument for the government's effort to de-institutionalize long-term care for the elderly. On the other hand, the question of the need of elderly people with disabilities for security and closeness, has not been seriously discussed in the public debate on public care. Institutional care can be said to give priority to helpless people's need for security, while home-based care services are associated with autonomy. Most people want both autonomy and security, and the dominant ideology of care seems to take for granted that – independent of how much help in everyday life the individual elderly person might need – it is possible to fulfil both kinds of needs adequately by reorganizing public care services and increasing home-based care services. In order to strengthen an elderly individual's economic autonomy, it is suggested that the individuals receiving services pay for them on a sliding scale according to income.

The leaders in the municipality studied found it difficult to implement the governmental recommendations for several reasons. The situation after "the great integration" was especially difficult, mainly due to financial constraints. The belief in being on the right track, however, made it possible for the leaders to cope with conflicts with care workers, clients and relatives. The leaders seemed to believe that they managed to implement the reforms because they invested a great deal of time in coordinating and discussing difficult cases and situations, and because they spoke with "one voice". What they meant was that they had managed to meet the challenges in public care services through what was called "a conscious organization": an organization able to change priorities and having shown its capability to formulate new priorities in a situation of great economic constraint. The leaders meant that, for the time being, there was reason to question the quality of services.

They were, however, convinced that the situation would have been worse if they had not changed the organization. According to the leaders, the most important change had been the increased chances for elderly people with disabilities to remain at home.

The clients we talked to did not have much knowledge about new methods for organization and management. What they did know was that the number of long-term places in institutional care had been reduced, and they felt this to be an unfortunate development. They underlined that they were satisfied with the quality of the help they received but were dissatisfied with not getting enough help, in particular with practical tasks. In addition, they felt it to be a problem that they had to relate to too many different care workers. Our study shows that clients who need a lot of care and help do not define and prioritize "autonomy" in the same way as the leaders of care services. They do not connect "autonomy" to living in their own home. What they evaluate as important, is to have some influence on when they will get help, what kind of help and how much help. They also attach importance to care workers not being so busy when they visit them, so that they, with the help of the care workers, can dress themselves and eat by themselves. Furthermore, there are many clients who find that, instead of having a lukewarm and relatively tasteless dinner delivered by "meals on wheels", they should have the right to decide, at least sometimes, what they want for dinner and to have it prepared in their own home according to their own wishes. In addition, the clients we interviewed responded very negatively to the idea of separating housing and services. This change led to some of them having to pay so much for services that they had less money left than if they had lived in a traditional nursing home.

Relatives argued that political and administrative leaders showed greater concern for efficiency reforms and cost-cutting than for individual clients. They also felt that the ideology of rehabilitation implied unrealistic expectations on the elderly's capacity for training and self-help. One consequence of this was that the relatives felt "forced" to take responsibility for elderly care in a way not in keeping with a welfare state. One of them, a woman who had her father living in her home, saw no other way to get more public care for him than to dress him, place him in his wheelchair, leave him outside the house, lock the door and call the police for help. After this episode, the father got a place in long-term institutional care.

The care workers argued that they had had little influence on organizational reforms. Protests against the content and speed of these reforms were allegedly met with expressions like "Don't be so negative". According to them, the most negative consequence of the reforms was greater time stress, implying more often the feeling of having much too little time with each client. One of them put it this way: *"There's no time to chat. Earlier, you could sit down or go for a walk. Back then you had a guilty conscience if you didn't have time to sit down or go for a walk, but now you don't think like that anymore"*. Lack of time had led to some clients not getting out of bed or being served breakfast as late as 11 in the morning. And over the weekends, some clients had to go to bed at 3 in the afternoon. It even happened that they had to call some of the "nicest" clients to tell them they would not get help at all, so they had to stay in bed the whole weekend. The care workers were tired of never-ending changes. Many of them felt that they were no longer able to protest against changes because, in their experience, it just did not make any difference. Many of them told us that for a while they took the problems home with them, took them out on their own family, and lost sleep over them. After a while, they said they had become "cold and cynical", went to work, did what they were told, and then went home. They felt it awful that they no longer cared for their clients as they felt they should. They felt, however, "forced" to act this way to survive on the job.

One conclusion of our study is that "quality" is defined differently by different groups within the care organization, and that there is widespread discontent with the effects of reforms among care workers, clients and family members, while administrative leaders and government authorities seem quite content with the changes. As defined by most other informants, quality had been reduced rather than improved because of the reforms. The leaders, on the other hand, see quality as having increased.

2   What About Efficiency?

Even if there are reasons to ask whether the reforms actually led to better quality, quality being understood as giving more individualized help, the reforms could be justified if they had led to public care services becoming more efficient.

When looking only at economic effects, our study shows that expenses per client had increased by almost 50%, mainly due to a reduction in the number of clients getting help. The reduction in number of clients cannot be explained by any "laziness" on the part of care workers. On the contrary, our survey comparing working conditions in several municipalities showed that care workers there scored highest on the burdens attached to their work. The reforms did not seem to have made home-based services cheaper. Home-based care services are cheap when they serve people who need only a small or moderate amount of help and care. When home-based services have to serve people who need more help and care, this service becomes more expensive than long-term care in institutions (Grundt, 1978). This is a finding not only from our study, but also from many others (see, for instance, Edebalk/Lindgren, 1996). The most important reason for the increased cost per client in our study appears to come about as a direct result of the new organization, i.e. the integration of home care services and institutional care, and the closing down of institutional care as a permanent service.

3 Discussion

Until the beginning of the 1990s, almost every Norwegian municipality had organized home-based care services and institutional care into two different units. Each unit had its own budget, management, care workers and different principles for organizing services. As already mentioned, the idea of "the great integration" is to have a joint budget, joint leadership and joint care workers for both kinds of services. The argument for this reform has been that an administrative separation implies a less flexible and more inefficient use of employees. The purpose of the reform is to achieve a more flexible, better-coordinated and therefore more effective and efficient chain of care services. So far, our study shows two important problems connected to this reform: first, the problems of integrating home care and institutional care; and second, the change in the number of leaders and their stance regarding direct work with clients.

The problems of integrating home-based services and institutional care for the elderly are connected to the fundamentally different traditions upon which these services have been built. One of the consequences of the new reform is that only elderly who need a lot of help and care, many of them suffering from senile dementia, are living in institutions for long-term care. For their well-being, it is very important to have just a few care workers for them to relate to. Our study shows that it is difficult to achieve this goal without stable staff who identify with "their" institution. In addition, it requires "know-how", both acquired and maintained through practice – not only for the care workers but also for municipal leaders – to give people with severe disabilities decent help and care. Giving decent help and care to elderly living at home also requires "know-how", but of the kind maintained through a different kind of practice.

In the municipality evaluated, the number of leaders was reduced when "the great integration" was implemented. As a consequence, one leader today has responsibility for about 70 employees, as opposed to about 20 before the reform. This change implies that it has become difficult for leaders to remember the names of care workers, and still more difficult to know the individual employees' skills, strengths and weaknesses in their work with clients – a knowledge crucial to their role as advisor. In addition, leaders no longer work directly with helping the clients. Practical problems experienced by care workers in relation to their clients therefore have become for the leaders almost impossible to cope with, since they know nearly nothing about these clients. Today, there is very little which leaders can contribute to solving practical problems: they can only contribute with their theoretical understanding.

Our study shows that the "managerial approach" towards reforming public care services for the elderly has not been successful in terms of bettering quality, if we define quality in the way in which most care workers, clients and relatives do. There are many reasons for this. First, the "managerial approach" lays great stress on formal, hierarchical knowledge, authority and routines. "Good care", however, is to a great extent a result of the individual care provider being resourceful enough to cope with needs, demands and situations almost impossible to foresee. This means that the care providers must have some flexibility to act according to the best of their ability, one based on at least some personal knowledge of the individual person needing care. The rationality of caring differs in many fundamental ways from the instrumental rationality upon which the managerial approach is based (Wærness, 1984; 1996).

Second, the "managerial approach", mainly developed on the basis of market-oriented activities, focuses very much on what the consumers want; and service quality is often seen as a measure of how well the service delivered matches the customer's expectations. This notion of the "consumer as king" can be seen as an appropriate basis for quality assessment on the market, but it is not fully adequate within the context of the welfare state. Public care services should serve the "needs" of individuals, and "needs" and "wants" are not always identical. Commercial enterprises serve those who are willing to pay the market price; public care services serve individuals who, according to commonly-accepted norms and values, really need these services and therefore have a legitimate right to charge the public budget. Different people may have different expectations of the same public service, and this represents a problem of fairness to public service providers. Questions concerning needs and need satisfaction in the context of the welfare state are both moral and political issues. Clients do not necessarily share interests but are often competitors who more or less struggle to get what they consider their legitimate share of limited resources. Being responsive to clients' expressed needs may lead, in a situation of resource-squeezing, to negligence of those clients who do not make claims; thus, the weakest or most vulnerable clients may emerge as the losers. In other words, to be responsive to clients in the way the market perspective prescribes, might have serious dysfunctions in the public sector (Vabø, 1996).

Thirdly, as is very well documented in Slagsvold's study (1995; 1996), the way of thinking which is a condition for developing "quality measures" according to the managerial approach, may lead to a *vulgarization* of care practices. "Vulgarization" means that care workers develop attitudes toward work with clients that are fragmented and decontextualized, attitudes which are contrary to what most people mean by a "caring attitude". Good care has its basis in "know-how" and is maintained through a kind of practice that the managerial approach is not able to grasp. Lack of attention to the conflicts between the rationality of caring and the instrumental rationality of the managerial approach, may lead to a decrease rather than an increase in the quality of public care services for the elderly. And this may, so to say, happen without planning and without political authorities knowing what has happened and why. "Quality management" in public care services should therefore be developed with the acknowledgement that public care services must be based on a different logic or rationality than market services. Rather than transferring the business approach to public services, a new approach based on the distinctive characteristics of good care has to be developed in order to achieve the goal of bettering the quality of public care.

Notes

1   This study is part of the project "Changes in Public Care Services". The project is financed by the Norwegian Research Council programme "Welfare and Society".
2   Government authorities nowadays seem to prefer the term "user" or even "customer", which is in accordance with the business approach. Since we are critical of this approach to public care, we prefer to use the traditional term "client" in order to stress the difference between the market and public sector.

References

Edebalk, P. G./Lindgren, B. (1996) 'Från bortauktionering till köp-sälj-system. Svensk äldreomsorg under 1900-talet', in: Eliasson (ed.), *Omsorgens skiftningar. Begreppet, vardagen, politiken, forskningen.* Lund: Studentlitteratur.

Grund, Jan (1978) *Perspektivanalyse for eldreomsorgen frem til 1990. Alternativer og forslag til en samlet plan.* NAVF Rapport nr. 4.

NOU (1992: 1) *Trygghet – Verdighet – Omsorg.* Oslo: Statens forvaltningstjeneste.

Næss, Sturle/Wærness, Kari (1995) *Fra pasient til bruker. Utviklingen fra tradisjonell kommunal eldreomsorg til rehabiliteringsorienterte hjemmetjenester i Hurum kommune.* SEFOS Notat 115.

Slagsvold, Britt (1995) *Mål eller mening. Om å måle kvalitet i aldersinstitusjoner.* NGI-Rapport nr. 1.

Slagsvold, Britt (1997) 'Can Quasi Quality be a Consequence of Quality Standards?', in: Evers, A./Haverinen, R./Leichsenring, K./Wistow, G. (eds.), *Developing Quality in Personal Social Services. Concepts, Cases and Comments.* Aldershot: Ashgate.

Vabø, Mia (1996) Commercial Thinking in Public Sector: Dysfunctions of Being More Responsive to Clients. Paper presented at the International Conference in Sociology "Sociology and Inequality", 5-8 September, Bergen.

Wærness, Kari (1984) 'On the Rationality of Caring', *Economic and Industrial Democracy* 5: 185-211.

Wærness, Kari (1996) ' "Omsorgsrationalitet". Reflexioner över ett begrepps karriär', in: Eliasson (ed.), *Omsorgens skiftningar. Begreppet, vardagen, politiken, forskningen.* Lund: Studentlitteratur.

CHAPTER 13

Quality by Users' Influence and Involvement in Denmark – The Logical Development of Social Services

Steen Bengtsson

In this paper I shall stress the importance of personal social services as it literally reads – that they are (1) social and (2) services. I shall start by defining these concepts and shall then draw a few conclusions from the definitions. There is a fundamental difference between social services and ordinary material production – and ordinary service production, too, which because of market conditions will remain of restricted importance in this area, both quantitatively and in relation to the social problems created in a liberal society.

Marxist social theory considers material production as the foundation of society, and social and cultural systems as belonging to the so-called "superstructure". The notion of economic primacy, however, has gained a much wider popularity; in relation to social protection, it is widely considered dogma that we must be able to "afford" them and that there is a "problem of financing".

In order to develop society to a higher stage, we must however not only expand social services much more than it now seems possible, but also combine and integrate them. A liberal job market will not be able to occupy a considerable part of the population, and mere cash provision does not make people an integrated part of society, anyhow. Therefore, job creation programmes must become an essential part of a social service system. Social service is already the main activity of many local societies and will shortly be the main content of our so-called "civil society". Producing social relations will take primacy over material production, which will serve society instead of forming it.

In other words, the prospect of social services is to develop into a new form of managing society as an integrated entity. With this perspective, the significance of user participation is obvious. Quality, I shall argue, is a concept with a content much different from its counterpart in material production.

1   Danish Social Services

For a considerable period, the Danish social protection system has been among the most developed in the world. Eurostat statistics shows Denmark for the period 1970-1993 in the more expensive half of EU and Scandinavian countries. Social expenses grew in the decade 1970-1980 from 20 to 29% of the total GNP; in the subsequent decade, the growth was nearly 0; and since then, it has grown to 33% of the total GNP.

As in other Scandinavian countries, services make up a greater part of Danish social protection than is the case in the rest of Europe, and cash benefits accordingly make up a lesser share. Especially such general services as home care for the elderly and nurseries for children 0-3 have been provided on a scale unseen outside Scandinavia. Perhaps this relates to the fact that female labour-market participation is high – second only to Sweden. Such benefits as unemployment benefits and old-age pensions, however, are not as high for Danish workers as for many other Europeans.

In reality, in the Danish social protection system these benefits have a social-assistance character and not so much of an insurance character. Joining the unemployment scheme is voluntary; but if you have the slightest risk, it is a favourable offer since the state pays more than 80% of the expenses. If you join the scheme and work for a year, unemployment benefits may be received for quite a few years, the period having recently been reduced from nine to seven years, including a number of job and educational offers. But once you have had a job for just six months, you may start the seven-year programme anew! Old-age pension is independent of work; and together with rent subsidies, it makes a modest living possible for pensioners with no other means independent of work, contributions or the earlier receipt of social benefits.

As in other countries, decentralization during the 1970s made possible the development of local social services. From the 1960s on, however, private non-profit social services were gradually taken over by municipalities or brought under very close municipal control. For this reason, and because of the broad autonomy of the municipalities, these have been more powerful than in most other countries. The National Association of Municipalities has nearly as much say in determining Danish social policy as Parliament, and much more than The Danish Council of Organizations of Disabled People!

Again, following the general trend, public bureaucracy in general has been attacked with a so-called modernization process starting in 1983. The first modernization occurred in the central government, but soon it spread to municipal bureaucracies, too. Inside the municipal frame, services have been further decentralized and integrated; and bureaucratic ways of management have gradually been replaced by more organic ones. In the so-called "second decentralization", individual municipal institutions received their own budget and a considerable degree of freedom within it. Danish municipalities can form their organizational structure just as they want, and administrative structures have often been changed so as to follow target groups, making a coordinated municipal effort possible. Compared to most other countries, it is my impression that this organizational development has been continual and radical. Often, economical reasons have legitimized these procedures; but real reductions have in most cases been avoided.

The 1970s were the decade of building up bureaucratic administrative machines, as the 1980s were the decade of developing these into effective and responsive service producers. By then, professional staff often defended the original bureaucratic system, talking of the rights of the consumer and the professional standard of the product. But it turned out that bureaucracy was not the right way to defend these issues and the organizational reforms were without any doubt beneficial to the users. Although a problem of municipal management no doubt still exists, merely strengthening management or repeatedly changing structure, however, would not be a solution. A continued development narrowly centred on management and structure would in fact put citizen's rights and service quality at risk.

Service quality and citizen's rights, as well as user influence and participation, are therefore some of the issues in Danish social service development today. The quality issue has become central and can no longer be an issue for the professional system alone; in accordance with Total Quality Management principles, it should be a central aim of management and a guiding star in all development as well.

At the same time, the debate for and against the privatization of social services has taken place for quite a few years now, mainly concerning elderly care. Public responsibility for and financing of their care have not been questioned, only the possible use of private care producers as has recently been seen in Sweden. Yet it is obvious that the private production of social services – be it elderly care, child care or whatever – faces the real problems of setting fixed quality norms and securing the equal treatment of citizens, for authorities as well as for politicians.

2   User Influence

Since the 1970s, new forms of democratic influence have been discussed, especially in connection with the emerging amount of administrative and public-service activities going on. Some social democrats began to see the "common man" – their electorate – not so much as "the worker" but more as "the consumer". Rooted in this image, the establishment of local social consumer's councils was proposed. This type of councils representing all social users was made possible in the social reform of 1976.

By then, municipalities were still so authoritarian that such "permission" had a function. Later on, they just installed the types of councils they wanted, continued decentralization having totally changed the relationship between state and municipalities. Some social consumer's councils were established; and later, a number of elderly councils and a few disability councils emerged, in some cases self-appointed but most often initiated by organizations and municipalities. We have even seen examples of municipalities having delegated considerable parts of their elderly budget to the elderly councils at a time when these bodies were not even mentioned in any law.

In 1991, I made a survey showing that 78% of the municipalities had at least some type of user's council. One third of these councils seemed to be dying because they had not met during the last year, but 50% of all municipalities had active councils. Most of the councils were elderly councils, with 40% of all municipalities having them. Often, there was more than one type of council, institutions or districts in greater cities often having their own user's council.

In the last five-year period, elderly organizations have been very active initiating elderly councils in the remaining municipalities, so that nearly all municipalities had got such councils by 1996. In some cases, the members are representatives of the elderly organizations (of which there are two major ones, one being a conglomerate of local pensioner's associations of a purely social nature, concerned with bingo and trips, but with an umbrella structure having a long tradition of national political influence; and the other being a modern publicity-oriented type of organization more appealing to active elderly). More often, however, their members are elected by all citizens of the municipality over 60.

A recent law has obliged municipalities to have elderly councils from 1997 on. This law has authorized the aforementioned model with an elected elderly council and will therefore get a number of municipalities to restructure their existing elderly councils. At the same time, the new law demands that appeal boards be instituted in every municipality to handle, among other things, decisions on home help which until now have not been possible to appeal. The elderly councils contribute with members to these appeal boards.

Elderly councils have no formal power, but the municipal politicians and administrations use them as a partner in determining their policy and in securing a degree of citizen participation in that process. They sometimes delegate parts of the elderly budget, and local user's councils are often in charge of practical tasks, such as making up a programme of activities in a centre.

Elderly-council members act as a link between authorities/politicians and the elderly population. In a number of cases, they have made systematic interviews to uncover the needs of the elderly population and especially those of the users of municipal elderly services, such as home aid and nursing. The hitherto non-compulsory elderly councils have had a very different impact, from being an important actor in the local elderly policy to being a discussion group of no importance.

The few studies suggest that the main condition behind an elderly council functioning more than formally is the attitude of the municipal officials. If they want the elderly council as a partner, if they understand how to make use of them as a link to the elderly population, an elderly council has a good chance to succeed. The attitudes of local politicians, as well as of the members of the elderly council, naturally also have some significance.

3 What Are Social Services?

No one should be shocked to hear that social services are services which are social. From this elementary fact, however, conclusions can be drawn which prove to be significant when it comes to quality control, both concerning the very concept of quality control (what is quality control?) and concerning the necessary methods to achieve it.

The organization or management of a *service* is different from the organization or management of material goods. A service product may be defined as a product whose production and consumption is the very same process.

In general, this means that the consumer experiences not just the product and his/her own consumption of the product, but quite necessarily the production process and the producer as a person, too. The service is "personal" in the double sense of the word: it is certainly *to* a person but is also *by* a person. It is "human" – and this human aspect is often considered a central feature. It may even be the main reason why some users want the service in the first place.

Hence, in any service production – private or public – this human aspect must be focused upon. The relation between producer and consumer should provide a considerable contribution to consumer satisfaction. On the other hand, social services should not replace social relations, which give much more than service. Home help should not crowd out family and friends; a nursery should not reduce the competence of the parents. If the need is partly or primarily a social need, the service should be designed to produce such social relations as needed – also between the users and other persons they can socialize with.

Commercial (not social) services even may take the form of "selling the users to each other", much as in a discotheque or a planned holiday. In these cases, commercial services come very close to the fundamental qualities of social services. A major difference, however, lies in the fact that these commercial services are used according to a function of demand, whereas social services are distributed according to needs – which is, for several reasons, a quite different notion. The social element in fact enables a further development of possibilities for creating social relations more inherent to services than to the commercial setting.

Social services are not just "services" in the everyday meaning of the word. An important dimension for classifying social services in fact concerns their degree of serving or mastering their clients. According to this first dimension, social services may be divided into three types: (1) mere serving, such as cleaning or shopping; (2) using professional knowledge, such as caring; (3) exercising a more or less mild societal pressure, such as in drug-treatment programmes or at-risk family provisions. In fact, the only difference is in degree: all social services involve all three aspects to a greater or lesser degree.

All three types of social services have their "art of service", i.e. methods of making it appear and experienced as a service and not as something done to the user by a huge inhuman apparatus – which it, however, in reality is, as we do not live in a tribal society where human wisdom can solve all problems! Nevertheless, it is important that social services do not appear to the population as just another form of police department.

A second important dimension is whether the problem solved by a service is common (as is the case with home help and child care) or not so common (as with disabilities or dysfunctional families). To solve a common problem, many votes may be mobilized, and the development of the services hence depends on how effectively the political system transforms a common desire into both decision and action. An uncommon problem does not hit or affect as many people, but often the persons who see the problems in their daily life and in their family will be that much more motivated to make an effort, and able to awake the compassion of others.

Together, these two dimensions produce a classification of social services based on relationships between service producer and service consumer, and between service consumers and other citizens.

There are many interpretations of the word "social" in connection with social services, but I shall argue that it at least involves production as production of a *common good*. To define the expression "social" as it is commonly used, there must be added "something" limiting the area (e.g. to old age, disability, sickness, family, unemployment, poverty). This last limitation, however, scarcely adds any conceptual content. Perhaps these areas can be said to be more reproductive than productive.

A distinctive feature of a common good is that it is more a good to society or collectivities rather than to any single person, that it not be possible or practicable to get direct consumers to pay and that a collective decision therefore be required to produce it. Examples are infrastructure or education, which contributes to production but in such a way that these contributions cannot be located or paid for.

Social services, however, generally do not contribute directly to production but most often are reproductive. Still, they make *activities that are wanted* by the majority, partially because they benefit direct users or clients, partially because a majority of the surrounding population wants these activities to go on. This concept of social service covers services which are seen as goods by nearly all of their users – such as home care – as well as services which are often felt in a more ambiguous way and perhaps not quite voluntarily used.

The commercial firm produces goods for the market, and the customer pays what he/she thinks the goods are worth. If it cannot produce at a suitable price, the firm will disappear. Public services produce goods that have some value for the user but, in addition to this, also some value to a number of other interested parties in the community. This may be reflected in a "user's ticket" which, in combination with public support, pays the costs of producing the particular service.

Social services, however, cannot be fully described by saying that they are common goods and activities that are wanted. This applies for quite a broad scale of activities. Something must be added about their content. Rather than just reeling off social areas (elderly, disability, etc.) social protection could be defined as activities with the primary aim of integrating people into society. It does so by overcoming obstacles and giving practical help so as to prevent isolation and, as previously mentioned, by putting a mild pressure on people. But it could only properly be called "social protection" as long as the integration and help aspect dominates the control aspect.

4   Organizational Development Methods and Quality Management

In accordance with the phases of development for social services mentioned in section 1, organizational or management development methods have naturally shifted. The rhetoric of the building-up period' was "planning"; the 1980s talked about "efficiency" and "service management", structure and management having been focus areas for more than a decade. No doubt this is one of the reasons why there is now a need to focus on the product itself and its quality. Moreover, structural changes easily become a sort of mania when not moderated by the overall aim of developing and preserving service quality.

To obtain a certain scale of social services, the tool of organization must be used. Organization is thus a tool; and a precondition that a tool can be used, is that it exists, which they only do when they reproduce themselves. Organizations therefore must always have their own preservation as one of their goals. Yet it should not be the only or even the main goal. Organizational methods may differ, but a central aim always must be to strengthen the owner's power over the organization, so that the organization to a lesser degree becomes its own goal, and the owner to a greater degree is able to use the organization for the purpose which is the real reason why the owner lets the organization exist in the first place.

Although this principle is common to all organizational counselling, it nevertheless explains very well the difference between solving the problems of an ordinary commercial firm and solving problems of a producer of a common good for the public. Although the problems may often seem quite similar, the situation of solving them need not be identical at all. The commercial firm has an owner or group of owners that is well-defined and whose interest is gaining a surplus. The owner is represented in the firm by a management often rewarded in relation to goal-attainment. Organizational development should have the same final goal.

The organization set up to produce a common good has an owner, too, but this is a formal owner, a political organization (e.g. municipality) representing all citizens. Some of them are actual users of the service; others have for some reason a serious interest in the functioning of this particular service (be it possible future use, or as relatives of users, or as groups outside the circle of users deriving some benefit from the service). But other citizens may be less serious supporters of the service, stressing more that expenses be kept low, or just wanting it to look as *if* the service existed. And even the worst social service does not go bankrupt! More precisely, we may distinguish an elitist (outside) and a risk (inside) view of social services. There is a conflict of interest between the group of those seriously interested in a service and those dependent on it, and the group who knows they never will come into such a situation.

The methods used over time reflect the changing need of the owner – the collective – to manage social services. After a planning and building-up period, the danger was that services would become inefficient "public" workplaces where uncommitted professionals passed their time in ritualistic behaviour – or just drinking coffee: therefore, the issue of "efficiency". Another danger was that the bureaucracy was the focus of attention, that professionals concentrated on pleasing their bosses and forgot the users (who their bosses could also easily forget): therefore, the issue of "service management".

Quality management is an organizational method with its origin in private goods production. There it focuses on the precise specification of the quality of components related to their contribution to the composed product, trying to get the desired quality to the lowest possible price in order to be competitive on the market. Used in the production of common goods, the concept of quality partially changes its character. Here, there is no later test against market realities; therefore, a concept of quality is here simply a *definition of the product* wanted, and quality control becomes a tool to shape the product.

Quality control (i.e. that the intended product be produced) has often been considered ensured by using public service deliverers and staff with special professional education. Non-profit service providers could also be motivated by a concern for quality, but then most often supplied with some public supervision or inspection. In such systems as the German, the contributions of welfare organizations likewise act as a sort of quality control. By these means, different forms of misuse of services have been hindered. These types of quality control have been considered sufficient as long as professionals came from layers of the population different from the layers of the users.

When quality *is* simply the definition of the product, two opposite consequences may be drawn:

1) Quality control is not necessary – there is no consecutive control.
2) Quality control is most necessary – there is no consecutive control.

Whichever consequence you choose depends on your attitude towards the service: elitist, or identifying with the group at risk. The ongoing development is a democratization of all social services involving much more identification with the users because the circle of users (among which we include former users of child institutions and future possible users of home help) over the past few decades has been extended to a great majority.

"Quality through user involvement" is suitable as the new trend of municipal organizational development for several reasons:

1) There is regularly a need for new concepts and new methods in organizational development – the old ones are simply worn out after a time.
2) "Quality" covers the old issue of efficiency – which is still relevant.
3) "User involvement" covers the old issue of service orientation. In addition, it covers a democratic or "civil society" angle, too.
4) Quality management in the context of defining services, in setting limits for quality, is necessary in a situation with a growing demand for the services combined with the need to limit expenses which must exist after the building-up period.
5) The content of the services is more important than ever before, simply because their volume is so impressive. Today, social services are often the greater part of local social life, the so-called "civil society". Some decades ago, the "neighbourhood" meant small local shops, housewives getting together and children playing in the streets. Today, the neighbourhood is the local elderly centre from where the home helpers go out, or the local birth group, kindergarten or school where you often find new friends among the other parents, and local employment projects.

As noticed, the users are not the only "consumers" of social services: there are other significant consumers, too. For elderly services, these other consumers may be the children who get rid of their guilty conscience or perhaps are relieved of part of the work they would have helping their parents if the services did not exist. For psychiatric services, it may be parents who can send their children out to play when the schizophrenic who went around shouting is given help in a centre. Some of these groups of secondary consumers are easier to define than others!

It can be seen from the preceding that both direct users and secondary consumers have interest in the functioning of a social service. In fact, there is no reason to prefer users' influence over secondary consumers' influence. Both parties are supporters and payers of the services. The political question is to reconcile their perhaps different interests and to distribute the burdens.

Professionals, however, play a totally different role and should not be considered an interested party in the same sense as secondary users. As a group, professionals are in the process of reconversion from managers of the social area on behalf of the elite, to becoming counsellors for ordinary people.

5   The Users' Choice of Service Supplier

Another trend in the organization of social services is the privatization of service delivery systems. As previously mentioned, Danish social service purveyors are nearly all public (mainly municipal) or strictly publicly controlled. Recently, the use of private suppliers has been very much discussed and has been made a hot political issue. Openly, concern is expressed for service quality and security; but it is obvious that social issues are discussed much more eagerly when labour conditions for great numbers of employees are involved than when it is just about the situation for the users.

Alternative service delivery could be combined with a possibility of choice for the user (an exit possibility), which could be seen as an alternative to users' influence or could be combined with users' influence. Thus, there is no simple relation between the issue of privatization (limited to service *delivery*) and the issues of users' influence or quality development.

If the development of quality is to be a success, the production of quality products must be made the guiding principle for all management and organizational development in the first place, in accordance with the principles of quality management. It is important to emphasize this starting-point in order to understand that user influence and user choice between different service suppliers are to be adapted within the frames of quality management. Quality by means of user influence is not a principle which excludes all others, but rather an asset to be used to reach the higher goals.

User influence and choice between different purveyors are both ways to get the users' opinion to affect which service is rendered. It should be expected that we get the most efficient and (for the users) most uncomplicated type of influence by means of a market-like situation where the users may choose between alternatives. The user does not even need to be aware why he/she chooses one rather than the other. The firms will guess what is the users' next wish long before the great majority of users realize anything themselves. We know the situation from the commodity market.

But perhaps a market is too efficient in transforming user wishes into concrete products? If the problems are solved before anybody realizes that they are there, problem consciousness is perhaps not created; and an important precondition for the citizens to support social policy and to see the sense in using resources for it, will be missing. Direct user influence is perhaps useful in expressing user needs, and thus making them politically visible. The participation of non-profit organizations with an attitudinal background in service delivery, may perhaps bring about much the same result.

User influence also has an effect on case officers as street-level workers providing a social service. Especially in areas where we not only make something *for* people but also do something *to* them – such as drug-addiction treatment, child removals, rehabilitation – it has turned out again and again that case officers and street-level workers have had difficulty in imagining what they could gain by asking people to give their views. And when they heard the users' opinion at all, it was often quite unexpected for the professionals.

It appears that case officers often use the assumptions of legislation as a model for how persons react, while the users in fact behave much more in accordance with what we call a "social science model for rational behaviour" (Uggerhøj, 1995). So social assistants may expect clients to tell them everything in confidence so that they can use it for the good of the client, whereas the clients sort out and give an edited version acting strategically as one would do in any other everyday encounter.

Often users' direct influence on social services is discussed in an altogether different way, which gives the impression that this should be a veritable revolution, a users' take-over of the services. Debaters put forth the question of whether it is acceptable that the power be displaced from the *citizens* and the parliamentary chain of government to the users. There is no doubt a theoretical point in this discussion; but in relation to the real situation, it seems quite hysterical.

In reality, there is no danger at all – or even a possibility – that the power over social services will be transferred to the direct user organs. They may at most be a counterbalance to the usual powers: public authorities, professionals, or institutionalized non-profit enterprises in the social area. But direct user influence can be an important element in quality control: an important aspect is that quality will always be quality as seen from the users' point of view.

The involvement of different service suppliers – provided that the public sector maintains unaltered its organizer and financier role – has primarily been discussed from the point of view of economy. And oddly enough, from two diametrically opposite points of view: on the one hand, that we could save money by letting private service suppliers compete; and on the other, that we could create an additional demand and therefore more workplaces by opening this field to dynamic market forces. Marketing both points of view at the same time requires the abilities of a tightrope walker; but calm down, it is never done without a safety net!

Competition does not merely entail lesser costs to obtain a given goal – which also may be expressed in such a way that more goals could be fulfilled for the given assets – but also that staffs work in another way. On the one hand, there is the danger that profit will dominate. On the other hand, we see that competition may involve a flatter organization and a greater zest for the street-level worker who is permitted to do what he/she and the user find is right.

Often, formal user influence and competition between purveyors are set up as alternatives – more scientifically called "voice" and "exit". There is, however, nothing to prevent the two methods of influence from being combined in different ways. No doubt, market-like forces in "exit" under some circumstances have a chance to create efficiency and to make the service live up to the expectations of the user. On the other hand, the participative mechanisms of "voice" may create political interest and support – which is necessary, too – and even produce political interest much needed in a time of general political disengagement.

6   Quality by User Influence

During the past few years, the experimentation and development culture has flourished in social services everywhere – not least in Denmark, where experiments and special funds are one of the methods used by the central government to influence an extremely decentralized social protection system. The central government has tried in different ways to stimulate experiments aimed at better quality for the same price, or a lower price for the same quality, involving a sort of user influence.

The methods of voice and exit, however, have hitherto been kept strictly apart in Danish debate and development. An exit possibility presupposes that there are different service providers: that is, that there are purveyors other than from the public (most often municipal) sphere. Non-public service production has been identified with "privatization" – a concept which could contain any cut-back you could imagine and is in any case a most bourgeois phenomenon!

The discussion has stiffened in an ideological confrontation between proponents for private service deliverers who want to economize, and defenders of the system of municipal social service. Because personnel in municipal and private social services are organized in different unions, the unions now organizing staff are naturally strongly against any change. The Social Democratic Party has strong support from the unions and from a majority of older members who are uncertain of changes; but on the other hand, there is a modernization trend in the party, as has been the case in other Western European countries over the past few years. The question of private service deliverers has brought about a lively discussion in this party – in fact, so heated that hardly any social-democratic municipality would dare to try them out right now.

For the moment, political confrontation will thus dominate if you make any experiments including exit possibilities for social users; and for this reason, you could not expect the results to express the potential of exit mechanisms in the social area in a more politically-neutral situation. In turn, there is broad political agreement as to formal user influence, through voice mechanisms, as worthy of being developed further. The necessary confrontations, however, will surely be taken in liberal municipalities; and after a time, we shall no doubt find a much more relaxed attitude to exit mechanisms in social services. This should give more possibilities to develop user influence by combining voice and exit systems.

A strong users' influence is exactly the means that could counteract and thereby conceal the control elements in social services, thus making them appear predominantly as expressions of solidarity for the user. As we have seen, the contrast between control and solidarity is a necessary feature if solidarity is to be more than an ideal: in other words, if it is to be institutionalized in a real society. Both aspects in this contrast must necessarily be present. Institutionalized solidarity has no meaning if it does not look like solidarity to the user, if it does not make society appear as the user's friend. But institutionalized solidarity is not possible if it does not contain a strong element of control.

When quality is to be controlled, the danger is obvious that a few things more will be controlled simultaneously. Most types of quality control strengthen one of the parties in the service system – this is an aspect of the very concept of control. Quality control through user influence has the double advantage of controlling quality at the same time that the solidarity element in institutionalized social solidarity is stressed and the social control element accordingly concealed or diminished.

Quality through user influence must be developed through a series of experiments and experiences. The Danish Social Department has initiated a project where municipalities and counties were invited to participate and where the Social Department partly finances the extra expenses of the participating projects. There are projects in four areas: rehabilitation, dysfunctional families, elderly, drugs. Projects cooperate in circles with three to four projects in each. There are two circles in elderly care, and one in each of the other areas. In all projects, each circle has a group of organizational counsellors, some coming from a great commercial counselling firm, others coming from the Municipalities' Organization. The project is named "evaluation" but is in fact explorative research, proper evaluation not being possible with no common design of the projects and no concrete goals specified for them.

The first step has been to describe the projects after one year (half the project period) in relation to the overall themes, to see what concepts were necessary for this. This has been used as a basis for a questionnaire to all projects (31 questions) to report experiences after the project period. In the meantime, we have gathered personal impressions from the different sessions in the projects. The aim of this research is to describe experiences which might illustrate what the concept of quality in connection with user influence could currently mean in the development of social services. The development of social services being considered an organic growth, the aim is to discover which shaping has been chosen and which experiences have been gained (as is seen by the projects themselves: we cannot scrutinize their reports and disclose if they do not report according to the facts).

As a first tentative result from this project, it could be mentioned that user influence has the potential to change the attitudes of professionals much more than they imagined at the start of the project; and it seems decisive for the realization of this potential that users be allowed to develop their attitudes and reactions in a process undisturbed by politicians and professionals before being confronted with these groups. This illustrates the main point of this article: that the users are not a powerful group in their interaction with the other groups in the social service system. However, their contribution has the potential of strengthening the service system and should therefore be protected and "green-housed".

References

Eriksen, Erik Oddvar/Weigård, Jarle (1993) 'Fra statsborger til kunde: Kan relasjonen mellom innbyggerne og det offentlige reformuleres på grunnlag av nye roller?', *Norsk Statsvitenskaplig Tidsskrift* 9: 111-131.

Hoff, Jens (1993) 'Medborgerskab, brugerrolle og magt', in: Andersen et al., *Medborgerskab – Demokrati og politisk deltagelse.* Herning: Systime.

Karlöf, Bengt (1987) *Kvalitetsfornyelse.* Schultz.

Larsen, Bøje (1987) *Kvalitet eller kaos.* Charlottenlund: Forlaget Sporskiftet.

Normann, Richard (1983) *Service Management – Ledelse og strategi i servicevirksomheder.* Schultz.

Pollitt, Christopher/Bouckaert, Geert (eds.) (1995) *Quality Improvement in European Public Services. Concepts, Cases and Commentary.* Sage Publications.

Socialministeriet (1994) *Socialministeriets Kvalitetsprogram – Information.* Social-ministeriet.

Uggerhøj, Lars (1995) *Hjælp eller afhængighed.* Aalborg: Aalborg Universitetsforlag.

CHAPTER 14

The City of Stockholm's Awards for Good Quality

Jonas Bjelfvenstam

1 Introduction

Autonomous local government in Sweden allows the country's municipalities considerable freedom in planning their activities to meet their specific needs. This includes the right to levy a municipal tax. The municipalities are responsible for a number of different activities, some of which the municipalities undertake voluntarily and others of which are stipulated by the state through special legislation mainly concerning social welfare.

In general, municipalities in Sweden are responsible for such activities as comprehensive and upper-secondary education, adult education, child care, elderly care and care for people with disabilities, individual and family care, road maintenance and town planning, recreational and cultural activities as well as certain environmental protection matters. The City of Stockholm has an annual turnover of approximately SEK 25 billion, and almost half of the City's total annual expenditure is in connection with social welfare, while almost a quarter concerns education.

The City of Stockholm is organized so that the City Council, with 101 members, passes the generalized principle resolutions with respect to the City's direction, goals, budget, tax rate and expenditure. The City Executive Board is responsible for implementing the resolutions passed by the City Council. There are also a number of committees and boards responsible for the City's various activities concerning such things as educational, environmental, and recreational matters.

From 1 January 1997, the City of Stockholm's organization is based on 24 geographically-demarcated district councils. The district councils are responsible for various social matters, child care, schools, road maintenance, etc. The City Council and the City Executive Board have the role of supreme, strategic, controlling authority. The district council reform has been introduced to strengthen democracy at the local level, as well as to improve the efficiency and quality of the City's services.

The austere economic climate of recent years has also left its mark on Sweden's municipalities. Reduced tax revenues as a result of growing unemployment, state cut-backs and increased expenditure due to structural changes, e.g. an increase in the number of elderly people in need of geriatric care, require good economic management. It is essential that each tax Krona is put to the best possible use.

Reduced financial resources constitute an important reason for the City of Stockholm to pursue a policy that promotes goal-oriented quality work. All experience shows that the systematic development of quality work should not only benefit customers and users but should also provide the opportunity to manage activities much more efficiently. The growing demands and requirements of the population also motivate the intensive development of quality work in the public sector. In order to defend a welfare system that is based on relatively high taxes, it is necessary for the authorities to provide the public with good qualitative services.

Matters relating to quality have also become a focus of attention in the public sector because alternative operational forms have been given greater freedom to compete with those of the public sector. If properly planned and carried out, competitive tendering can lead to lower costs and incentives to develop activities. This is why the Stockholm City Council believes that there is good reason for the district councils and committees to utilize this new tool.

Competitive tendering means that the City allows private contractors to take over such things as the management of service blocks and snow clearance. Of course, this is on the condition that the private contractor can do it more efficiently than the City. It is still the City that has to foot the bill. A procurement can also be concluded with the assignment remaining within the City's own organization. But even then, competitive tendering provides positive results, as competition promotes more efficient working methods.

Competitive tendering is already a regular feature of the City's operations, particularly with respect to the technical sector. During recent years, personal social services have also been exposed to competition. We have become increasingly adept at drawing up contracts to ensure that standards of quality be maintained and developed.

On 20 May 1996, the City Council passed a resolution for a new strategy of competitive tendering. Stockholm's 24 district councils and committees will now have another instrument upon which to model the best possible services for

Stockholmers using the resources at their disposal. The resolution was preceded by a comprehensive programme of research as well as a number of evaluations. Exposure to competition has resulted in a number of positive effects: it has led to the improvement of City activities. It is also compatible with the principles of general welfare policy. This is why the City Council considers it to be of strategic importance for the City as a whole that the district councils and committees use competitive tendering more than before. The City's leadership encourages this in a number of ways.

Municipally-financed and -run day care centres, or homes for the aged run by private service providers, increase requirements for orders containing detailed specifications. This means that municipalities have to define their quality goals better than previously, and also to follow up on contracts with e.g. contractors providing elderly care. Consequently, multiplicity in the production of municipal services contributes to developing quality.

2   City of Stockholm Awards

The City of Stockholm has been engaged in a relatively comprehensive programme of quality work over the last few years. It was initiated in the wake of intensive debates regarding privatization and the exposure to competition; as previously mentioned, some of its components can be linked to these debates.

Quality work in the City is carried out in accordance with three principal guidelines. The first concerns a high degree of integrating financial and activity management in a coordinated, goal-oriented system. Therefore, an intensive programme of work to formulate goals based on a common structure is currently in progress at all levels and in all activities.

The second concerns a special programme carried out for quality development, aimed at improving the internal operation of the various activities. This includes the development of common terminology, training programmes and central support to those wishing to initiate quality work at their workplaces. This can be done by means of such methods as utilizing special internal consultants. A number of projects aimed at involving users, through so-called "user influence", should also be given prominence.

The third concerns guaranteeing so-called "result quality" in various ways, i.e. to ensure that such factors as the quality of care are achieved or that contracted snow clearance is carried out. This requires efficient methods of follow-up as well as drawing up contracts possible to follow up. This entails a great deal of effort, not least of all with respect to the so-called "soft-sector" services.

The City of Stockholm's Awards for Good Quality constitutes one important component of the City's quality work. Considering how to improve the City's customer orientation and efficiency in work processes, the City's leadership looked abroad for different methods to strenghten management and to change traditional public-sector attitudes towards citizens. It was considered especially important to find solutions within the area of personal social services, among other reasons because of the well-known problems to assess quality in this area.

The awards are based on internationally- and nationally-tested methods with various designations: e.g. TQM; seven instruments; offensive quality development. The basic concept, however, is the same: all the processes contained in an activity are included in quality assessment. Customer satisfaction is therefore central. The American Malcolm Baldridge National Quality Awards and the Japanese Deming Awards are based on these methods. Sweden's national awards, which so far have mainly involved trade and industry, are also based on these principles. The National Swedish Awards for Good Quality were established by the Swedish Institute for Quality Development (SIQ). The SIQ assisted the City in establishing its own quality awards.

The awards for good quality are a part of the City's programme for quality development and are intended to stimulate quality development, highlight good examples and facilitate the possibility of making comparisons. The competition itself includes a great deal of self-assessment documented by the participants, examined, and awarded points by a team of specially-appointed examiners in accordance with a strict evaluation technique.

The third round of the competition was held in 1997, and the participants consist of nominated units from municipally- or privately-run activities in the following categories:

- schools;
- child care;
- elderly care;
- other care and welfare activities; and
- an open category for the City's other activities.

An award for each category was presented at a formal ceremony held at the City Hall. All the units participating in the competition were invited to attend this ceremony. The winning units each received a diploma and a prize of SEK 5,000 per employee. The prize money can be used in any way the unit sees fit in order to continue developing its quality standards.

3   Procedures

The units participating in the competition have been nominated by the respective political committees responsible for them. From and including 1998, the City's activities carried out in corporate form will also be invited to participate, e.g. Stockholm's energy corporation, refuse and recycling corporation, and housing corporations. The number of units that can participate in the competition is limited, and this means that many committees cannot nominate all those who would like to participate. The process of selection for the committees' nominations varies; however, in all cases it is the administrative leadership, as well as the committee's politicians, who decide on the candidates. This procedure forces politicians and administrators to discuss and define their opinions on what constitutes good quality. In doing this, quality issues are put into focus in a different way than before.

The criteria used by the units for compiling a description of their activities, form the basis for the awards. These criteria do not only form the basis for assessment in connection with the competition. They are also an excellent device for self-evaluation and should function as an instrument for creating common methods and concepts that can be used in the City's quality work.

The criteria contain a number of basic values regarded as characteristic of successful organizations, as well as seven question areas: basic criteria regarded as reflecting each of the activity's main aspects.

The basic set of values must not only be known but also applied in an organization. They are, for example,

- client/customer orientation;
- committed leadership;
- participation by all concerned;
- social responsibility;
- process orientation.

4 The Seven Main Criteria

The seven main criteria contain 28 parts. The main criteria have been rated and awarded points. Customer satisfaction has the highest rating. Any description of the activity should be based on the criteria. The seven main criteria are as follows:

1) Leadership for Constant Improvement

This describes how leaders create the conditions for working with the right things, in the right way and in the right direction.

2) Information and Analysis

This describes how you ensure that the right information is available in the right place at the right time.

3) Strategic Planning

This describes how you plan for the development of goods, services and processes, as well as for the development and improvement of the activity itself.

4) Employee Development

This describes how you develop the personal attributes and competence of employees, as well as the collective competence of the activity from a strategic angle.

5) Activity Processes

This describes how all the activity's processes should develop and be managed, in order to ensure that everything is done in the right way from the very beginning.

6) Activity Results

This shows the results of the activity's various processes and includes such things as the attributes of the processes' goods and services as well as productivity, efficiency and capability.

7) How to Satisfy a Client's Needs, Demands and Expectations

This describes how you establish what expectations and experience the client has with regard to the quality of the activity, as well as what "method of attack" you should use to gain the most benefit from this information. You can also give an account of how satisfied or dissatisfied your client is.

The description should, in principle, be based on four key questions:

- What do you do?
- To what extent do you do it?
- What does it lead to: results?
- How do you evaluate and improve what you do?

It is a demanding task to prepare an activity description, but it is well worth the trouble.

The result not only consists of a competition entry but also provides a comprehensive view of how the organization functions. At most, the description should consist of 30 pages.

5 The Evaluation Process

The next step starts with the examiners' work. The examiners are specially-trained people who, in everyday life, are salaried employees working in various posts – most often at middle-management level – in the City of Stockholm administration. At present, there are some 80 such people who, because of their specialist training in quality management, also represent a valuable human resource for their own activities.

The examiners evaluate and assess the strengths and possibilities for improvement of each activity, based on the unit's activity description. The evaluation is aimed at establishing how systematically the organization works and what preventive measures it employs, as well as what methods are used to evaluate and improve the activity, and to what extent the methods are applied. Consequently, there are three bases of evaluation:

5.1 Method of Attack

This assesses whether or not the "method of attack" reflects the basic values and whether

- it is systematic and consistent;
- it is preventative;
- it is regularly evaluated and improved.

5.2 Application

This assesses whether the method of attack is applied

- to all goods and services;
- in all internal processes and activities; and
- in connection with all cooperation with clients/customers, suppliers and society.

5.3 Results

This assesses such things as

- the level of quality achieved;
- the tempo of improvement work;
- quality improvements in all parts of the activity;
- comparisons with organizations that are leaders in specific fields, as well as comparisons with competitors; and
- the organization's ability to prove that the results are derived from the application of the method of attack.

A balanced assessment of the three evaluation bases is made according to the following matrix:

	Method of Attack	Application	Results
100%	Systematic, under constant improvement	Always, in all relevant processes	First class, continuous
0%	Anecdotal	Not applied	Not accounted for

Assessment is done by awarding percentage points. All ten percentages, by which every criterion is finally assessed, make up the proportion of the accumulated points that each criterion can receive. The maximum number of points is 1,000. This sum should be regarded as a utopian, ideal state. Not even the most successful and well-functioning organizations manage to receive full points for all the criteria and parts thereof.

The examiners work in special teams. Each examiner first makes his/her own assessment of the candidate the group is to assess. Thereafter, a "consensus process" is initiated to ensure that each group will be unanimous in its assessment of the candidates. As the number of candidates is large in relation to the number of awards, there is an elimination round after which the examiners' assessments are submitted to a special committee of judges for a final decision.

The points awarded to each unit are confidential; however, each participating unit receives a "feedback report" from the examiners. The feedback reports contain details of the strengths and improvement possibilities of each school, day care centre, etc. The examiner hands over the written feedback report during a visit to the unit and is therefore able to discuss the contents of the report with the unit's employees. Even if a participating unit does not win an award, it has made a comprehensive analysis of its activities and has been assessed by outsiders. The feedback report acts as a type of consultant's report that provides the unit with tips and guidelines for improving its future work. This means that all participants are winners.

Although the points awarded to the individual units are confidential, they provide the basis for the City's leadership to gain a picture of the quality standards of the various activities. For example, last year's competition established that the criterion "leadership for constant improvement" was better fulfilled in the City's schools than in its care for the elderly. Results confirmed a commonly-held opinion: because of such things as traditional, organizational-cultural and educational factors, schools in Stockholm have a more modern leadership than other activities. Consequently, these types of indications provide the basis for the decisions the City's leaders make with respect to various strategic measures to strengthen certain of the activities' weaknesses.

5.4 Examples: Average Results Achieved from Those Possible in 1996

The awarding of points can also form the basis of a benchmarking system in which

- the different units can compare their points with those obtained by the best units;
- the different district councils can compare their units with the best districts; and
- in the long term, different cities can compare themselves with each other.

When the "Glada Björnen" day care centre compares itself with the "Bullerbyn" day care centre – last year's winner in the child-care category – the natural question to ask is, "What do they do that we don't?" And, at best, the conclusion follows: "We should also be able to do that – if we do this or that, then we can be just as good." In this way, we reach the nucleus of all quality development: to compare oneself with the best in order to obtain leverage in one's own improvement work. Comparison with the best is therefore a prerequisite for the possibility to carry out successful quality work aimed at continuous improvement.

Figure 1: **Average Results Achieved from Those Possible, 1996 (in %)**

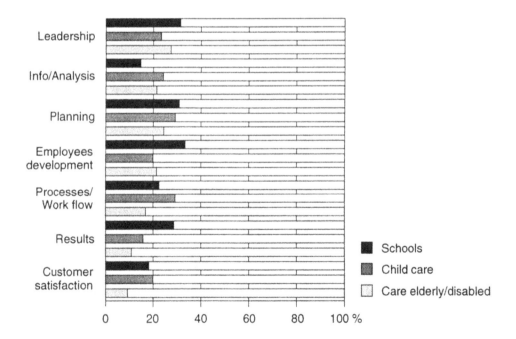

Figure 2:   Elderly Care and Care for People with Disabilities, 1995-1996 (in %)

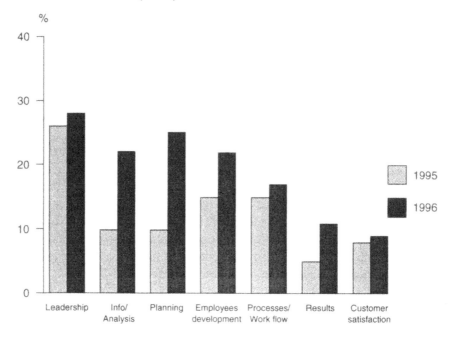

Figure 3:   Child Care, 1995-1996 (in %)

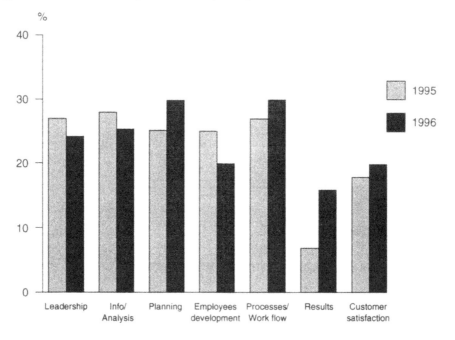

6   Evaluating the Awards

The City of Stockholm's Awards for Good Quality is a development project. The first round culminated in February 1995 with a prize-giving ceremony attended by 1,200 people from 33 participating units. Since then, the number of participants has steadily increased as more and more activities have been invited to compete. From 1998 on, all of the City's activities will have the opportunity of being candidates.

For the further evaluation of the competition and its TQM concept, a special survey was done during 1996. Three key questions were put to units participating in 1995 and 1996:

- Has the work with the criteria promoted development and planning, participation by those concerned, and evaluation of results?
- Has the unit's work been observed by others, and has there been an exchange of experience with other units?
- How was it working with the criteria? Was there enough support?

The evaluation shows that most units find the criteria difficult but nevertheless interesting. The units have also stated what positive impact in their daily routines the work with the critera has given. A problem for those units participating in the award competition was lack of time. Most units therefore request more support from the administrative leadership in their own district administrations.

Of the responding units, 38 out of the 43 in the survey claimed they would use the criteria in the future, primarily as a tool for evaluation and improvement.

All units informed their customers/users about their participation in the award competition. Parents with children in child care units were particulary interested in the event. Many children and parents were proud that "their" unit was competing.

The majority of the units responding had not noticed more than a limited interest from other units in exchanging knowledge or requesting study visits. On the other hand, the interest from units in other Swedish cities has been more intensive. The survey also shows that candidates are most willing to share experiences, give lectures and in other ways contribute to furthering quality development in the city.

The participating units describe, both in writing and in interviews, that the quality work has contributed to deepening their knowledge of their own activities. They also feel joy and pride in seeing all their daily work and activities written down in a systematic manner.

7   Further Development

The possibility of using the criteria and evaluation methods outside the competition involves a development process that will stretch over many years. The City Council has adopted a resolution on a basic structure for following up on the City's quality standards. Part of this resolution concerns the creation of a uniform goal structure, as well as the possibility to follow up on the activities' goals. It is essential that financial and activity management, as well as follow-up procedures, be integrated in a better way.

Another part of the resolution concerns ways in which the criteria and awards can be used. The City Council's resolution constitutes that, in 1997, the City will start following up on the number of units within each committee's area of responsibility which have worked themselves through the criteria. In the long term, the City Council will have a chance to select a number of units at random from each area of responsibility which will then be required to draw up a complete description of their activities and undergo an examination. This will be done completely independently of the competition itself. The ultimate purpose would be to set up a type of "quality index" to form the basis for benchmarking and for a total assessment of the City's quality standards. However, the methods involved require further consideration and work to develop them.

Many people were sceptical when the quality awards were established in 1994. This scepticism was partly politically motivated, and partly due to ignorance of the methodology. "How can you compete with quality?" or "Why should we compete with quality when we are being subjected to cut-backs?" were common arguments. I was a sceptic myself. But with time, the awards have become more accepted. In general politicians agree that the criteria are an excellent instrument in quality work. Most of the employees who have worked with them are enthusiastic.

As far as the City is concerned, it is obvious that the awards have had positive effects in at least three respects:

- The awards and criteria work have stimulated quality development within the participating units.
- The winners and candidates have become models and good examples for the City's other activities, and therefore also stimulate quality development in non-participating units.
- A basis for assessing the City's quality standards, as well as for development and benchmarking, has been established.

The use of quality awards based on the TQM philosophy has been spread all over the world as an efficient tool to improve organizations of the most different kinds.

Among local government in Sweden, there is an increasing interest in quality development; and some cities have introduced awards similar to the Stockholm model.

There are no simple solutions to the debate about quality development and how the public sector should tackle quality work. Quality is a concept that is difficult to define and which ultimately comes down to subjective values. One often says "beauty is in the eye of the beholder". Those of us who work in the public sector are confronted with a number of problems in this respect, as our activities are directed towards many different, and often heterogeneously composed, categories of customers. Neither is it certain that the taxpayers' interests are the same as those of the users. However, the more systematic quality work carried out in the public sector in recent years has been important inasmuch as it aims at orientating activities with users to a greater extent, which in turn facilitates efficiency and ultimately benefits the taxpayers. Offensive quality development and constant improvement work are therefore necessary for maintaining a well-functioning public sector and general welfare system. We must realize that whatever stops improving will stop being good. If something stops being good, nobody wants it.

CHAPTER 15

Quality in Home Care and Nursing?

Karen Christensen

1   Introduction

During the last few years, "quality assurance" has become a catchword in Norwegian public care for the elderly and for people with disabilities. This catchword has emerged in a period with two central characteristics: a growing population of old people needing more care and nursing, and increasing financial constraints in the public sector. Statistics about the development in public home care and nursing services show that it has become more difficult to get such services in Norway during the past few years (Olsen, 1995). So if, as a first definition of improving *quality*, we think of giving the recipients more individual care – that is, taking the needs and wishes of the individual recipient more seriously – it looks like the possibilities for this are reduced. Thus, there are good reasons for not speaking of rising quality these days; and the catchword of "quality assurance" is thus in a way discordant with the general development in public home-based care services.

I want to discuss how to analyse "quality assurance" in home-based care and nursing on the basis of a sociological study of these services in a large Norwegian city, Bergen. The data was gathered in the years between 1988 and 1994 and consist of interviews and participant observation. The informants were home helpers, professional and practical nurses, and some pensioners. The abovementioned study shows that the discussion about rising quality needs to be analysed from different points of view. We can discuss it from the outside and ask, "What has been done to advance quality?": for instance, through the way the work is organized and through different strategies for organizing it. We can, however, also discuss it from the inside and ask, "Do old people and people with disabilities get more individual help? How has quality been assured in the caregivers' work?" The inside has two levels of quality. Improving quality not only can be defined as a question of giving more individualized help to the old and to people with disabilities; it is also a question of putting the caregivers in a position to give help in a more individualized way.

2   Quality from Outside

The extensive process of reorganization of the public home-care and home-nursing services in Norway during the 1970s and 1980s can be summarized by four keywords: *decentralization, coordination, flexibility* and *"homemaking"*[1].

Decentralization has been promoted by a new law passed in 1984, which moved the responsibility for public care from a higher administrative level to a lower local level, the municipal level, thus providing possibilities for managing both institutional and home-based care from the same level. The municipality did not get more power under this law but instead got many more functions to perform. One of the most important arguments for this new law was to give old people and people with disabilities more equal opportunities for getting help, independent of where they lived, by bringing the services nearer to the recipients. To realize this, the responsibility for decisions about how much and what kind of services the individual client should get, was moved from the administrative leaders at a higher level to new leaders on a lower level in the organization.

Another part of this law is related to the *coordination* of services. Until 1984, home-care and home-nursing services were part of the local social service departments and had separate administrations. These two services became organized in a special department of Nursing and Care Services after 1984, independent of both health and social services. Their development has since then been characterized by an increasing integration between these two services. This has had two parts, the so-called "big integration" and "small integration". The "big integration" deals with coordinating institutional care for old people and people with disabilities with home-based care services. The "small integration" deals with coordinating home-help and home-nursing services. Until this coordination was realized, home helpers and home nurses did not know each other; they worked separately and only had a few formal common meetings. Now they are gathered in groups and coordinate their daily work. There have, however, been different opinions about *how* to integrate these services. Two models have especially been discussed. In the first model, the two services are organized parallel to each other, meaning that home help and nursing work are separated, with no real collaboration between nurses and home helpers. The other model is called "the integrated model". Here, employees in the two services are gathered into small groups with responsibility for clients in a specific geographical area. The last one is a more integrated model than the first, because the home helpers and home nurses are working together in their daily work. But also in this model, different solutions are being discussed: for instance, having one or two leaders. If there is to be only one leader, it has to be a professional nurse, since professional nurses are theoretically the most qualified among the three groups mentioned. This means, however, that home helpers have no leader for their work activities, since these are different from nursing activities: while the home helpers use most of their time with the client for housework, the nurses concentrate on medical tasks. Under this process of coordination, however, some of the nurses' routine tasks have been transferred to the home helpers. There have been different solutions to the problem of which kind of leader to have. In the area where we concluded our study, they had chosen a model having one common leader for the whole group – a professional nurse – and a subordinate leader for the home helpers. The process of coordination has thus also brought more hierarchy into home-based care, particularly by giving more leadership positions to professional nurses.

The strategy of coordinating services, however, is not only about coordinating home help and home nursing and, on a higher level, coordinating home care with institutional care. It is also about cooperating with individuals or organizations giving informal help to the old and people with disabilities, especially family members and voluntary organizations. This part of the strategy of coordination can be seen as a public acceptance of the fact that public care often is coordinated with informal care, and that this informal care is actually given to a great extent (Lingsom, 1985). Thus, coordination means coordinating home help, home nursing, institutional care and even to some degree informal private care.

The third keyword, *flexibility,* follows the process of coordination, because the process of coordination makes flexibility possible. It leads to greater flexibility between getting home-based care and institutional care, and between public care and private care, from family members and others. From the recipients' point of view, we get more flexibility as to who can receive care, how much care to receive and at what time. Earlier, the home-based care mainly served people needing little or relatively little care; and such care services were given only in the daytime. People with mental disabilities, for instance, could not get home care because their needs were evaluated as too great for the system to manage; they therefore had to be cared for in institutions. But all this has changed. Now even people who earlier were clearly defined as institutional cases, can get home-care and nursing services; and they can get help both day and night. Most of the services are still given in the daytime, but in the evenings they are concentrated with smaller groups helping people, among other things, to go to bed. During the night there are night patrols giving emergency help but also having such routine tasks as, for instance, catherization[2]. For the recipients, flexibility means that more different groups of people needing care have opportunity to get care in their home. But it also means that the control over what they get has to become tighter. Earlier, persons who got public home help could be sure of receiving this service for a very long time, sometimes for the rest of their life. Now this service can be removed when the recipient, for whatever reason, is evaluated to have become more self-sufficient, as the new home-care service is also a more concentrated help with the aim of making clients more self-sufficient. For the home helpers, these changes have brought in a new demand for competence, which also implies that they have to be more flexible. Home helpers have, until few years ago, primarily been recruited among women with a lot of household experience; but now there are more young girls without this experience working in this service. This development has come at the same time as the demand for qualifications in the home-help service has increased. Also, the work of the home nurses is on the way to redefinition. Until this process of attaining flexibility, home nursing has been seen as work with very few medical tasks but a lot of routine tasks, as compared to institutional nursing. Now, much of the nursing work earlier done only in institutions also has to be done in private homes. This has to do with another important part of flexibility, namely the closer collaboration between institutions and home care, providing more possibilities for sending people home quickly after a stay in hospital. And it also gives more possibilities for giving people a short-term stay – a so-called rehabilitation stay – in institutional care. The transport between institutions and home care has thus become much more fluid.

Finally, the fourth keyword, *"homemaking"*, implies that during all these changes, staying at home has become a norm for all old people and also all people with disabilities independent of how much help they need. It is taken for granted that old people want to live at home as long as possible. And to meet the demands following this norm, the housing situation for old people and for people with disabilities has been changed, by building more special residences adapted for them. These changes have thus made the line between private homes and institutions much more fluid. An important ideology behind this process of "homemaking" is the ideology of rehabilitation. The idea is to avoid looking at old people as ill, weak and dependent on others, but to look at them as at other people (read: younger) having a chance, for instance, to become more self-sufficient. The aim of helping people is then to provide them with more possibilities for doing more themselves.

As one of the reasons for these changes has been to give people more equal chances for getting help – which is an argument about justice being one of the keywords in the ideology of the welfare state – we can see these changes as an attempt to improve the quality of these services. Already on this level, however, there are some paradoxes, and I want to mention two of these. The first one is about homemaking and the part of it called "rehabilitation". Many of the intentions behind this strategy are positive. It is positive to look at old people as people with resources, when the common view is that these people are on the periphery of society, no longer a part of production. The paradox first becomes visible when we look at the people it concerns. As I mentioned in the beginning, it is an extensive and important trend that there are more old people and thus also more people with disabilities. And a supplement to this is that there are more people living in single-person households, meaning that they are more dependent on public help. Kari Wærness has called care for elderly *a care without results (a "resultless care")*, meaning care that cannot be defined by results, in contrast to care given especially in hospitals, where the patients are sent home after treatment (Wærness, 1982). This means that a strategy with rehabilitation as its ideology, is of very restricted use for old people, since it is generally not realistic to expect much improvement.

The other paradox I want to mention is about *"homemaking"*. Also this strategy is initially positive, because it gives people several possibilities for deciding the type of home they want to live in when they are ill and old, whether they want to live alone in a private home or close to other old people. But giving help to still more people with disabilities and more old people means building new types of homes, putting a lot of necessary things into these homes (like special beds, lifts, etc.) and trying to gather these homes where the caregiver office is located, and so on. In many ways, this is, however, just another way of making new institutions or institutionalizing private homes.[3] Trying to realize a strategy of homemaking for old and ill people thus means making new kinds of institutions. Here we have the other paradox.

3   Quality from Inside – The Caregiver Side

During our research, we found two dominating processes in home-care services, along with all the changes mentioned above: one for home help and one for nursing. The process for home help we call *professionalization*. The home helpers no longer just have experience from household work from their private home and family situation: improved training is a general trend for home help. In the 1980s, they were offered a three-month course. Many of the home helpers did not, however, take this course. Then, in the late 1980s, a course of one year's duration was offered. And now, in the 1990s, a new training programme (for "care workers") has been built up which has stopped the process of setting-up specific training just for home helpers. The new training is of four year's duration and it is important that this new training be in accordance with one of the central points coming from the new way of organizing home care, namely the demand for flexibility, because it is general training. This means, among other things, that after finishing it, one can work both in institutions and in home care; and one can work not only with children and old people, but also with people with disabilities. Thus, the "care worker" is seen as a more flexible worker than the home helper. But it is also important in this context to mention that home helpers in general already have more training for doing their work and in the future will have much more training for doing this work because of more opportunities for care-oriented training. Other changes are that home helpers are more interested in organizing themselves; they more seldom take part-time jobs, and they want to have a stronger separation between their work and their private life. The traditions for doing unpaid work for care recipients have become weaker; and during this period, it also has become more important to define the content of home-help services as different from home nursing, especially when working more closely with each other. First of all, nurses define exactly what should be home-help work and what should be nursing. Thus, professionalization is not only about having more training and focusing more on it; it is also about bringing a new culture into this service, a culture with central principles from the labour market in general. One of the major changes bringing home helpers to this new position and new subjective view of their work has been achieved by changing the work from individual work to group work. On an organizational level, this process has been accelerated by placing this work closer to home-nursing services, professional nurses being the most professionalized.

Also in home nursing, a process of professionalization has taken place over time; and this process has come much further because professional nurses and practical nurses, for instance, have more education compared to home helpers (three and one year[s], respectively). They have more traditions for unionizing and more full-time jobs. However, we do not find professionalization as a key process in home nursing. Instead, we find a process we call *institutionalization*, meaning that home nursing increasingly becomes nursing in institutions because of the institutional culture coming into home nursing. Two elements similar to this process we call "fragmenting of work" and "predictability of work". Fragmenting has come, for instance, as a consequence of separating practical activities from administrative tasks, accomplished by getting a nurse to be leader of the working group. Earlier, home nurses did all the work for the care recipients. They did both medical work and administrative work: applying for a place in an institution, contacting family members, etc.; and they had a great deal of knowledge about the life of the recipients. Maybe many of the nurses also have much of this individual-history knowledge of their patients today; but in fact, it no longer has the same function. It is no longer necessary to have this knowledge, as administration work is done by a leader at a low level. Decisions regarding recipients have thus been moved to these leaders, in spite of the fact that these leaders can never have as much knowledge as the group members about the recipients. Therefore, decisions about help have become more theoretical and more bureaucratic. Another part of this fragmenting of work has come about as a result of the use of computers. Earlier, the exchange of knowledge between nurses took place during meetings, where they talked about the life of the recipients. But now, every group member puts her information into the computer and the leader checks it. The computer has thus reduced the importance of verbal communication, because a part of this is now done by putting information into and getting it out of the computer.[4] This process has thus also reduced the possibilities for what this communication is about, because putting data into the computer also means following standards for doing it.

The other part of the process of institutionalization which I would like to mention here is the new predictability of service. It is characteristic for home nursing, compared to home help, that the help is much more concrete and organized in detail before the nurse meets the patient. This difference between services also has something to do with the much shorter time nurses stay in the home of the recipients as compared to home helpers. As a trend, this means that the work for the recipients is concentrated on doing special tasks decided on beforehand and nothing more than that, because time is so limited.

If we mean by "quality assurance" better working conditions due to nurses and home helpers, there has been some improvement due to these two processes. Professionalization has reduced the risks for subordination of the home helper: the home helper has a work history with two roots, the work of the housewife and that of domestic servant. This means, that the work, from a historical point of view, is very subordinated. When comparing the home helper with the domestic servant, it is an improvement that the role of the employer is moved from the recipient to a third party, the public authority. This difference, however, does not mean that subordination is no longer a problem for home helpers; but professionalization has helped the home helpers to have more control and influence in their work situation. When I compare this study with a study conducted by Kari Wærness about ten years earlier (Wærness, 1982) in the same part of Bergen, I find that the relationship between the home helpers and the recipients during this process of professionalization has changed quite a bit. It is no longer isolated but has become a much more public relationship, by which I mean more open to scrutiny. The concrete tasks are defined and limited, a leader coordinates the work between the home helpers in the working groups, and the individual home helper is not indispensable, meaning that the same work can also be done by another home help for the same client. These are some changes showing that the risk of subordination has become weaker but has not been eliminated. The process of controlling working conditions, seen from the employee's point of view in relation to the client, has been and still is individual. The home helper is, however, no longer standing alone in relation to the client but has colleagues and has become a member of a group with the same kind of rights as other employees.

The institutionalization process has also had positive effects on home-nursing work. This work has had from the beginning a lower status than nursing in institutions, which has to do with the history of home nursing: one of the important arguments for starting home nursing was to relieve the pressure on institutional care (Nordhus/Isaksen/Wærness, 1986). In the late 1970s, home nursing was given to people who could easily be at home with just minimal help from public services. Now this, for different reasons, has changed very much. Patients are no longer "only" old; some of them are younger, with physical disabilities; some have mental disabilities; many are senile and several more are very ill. Some of the work done earlier in institutions now has to be done in the home-care sector. Hence, there are different changes pointing to the fact that the status of home nursing will become higher as the demand for nursing skills becomes greater. In this study, we find that the nurses themselves have internalized the norm of traditional institutional nursing being more prestigious, maybe not least because this is a part of their professional socialization process. Especially professional nurses, compared to practical nurses, choose to work in an institution before they go into home-care services, because the institutional work of the nurses themselves is seen as more prestigious than home-nursing work. Probably the new changes will give the home-based care a greater prestige and improve the vocational possibilities for nursing careers. Thus, the dominating processes, in some way, mean more orientation towards improving quality – which implies less possibility for subordination and greater possibility for giving care workers higher status.

However, if we define better quality in these services as more personal individualized help, we do not really find the dominant processes leading to better quality. Instead, we find quality assurance in the resistance to these dominating processes. The process of building this resistance, we call *deprofessionalization*. This is there because it takes time to build a new awareness, and a lot of our home helpers still have housewife awareness; they are very altruistic in their way of helping the old and people with disabilities. This altruism means wishing to help others, which implies that they in different ways not only act as employees but also as housewives. We still find examples of unpaid work for clients, going to work when ill, or doing things for the clients they do not have to do: for instance, things clients could do themselves or tasks which are not mentioned on their list of tasks. Ten to fifteen years ago, these things could be done on a larger scale, because the care relationship was much more private (Wærness, 1982). Today, it can be done only by breaking rules. For instance, it is a central rule today not to do things care recipients can do themselves, because the work is now defined as "help-to-self-help" work (the ideology of rehabilitation). Thus, these elements of deprofessionalization conflict with the dominant process: home helpers therefore often get into a dilemma between doing things in favour of the recipients, and doing things in favour of themselves as employees.

Also in home nursing, we find a process of resistance to the dominating process of institutionalization. And here, it has to do with elements not in harmony with the institutional elements. The caregiver role as an authority with a long tradition of institutional care does not harmonize with giving help in the patients' home, because here the patients have their own rules for living.[5] The role as a treater does not harmonize with a patient who has much more than a bed and a few personal things on a bedside table. In the home, the nurses see family pictures, get to know family members, and so on. It is more difficult just doing medical work and then leaving again. It is much easier in a hospital or another institution to go from one bed to another, from one patient to another, because here the patients have not constructed their daily life and routines themselves; these are part of the institution. But in homes, the recipients have constructed their routines themselves. This means that doing home nursing work often implies to break these routines of the recipients. So it is different coming to and leaving a home, because it is more difficult not becoming involved in some way. The contact with the home makes it more difficult to perform one limited task, and the work is much more unpredictable.

The development into home care has made these dilemmas both stronger and more actual. The consequences of the dominant processes have made the distance between caregiver and recipient greater. These dilemmas have also revealed that there are some important elements in home-based care for giving personal individualized care, and that this is coming from resistance to the dominating process. Thus, the new dilemmas are also showing chances for giving personal individualized care. The home help in our study tends towards altruism. We find much of this altruism because many of the home helpers have long experience as housewives. In the future, the possibilities for nearness to the recipient will depend more on organizational possibilities in the actual work for coming closer to the recipient. In home nursing we find possibilities for personal individualized service in the chance to see the recipient not only as a patient but also as a person with different kinds of needs and not least with an individual life history. For anyone helping, this means giving more adequate help by placing the task into a framework of a life history.

4   Quality from Inside – The Care Recipient's Side

If we finally consider the recipient's side and look at "quality assurance" from this point of view, it looks quite different. In spite of the fact that home-care services during the process of decentralization have come closer both to recipients and potential recipients, not only fewer get help but it is more difficult to keep the help (Olsen, 1995). As I mentioned earlier, it follows from the reorganization that the work is now more controlled. Seen from the recipient's side, a central part of this control has come about as a result of contracts through which the care relation has been formalized. By having a contract, it is easier to change (read: reduce) the help, because the contract can work, for example, for a few months and then has to be renewed. If the recipient can do more things now, maybe the contract will terminate and the help will be removed. This happened very seldom before reorganization. The contract also implies that the work both of home help and home nursing is becoming more limited. From the recipient's point of view, this means that he/she cannot demand work not mentioned in this contract. On the other hand, the recipient can complain if the work mentioned in the contract is not done. The contracts have thus concretized the chance to complain. This means, for instance, that in any disagreement about help, one no longer has to find solutions during (informal) discussions between caregivers and recipients and sometimes a leader; this now is placed on a higher administrative level. As home help and home nursing are connected to different laws, the complaint cases have different administrative methods to follow. In this way, contracts have brought more bureaucracy into home care and have formalized the care relationship. If this is seen together with a situation where the time for help has been reduced and more different persons are going in and out of the homes of recipients, we have a situation where the possibilities for distance between caregiver and recipients have become much greater. If I compare my results about giving home help with Kari Wærness' from the late 1970s, I find that the time has been reduced from up to 6 hours per week in 1979, to up to 3 hours per week in 1989; and that the number of regular clients per home helper has increased from between 1-2 to 4-8, i.e. four times more. So if we talk about bettering quality from the inside, we find that recipients have more formal rights, but that these rights are also more difficult to get. If a recipient is very old and senile and has no family members helping him/her, he/she has rights but no opportunity to use them. Thus, we find that the new rights have given greatest influence to the old and to people with disabilities who have the largest resources.

Together with the dominating changes in home care, recipients are no longer called "clients" or "patients" but rather "users": they are now users of the services. Our study shows that the old terms are actually more realistic than the new one, which attributes resources to the recipients which they do not actually have or which only a minority among them have.

5   Conclusion

Putting the catchword "quality assurance" into home-based public care makes it possible to create standards which can assure quality. Inside the welfare state, this can be done to some degree, given economic help, because the welfare state can give the same amount to all; and some will call this just. When talking about social services, however, the discussion about objective standards is much more complicated, for many reasons: among others, that here it depends on subjective perception. High quality of care cannot be assured completely, and especially not by setting up standards; but care can be organized in a way which makes it possible to improve quality. Thus, the quality of care has to be evaluated almost continuously, as the subjective perception is unpredictable; and this evaluation has to consider the different points of view, because looking at quality from the outside does not necessarily mean the same as looking at it from the side of the recipients of the services or the caregivers. This study showed that the dominating processes, in spite of their good intentions, have not raised quality from the recipients' point of view. But quality has improved to some extent if seen from the caregivers' point of view. This is only partial, as the changes have also made the work less autonomous compared to the situation before reorganization. Whereas work used to be characterized by more autonomy, it now means following rules, common standards and orders from leaders. But there is still resistance to all these changes, and it is in this resistance that the real possibilities for individualized care are found.

Notes

1 The idea to use the last of these four keywords is taken from Bjørn Olsen, who is asking for " 'Homemaking' for the care for old people in the 1990s?" (Olsen, 1995).
2 Some old people or people with disabilities who cannot urinate are being catheterized.
3 Greta Marie Skau (1994) and Anders Bergh (1993) have also called attention to this problem.
4 This process of the "computerization" of nursing has also been problematized, for instance, by Ingunn Elstad and Torunn Hamran (1995) and Marie Cambell (1992).
5 Also Ritva Gough has shown this very well in her study about people with disabilities (1996).

References

Bergh, Anders (1993) *Mänskligt, kvinnligt, manligt. En etnologisk studie av mötet mellan vårdbiträden och gamla i de gamlas hem och vid en sjukhemsavdelning.* Rapport nr. 16, Forsknings- och utvecklingsbyrån, Stockholms socialtjänst.

Campbell, Marie L. (1992) 'Nurses' Professionalism in Canada: A Labour Process Analysis', *International Journal of Health Services* 22 (4).

Christensen, Karen (1990) *Professionalisering og modprofessionalisering i et omsorgsarbejde.* SEFOS notat 34.

Christensen, Karen (1992) *Slutrapport fra projektet: "Endringer i den kommunale hjemmebaserte omsorgen".* SEFOS notat 69.

Elstad, Ingunn/Hamran, Torunn (1995) *Et kvinnefag i moderniseringen. Sykehuspleien mellom fagtradisjon og målstyring.* Oslo: Ad Notam Gyldendal.

Gough, Ritva/Modig, Maria (1996) *Leva med personlig assistans: vårdtagare blir arbetsledare.* Stockholm: Liber Utbildning.

Lingsom, Susan (1985) *Uformell omsorg for syke og eldre.* Samfunnsøkonomiske studier 57.

Nordhus, Inger/Hilde, Lise/Widding, Isaksen/Wærness, Kari (1986) *De fleste gamle er kvinner.* Bergen/Oslo/Stavanger/Tromsø: Universitetsforlaget.

Olsen, Bjørn (1995) ' "Hjemliggjøring" av eldreomsorgen på 1990-tallet?', *Samfunnsspeilet* 4.

Skau, Greta Marie (1994) *Mellom makt og hjelp.* Oslo: Tano.

Wærness, Kari (1982) *Kvinneperspektiver på sosialpolitikken.* Oslo/Bergen/Tromsø: Universitetsforlaget.

CHAPTER 16

Promoting Quality of Life for Older People in Institutions

Carla Costanzi

The aim of this paper is to explore the specific cultural context in which Italian public administration tries to promote quality development in services for older people, here focusing particularly on institutional care. Currently, the evolution of the service system is at the stage where it puts priority on measures for developing quality within the sector of old-age homes: in Italy, these are the main formal answer to the needs of older persons. I shall exemplify these considerations in the light of an innovative project in the Italian municipality of Genoa. This project illustrates an experimental approach in the Italian context, i.e. the role of the public administration towards third parties, in particular by setting priorities, developing a definition of standards, new guidelines and incentives, new control mechanisms, and user involvement.

1   Quality of Personal Social Services in the Italian Context

In Italy, the concept of quality has emerged rather slowly in the field of social services. This is due to the relatively brief history of welfare provision in this country. Having been created decades later than those of other European countries, Italian social services have just emerged from a pioneer period of expansion and identity-building. They have therefore only recently been able to come to grips with the question of quality. Concerning institutional organization and the research connected to it, there were always uncertainties with respect to the relevant legislation and its slow implementation. Furthermore, during the last 20 years revisions and replanning were frequent in the social services. During this period, a number of important issues emerged relating to, for instance, programming techniques, organization, different approaches to management, and tools and methods for evaluation. To some extent, all these issues are preliminary to quality development.

However, an increased awareness of quality issues could be observed during recent debates within the various professions active in the field of health and social services. Private research centres (rarely universities) have also been involved in this debate. In addition, grass-roots movements have played a significant role in inciting the debate by making explicit demands for more participation in and control over services. In recent years, a further boost to innovation came from the public administration which, from the beginning of this decade, has paved the way with new legislation aimed at protecting the rights of the citizen.[1] The most recent result of this innovation has been the Public Services Charter,[2] which, if properly enacted, will produce basic improvements in quality. The development of social services in Italy has also been influenced by international stimuli, to which Italian services have become increasingly attuned.

As a corollary, one can say that quality development in Italy – in particular its methodological aspects, strategies for quality promotion and methods for evaluation – has also become an important issue. Nevertheless, Italy is still a long way from establishing general practices related to quality. Currently, the debate is whether experiments with new proposals are to gain ground or existing methods should be elaborated, or even whether relevant routines are still to be implemented. It is, however, possible to speak of a "quality trend", by which we mean the constant flux of a process that can never be concluded or rigidly defined.

2 Different Approaches to Quality Issues

2.1 Professional Approaches to Quality

Quality Assurance activities were first introduced in Italy during the 1980s, primarily within the hospital system under the title "Verification and Review of Quality" (VQR). Today, this system is being used extensively outside the medical field, above all in the provision of nursing care.

With the development of self-assessment initiatives in the field, criteria for standards have been established that allow the care provider to assess his or her professional work. Furthermore, other strategies using inspections have been developed in other health contexts to verify whether predetermined quality standards exist throughout the system. Very recently, some regions in Italy have introduced so-called "accreditation mechanisms" for providers of old-age homes, with such quality objectives as the promotion of a culture of continuous improvement. However, at the moment, the system of accreditation is usually restricted to old-age homes.

2.2 Business Approaches

Alongside these professional approaches to quality, specific strategies termed "business matrix techniques" (i.e. ISO 9000 and Total Quality Management) have been developed in other operational contexts. Even if the diffusion of these techniques is relatively new, having been developed only during the past few years, the models, the operative applications, and the overall concepts inherent to them now seem to be predominant in the area of private business.

With specific reference to the realm of health and social services their application has been initiated in the fields of hospital cure and care. Bologna was the first public administration in Italy to conceive a Total Quality Plan for home care and old-age homes. Apart from these approaches, it is now possible – in our opinion – to consider a third approach to quality issues, which we will outline in the following.

2.3 Quality and Personal Social Services

For some years now, we have witnessed a gradual shift from a system of social protection based on state intervention, to a mixed system in which the market has assumed a more significant role, either directly or indirectly. Of course, this can also be observed in quality issues and in approaches to quality development.

There is one basic question, however: what effects may result from introducing criteria, organizational solutions and communicative strategies that seem so far away from conceptual and idealistic paradigms and values propagated by the welfare state, when it comes to defining and promoting quality in personal social services?

Of course, such factors as appropriateness, efficacy, accessibility, fairness, and efficiency have to be considered as important elements in regulating the quality of personal social services. Given the specific nature of the latter, those variables that illustrate a system based on social justice and protection of the weaker members of society are becoming ever more important.

Thus, the evaluation of the possible effects of increased marketization on the specific peculiarities of personal social services is of growing importance. Such an evaluation has to start with a proper definition of those features of social services that make them unique.

If we wish to characterize the quality of such non-material products as services, we must bear in mind aspects with strong subjective connotations: the perspective of someone who provides a service is radically different from that of someone who provides a manufactured product. The quality of a service is measured in terms of its function, which, although variable, has a consistent symbolic connotation. The image of a service is, however, tied to predominantly intangible elements whereas the value of a service is expressed in terms of how it is performed.

When we talk about social services, the discussion hinges mainly on the characteristics and the conditions of the specific interpersonal relationships that compose or support the service offered. We are speaking of a specific type of relationship, peculiar to a care relationship.

The service is offered as a response to a request from someone unable to create or maintain a normal situation without the active intervention of other people, namely the service is conceived as a response to a situation or problem that is centred on a state of dependence possibly related to different types of disabilities, i.e.

- the lack of functional autonomy (difficulty/inability to manage as in the past);
- the lack of psychosocial autonomy (difficulty/inability to conceive, construct and sustain one's own life, to manage emotional and intellectual relationships); and
- the lack of ethical autonomy (inability or refusal to make free choices about the direction of one's own life following proper norms or ethical principles) (cf. Nelisse, 1993).

The more serious the level of the problem, the more difficult it is for the person in need of help to determine the characteristics and conditions of that help, and the more he/she loses the capacity to manage the whole situation. It is necessary to underline that all different types of dependence are to be found between residents of institutions; but it is, above all, respect for the ethical autonomy of the individual, respect for his values and the ability to make up his own mind that are the most fundamental prerequisites for a good relationship at a professional level. There is always the risk of substituting one form of lack of autonomy for another (dependence on the professional); this kind of risk cannot be totally eliminated, but it can be regulated and kept within reasonable limits.

We can conclude that the quality of the service lies in overcoming the paradox inherent in the relationship between professional helper and the person being helped. The correct professional relationship does not lie in the guarantee that the provider of the service can distance himself from an eventual emotional involvement, but it will be better guaranteed by his ability to comprehend, in a literal sense, the subjectivity of the helped person and so help to maintain the ethical autonomy (the ability to act according to his/her own will) of the beneficiary of the service.

Following these considerations we could define the promotion of quality in personal social services as the creation of an environment in which the user of the service, in our particular case the elderly person, can freely express his or her own point of view, beginning, for instance, with an explicit agreement on the content and form of care and expecting to eventually give his or her assessment of the care received.

This approach to quality, which is based on the point of view of the user defining requirements and parameters of quality according to his/her expectations, can be considered an evolution of the "active client" concept. The expression "prosumer" (producer/consumer) has been introduced into marketing language to remind us of the interaction between producer and consumer.

Involving the client in the development of a service needs to be better defined within the specific context of care of older persons. The active client is, from this point of view, not only an active participant in the proposed initiative, but he/she is considered to be the one who is best able to express his/her will and desires, at least regarding the way in which his/her needs are fulfilled.

In contrast to the client purchasing products or usual services, the older person making use of social services has one or more handicaps (cultural, social, psychological, physical, etc.) which must be resolved at a basic level in order to empower him as a person with precise rights, opinions and choices. Thus, promoting quality in personal social services is closely related to maintaining what are considered to be our inalienable moral rights (personal liberty, freedom of religion, freedom of thought, individuality, privacy); whereas in the market-place, the inadequate quality of a product/service will be judged much more by standards that are other than moral.

In light of the above, the quality of a welfare service is directly proportional to the degree to which this service creates and protects ethical autonomy. The person who decides on the form of care must have the ability to act with great discretion and elasticity, even to tailor original solutions wherever necessary. This scenario indeed requires a radical break from the traditional thinking of professionals in social services. Providers of these services have to deal much more with uncertainty and continuous innovation rather than to simply provide routinized and standardized services.

2.3.1 Quality and Institutions

Within the realm of welfare services, old-age homes have many particular features which need to be discussed. First of all, there is the question of whether residents of old-age and nursing homes are really able to play an active part in the actual service provision, be it at the different stages of decision-making,[3] or be it with respect to advocating their own interests. While the elderly may have experience and even expertise with the performance of home care services, experience with residential services is obviously scarcer. Furthermore, the user usually lacks the skills necessary to evaluate these services. This lack of expertise on the part of the user – and his/her family – is closely interwoven with a second weakness typical to institutional care. The frail older resident has no definite expectations: he/she rarely anticipates entering an institution, nor can he/she express him/herself effectively on this traumatic event in his/her life. As a corollary, institutionalization is nearly always an event suffered passively. Thus, it is difficult for any resident to formulate questions or proposals with respect to an event that he/she had not planned, not expected, or not even thought about.

A third specific condition of institutions for the elderly concers the operational structure of this kind of service. From the point of view of the operator, we are dealing with a service of high professional risk. This is due to the type of service provided, the very stressful interpersonal relationships, the heavy workload, and the widespread lack of cultural awareness of the ageing process. This latter aspect not only affects society as a whole, but in particular affects professionals, in case of lack of proper training and of the necessary "know-how" or systematic supervision.

Business matrix techniques can be of great help when they define the total quality objective to everyone's satisfaction: social workers, suppliers, shareholders and the ecosystem. In other words, quality can only be found in an approach that involves all the parties concerned in the process of promoting quality.

However, the needs and expectations of the social worker become a determining factor in the global quality strategy, because his sense of dissatisfaction or discomfort inevitably affects the quality of the whole service in a significant way. The horror stories that we read about providers in the sensationalist press do not necessarily refer to concentration-camp style institutions; sometimes good architecture and furnishings hide degrading working conditions which breed inadequate, cynical or even violent behaviour towards the residents. Very often, the administration, devoting its attention to the material comfort of the residents, overlooks or is not cognizant of such perverse tendencies.

2.3.2 Involving Older Users in Promoting Quality in Social Services

We have seen that quality development in the social services, in particular with respect to institutional care, is a very complex concept. This complexity is not just derived from its numerous components, which can vary considerably from one context to another, but also from the unstable nature of these components.

The involvement of all parties concerned in the development of quality, needs to be specifically planned and organized in advance: they all have to continually redefine the content, stages, minimum acceptance levels and all other aspects related to the specific goal. Therefore, it is essential that all parties be able to participate from both a formal and a substantial point of view. This prerequisite is still difficult to fulfil with respect to the client/user. The participatory system in operation until now in some local administrations has given citizens a consultative but not an active role. The idea that has inspired these forms of involvement does not put the person but rather the administrative document at the centre of activities of the public administration; that is, putting "taking charge" above results, i.e. responding to needs.

The meaning of participation must therefore be particularly extended in the direction of controlling service quality. However, an important precondition is the ability to perform this function. A client cannot exercise any real choice between the different options that the entire supply system offers: he lacks the specific competence and the information or "training" necessary to distinguish the more relevant aspects from the more easily definable in any given service. What kind of control will he be able to successively exercise? Overcoming the purely formal practice of participation requires educating the population on the questions and problems of care for the elderly and, more generally, on the ageing process.

In this field, another area for public sector intervention is promoting public awareness, with the goals of stimulating public consciousness of the problems and issues and of inculcating cultural patterns.

2.4 Evaluating Quality as a Strategy for Promoting Quality

To achieve the quality mentioned above, we need two phases: in the first stage, we need to define the empirical components of the concept of quality. In the second stage, we have to define those techniques and procedures necessary to evaluate it. In the following, we will make some general considerations, rather than merely presenting technical tools.

The first matter to be considered is the question of who is in charge of evaluation. The problem is not so much the internal or external placement of the evaluator, but rather issues surrounding the promotion of this kind of process as well as the importance of evaluative interventions within the global panorama of what is being done to satisfy the social request.

It is obvious that, if the public administration changes its role from provider to purchaser and strategic supervisor in the welfare system, the maintenance of adequate levels of protection can only be guaranteed by three things: the implementation of control mechanisms, the definition of quality standards for the type of care given, and proper evaluation. In Italy, the culture of public administration has not yet developed such mechanisms, so that, for instance, any project is automatically concluded by an evaluation, from which positive or negative results and, if necessary, suggestions for improvement can be gathered. Currently, the role of the administration is only seen as initiatory, and its proper activity is regarded exclusively as the verification of the proposed intervention and the existence of sufficient funds. We still lack adequate examples of appropriate or "good" practice with respect to monitoring and evaluation. A necessary precondition would be that public authorities be both capable and authorized to assume some control over both profit and non-profit private enterprises. At the moment, Italian public administration risks to confuse the evaluation of quality with the bureaucratic procedure for approving public financing rather than a constant improvement of quality. In the following, however, I would like to give a positive example for a more adequate approach to quality development.

3   An Example for the Evaluation and Promotion of Quality in the Municipality of Genoa

The fact that the city of Genoa has the highest values on all the national indices describing the ageing of the population, explains why the local administration has promoted a quality project aimed at this group of users.

To highlight the size of the problem, it is sufficient to say that last year, for example, expenditure for this group amounted to 58% of the municipality's budget for social services. The choices made in the programme "The Quality of Life of the Elderly Receiving Care", established in 1995, attempted to match the "techno-methodological" aspects with the managerial aspects of public administration. The actual dimension of the problem of providing care for the elderly, as well as the expected increase in both short- and long-term applications for care, highlight the urgent need for effective service coordination for these citizens.

The particular demographic characteristics of Italy will necessitate a steady increase in the provision of residential care, even with improvement of the different welfare services permitting the elderly to stay in their home or with their family. Not only is Italy faced with a great increase in the ageing of its population (percentage of those over 60), as are all the developed countries; Italy is also faced with one of the fastest growth rates of those over 80, the number of whom is expected to double between 1990 and 2025. Because most requests for residential care (between 60 and 70%) come from this age group, even by the most conservative estimates,[4] a city like Genoa will need an additional 500 beds in the next decade.

It is evident that the municipality cannot satisfy the total demand directly. This will make it necessary to turn to a third party to supply the required services. The consequent decisions reflect the criteria that are the basis of municipal social policies, one which intends to undertake the following responsibilities:

- to give guidelines and priorities by which to organize all social services;
- to promote innovation among other groups and agencies in the field: taking an active part in the stimulation and coordination of quality improvement, and providing cultural development in which all parties must be induced to participate so as to bring about significant and synergetic results; and
- to evaluate and check the performance of the third parties involved, laying down clear guidelines on binding conditions for proper evaluation.

Therefore, the target of the activities described in the following are not only public workers and service users, but also the third sector and the population in general. At an operating level, this translates into the objectives listed in Overview 1.

Overview 1: Objectives and Methods of the "Genoa Project"

Objectives	Methods
1. To give priorities for interventions	McKinsey Matrix
2. To define the minimum levels of care in institutions	Working group
3. To survey the problems that workers see as obstacles to effectiveness and efficiency	Delphi consultation
4. To promote opportunities of confrontation, documentation, information for institutions	Seminar and exhibition
5. To improve admissions to institutions	• Decision support • Admission by assessment • Individual care plan • Staff training and supervision • "Assigned" operator
6. To raise the level of information on services in the population	• Services database • Television broadcasts
7. To recognize and promote the rights of the resident	• "Observation scheme" • Working groups to raise professional awareness • Enforcing the rights of the elderly in institutions

3.1 Giving Priority to Intervention

The first step in this process was characterized by the prioritization of different categories of social problems and their respective services in such a way as to allow for successive evaluation of their appropriateness.

With this aim, the McKinsey Matrix (see Figure 1) was applied to compare the programmes of intervention based on two judgements: the number of people interested in the service/intervention, and the seriousness of the problematic phenomenon which the intervention intended to contrast/contain.

**Figure 1:   Matrix for a Comparative Evaluation of the Needs
of the Elderly**

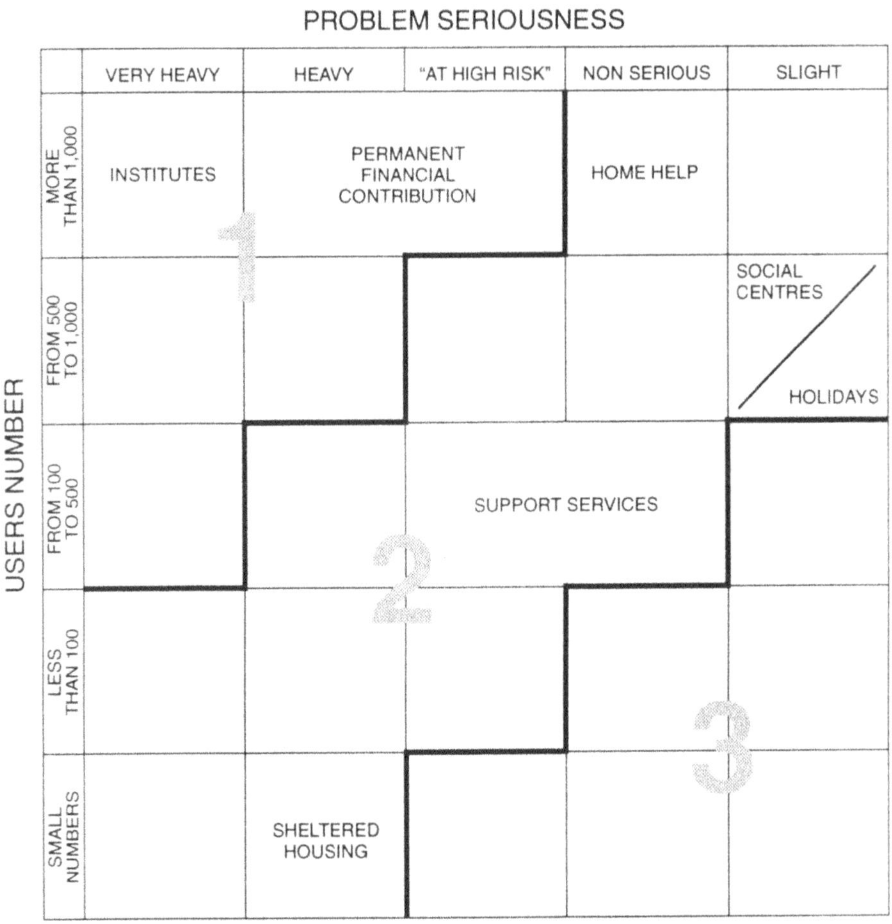

PROBLEM SERIOUSNESS

	VERY HEAVY	HEAVY	"AT HIGH RISK"	NON SERIOUS	SLIGHT
MORE THAN 1,000	INSTITUTES	PERMANENT FINANCIAL CONTRIBUTION		HOME HELP	
FROM 500 TO 1,000					SOCIAL CENTRES / HOLIDAYS
FROM 100 TO 500			SUPPORT SERVICES		
LESS THAN 100					
SMALL NUMBERS		SHELTERED HOUSING			

USERS NUMBER

Zone 1 incorporates areas of intervention to receive priority; Zone 2, areas of medium importance; Zone 3, deferrable areas of intervention.

Two areas of intervention have been pinpointed as priorities: institutions and economic intervention. Here, one must consider the type of intervention, which will require a more complex working plan: firstly because of the internal organization and the tools required, and secondly because it can serve as an initial step in a chain reaction involving other sectors.

Within the field of quality development in residential structures, the most widespread experiences have been based on a low number of variables; the approach chosen here, on the contrary, emphasizes the multidimensional aspect of the service by including in its working plan a high number of variables for simultaneous intervention and thus foreshadowing a project flexible enough to allow adaptations during its operation. Even though there is a wide range of standards within residential care in our city, the situation can be described as very similar to the national average. We are convinced, however, that the guarantees provided are not sufficient to create acceptable living conditions in our institutions.

In this sector, we tolerate considerable cultural backwardness; for example, the law requires precise organizational and structural standards in institutions, but there is a lack of systematic thinking and tools to allow for the evaluation of the qualitative aspects of care and treatment.

In order to establish a preliminary definition of the quality of institutional care, we undertook a survey that collected and collated the different types of expertise, both professional and non-professional, user preferences (though indirectly) and suggestions from anyone else who wished to contribute.

3.2 Defining Minimum Levels of Institutional Care

Defining minimum levels of care as well as other parameters inherent to the concept of quality of life for the residents in old-age homes, should enable us:

- to list significant elements for defining the quality of care, measurable ones that we can use in future contracts between the municipality and private institutions;
- to provide guidelines for non-measurable parameters to supplement existing laws that only establish structural and organizational standards; these new guidelines should take the form of "recommendations" to be used as criteria that focus on the needs of the user;
- to create "cultural" prerequisites that protect the rights of the elderly in institutions; elderly people under care are often exposed to deceit, neglect and abuse – protecting them requires both a broad knowledge and direct experience with life within the residential system. The first working tool in this programme is the development of an "observation scheme" that considers all aspects of how their protection is to be organized, with the aim of creating a board with recognized protective powers.[5]

3.3 The Delphi Consultation

Strategies within the professional approaches for the promotion of quality are traditionally based on recording of problems that operators consider in need of improvement for an efficient and successful activity or intervention. From this realization, a sequence of actions for training, improving and verifying the quality of the service can be initiated. The consultative action we are about to discuss can undoubtedly be included among the examples using these tools. However, it can also have other meanings. The purpose of this action is to use the existing knowledge explicitly – and description of the problems and difficulties that the operator may meet is certainly an extremely important aspect of professional expertise. This knowledge is also a source for innovation, but usually it does not become the collective inheritance of a whole service system.

As part of the project "The Quality of Life of the Elderly in Institutions" a working group was established consisting of representatives of the municipality and operators from private institutions contracted and reimbursed by the municipality.

This group has started a series of activities and brainstorming sessions with the objective of improving the intervention given in residential structures. One of the main results was to improve contact with the outside environment: that is, the community and its services and operators. Another finding of this working group was the low level of understanding within the group, particularly regarding the needs that constrain particular choices and professional behaviour. The group concluded that substantial benefits could accrue from an exchange of information between operators and services. It therefore decided to organize a conference with the aim of designing a "map" of the main obstacles to efficiency in residential services, in particular concerning their qualitative aspects. These "maps" were a common starting point for formulating proposals to improve the conditions of all involved persons and organizations.

This of course introduced another important aspect of the consultation. The quality of a welfare system results from a sequence of actions and interventions that are closely linked to each other and thus from the cooperation between different organizations and professions serving the same client. It is therefore necessary to create preconditions that facilitate collaboration between these agencies and individuals. In the group mentioned before, various possibly conflicting perspectives and needs required an exchange system that would permit the expression of all opinions without creating difficulties and tensions.

These considerations have justified the choice of the Delphi Technique, which is, briefly stated, a method for gathering and comparing evaluations and judgements through *ad hoc* questionnaires within the group in a systematic and non-confrontational way.

The first questionnaire usually contains general questions: every successive one summarizes the acquired information, as well as proposing further questions to clarify and deepen the discussion of the different positions raised. This process ends when consensus has been reached among the participants or when a sufficient exchange of information has taken place. From this general description, it is possible to understand the potential this technique has for the full and equal participation of all individuals involved in the different phases of selecting and defining problems.

In fact, the answers are anonymous. This allows for reviewing one's own opinion through continuous feedback, which may lead to revising or abandoning what had been sustained before.

As with other techniques for non-conflictual group discussion, the Delphi Technique also allows for using time in the best possible way: it produces considerable information as well as a deeper understanding and development of thought. Operators from community services, institutions and the main city hospitals were all invited to participate.

The first questionnaire asked for a description of the respective professional requirements, on the one hand, and the conditions and restrictions prevailing in their daily work on the other, in particular with regard to the following phases of intervention:

* establishment of procedure;
* waiting period for admission to an institution;
* patient information; and
* case management after admission.

The responses to the questionnaire gave considerable detailed information. Going beyond what was requested, the participants did not limit themselves to indicating problems, inadequacies and shortcomings in each of the four categories above: they also formulated proposals to resolve them.

The second questionnaire took these elements into consideration. The responses were reorganized into thematic areas, putting together problems or operative proposals that were thematically linked. This list formed the basis of the second questionnaire, which asked for an evaluation of each area as to its importance (using a score from 0-10) and also asked for a verification of its completeness and additional pertinent details. The participants were also asked to give a quantitative score on their level of agreement with the operative proposals (these, too, were organized into thematic areas) and, again, to include other proposals.

The message that the operators gave us through their replies clearly showed that they were being forced to rely on personal ability (the ability to shift for oneself) rather than on adequate tools and resources when confronting their daily tasks. The replies also underlined the fatigue and stress under which they were working: stress brought about by anxiety, overwork, a feeling of impotence, and loneliness. This condition is in some aspects very similar to that of the elderly for whom they care.

Beyond any specific features, these feelings were distinctive throughout the entire system, regardless of function and profession. The numerous criticisms can be reduced to four specific points:

a) professional role of the social worker;
b) resources and work organization;
c) relationship between boards and offices; and
d) repercussions for the elderly.

A detailed analysis of these points is omitted for lack of space (see Costanzi/Ferrari, 1997). In any case, the conclusions show a clear need for the establishment of better cooperation and synergy between the different elements of the social and health care system. The potential task of each agency in constructing this cooperation is listed in Overview 2.

Overview 2: Actors and their Responsibilities

Actors	Tasks
Professionals	• To find opportunities for training and support, for recovering technical space and for reinforcing professional identity
Local administration	Revival of sector policy through – defining intervention priorities (prevention and discouragement of institutionalization) – revising the rules, criteria, and parameters of eligibility, of operative tools (case histories, data cards) and procedures – reviving working models based on projected models and networking – coherent organization of resources with specific priorities (intermediate structures and temporary reception centres) – cooperating with the health services to recreate operative protocols for a welfare policy that is not purely residual – formalizing the level of collaboration and different tasks of institutional operators (inspections, verification, etc.); joint training of professionals in community care and institutional care
Institutions for older persons	• Adherence to established quality standards; definition of operative protocols
Hospitals	• Defining minimum levels and modes of care; collaboration with the entire hospital system through operative programmes

3.4 Promoting Opportunities for Confrontation, Documentation and Information for Institutions

The actors involved in the quality-promotion process can be envisioned as concentric circles, the innermost representing the municipality, and the outermost the private sector, both profit and non-profit. It has to be stressed that, in Italy, residential care for older persons has been booming for quite a few years now, particularly due to private providers who often lack specific competencies in the field. Thus, regulations defining organizational structures do not suffice if quality is to be promoted. This means that additional initiatives have to be started. One of these was a seminar on the promotion of quality in old-age homes (February 1996), designed for managers of residential services, including an exhibition of architectural projects with innovative structures, products and experiences.

In order to elaborate on the functions of the projected "accreditation commissions", a working committee was started. By including representatives of the health and social professions operating inside institutions or in the field, its goal was to produce operative protocols as well as other sound professional support measures to improve service quality. In the present stage, these commissions may intervene only in those institutions that have been contracted by the municipality. The results of this interprofessional work will be shown in a seminar open to the whole sector.

3.5 Improving Admission to Institutions

Doubtlessly, frail older persons prefer alternative solutions to residential care which, in many cases, are also less expensive. The latest laws in Italy, however, privilege residential care by allocating important financial means to the modernization of existing structures and the conversion of small hospitals into homes for long-term care. Thus, some mid-term strategies are needed, one of which would be to improve assessment procedures prior to admission to residential care. By doing so, it could be ensured that only those who cannot be otherwise assisted be admitted. At the same time, the process of "choosing the right service" could be improved. Actions planned within this intervention are staff refresher courses, new forms of counselling (protocols), and regular supervision of operators.

Some organizational innovations within a few old-age homes in Genoa are concerned with the stage directly following admission. One of these innovations is the chance for admission "by degrees", in order to ease the trauma suffered by older people when they have to move away from their own home. Another one is the establishment of a partnership with an "assigned" operator during the first few weeks in an old-age home. Given the positive results, the local administration is trying to extend those innovations to other old-age homes as well.

The most committed initiative in this area is the introduction of the "Individual Care Plan", a tool which combines the planning approach with a multidimensional evaluation right from the moment of admission. The multidimensional evaluation provides evidence for residual abilities, hidden potentials, and problems which need to be restrained or monitored. Starting from this dynamic description, an individual care project is developed, which will be verified and arranged periodically. During the next stage, all institutions contracted by the municipality will be involved. Initial training of the operators on how to manage the Individual Care Plans will be provided, and care planning will be made compulsory within all new agreements. Our goal is to improve the quality of service in all public and private old-age homes, linking the right of the citizen to choose the services desired with the guarantee of adequate conditions throughout the entire system.

3.6   The Elderly as Frail Partners

The last two aims mentioned in Overview 1 are both related to measures on how to overcome user weakness. One aim is to improve public information offered to citizens about services for older people. In March 1997, two actions targeted at this aim were started:

* firstly, a sequence of television broadcasts on a local network explaining new services for the elderly;
* secondly, testing in two town districts of a PC database containing information on local health and social services, both public and private.

A further aim of the project will be to raise the awareness of personnel regarding the rights of the elderly – from self-determination to privacy to recognition of their individuality – and to promote this cultural attitude both in and outside the institution. We must deal with a particular group of users who are not able to express their needs in a coherent way and who will not be able to evaluate the relative merits of any initial contract.

The actual consumer is forced, because of his incapacity or "ignorance", to delegate his choice to other people who may well have needs very different from his own (both relatives and operators may have difficulty in considering the situation from the user's point of view rather than their own). With the passing of time, the elderly in an institution gradually lose their rights as citizens, becoming victims of different forms of manipulation, disrespect and even violence. This project aims to provide the specific training necessary to ensure respect for the rights of the elderly, from both inside and outside the institution.

With regard to this last point, the project sets up an observation scheme that considers all aspects of protection, involving workers by means of working groups and establishing an authority to safeguard the rights of the elderly in institutions.

3.7 Future Stages

To close the review of the activities we started, we have to stress the complexity of any quality-promotion process: it needs not only specific actions planned for single and limited aims, but it is also in itself the beginning of a cultural renewal.

Therefore, relevant investment in training has been made over the last two years, under the assumption that more professional competence is a prerequisite on which to build quality. Among the issues on the agenda, the most relevant ones are "working by goals", "networking", and "setting up and managing the Individual Care Plan".

Furthermore, we have to pay attention to the global environment: this means not only monitoring the observance of the law, but even promoting better conditions, also through inspection activities. This role of the public administration to promote innovation and to support other agencies is a positive new direction in the Italian context: it usually shows the state setting up against the private sector in a view able to produce some positive effects only in case of a competitive situation. Attention needs to be directed mainly at the middle-low segment of suppliers who are not in a competitive situation but rather survive through user incompetence or because they benefit from protected niches in the market.

The most important goal is to provide a proper service network, creating and/ or developing intermediate solutions between one's own home and residential care, to guarantee that only the elderly who cannot be helped in any other way need to move to an institution.

We intend to follow two social policies within our institutions. The first is to provide occupational therapy, an activity that seems to be sadly lacking in the daily life of our institutions in both formal and experimental or educational channels. The second, which still requires considerable planning, is to stress safety and personnel training, to enable staff to confront the various emergency situations that can occur inside institutions or befall both patients and personnel. This type of preventive measure is rarely taken; but it is obvious that without minimum safeguards, there cannot be quality.

4   Conclusions

The practical experience gained from this project has shown that the process of improving quality in the system of social care services in Italy has to take root within the status quo, i.e. where operators, professionals, officials and users currently are. Given the lack of legal operational regulations and standards, lack of training, shortage of personnel, and insufficient information on the part of users/citizens, the direct introduction of management tools developed in the area of private business would disturb the current system to a degree that cannot be predicted. We cannot omit furthermore the discussion presently going on in Italy during the last months about the reduction of the welfare state towards the delivery of basic services to poor people only. This scenario, of course, does not support quality improvement. Therefore, while waiting for clear guidelines from politics, in our mind the most feasible way seems an "incremental" one: to introduce tools which prepare the cultural background for future innovations.

Thus, "soft" tools, e.g. those based on the Delphi consultation that start from the expertise and experience of the actors involved in the field, seem to be a wise idea when it comes to designing the initial steps towards quality improvement.

The project in Genoa has shown that those working in the field are well aware of the necessary adaptations as well as of the need for professional training. In particular, skills for networking between the public and the private non-profit sector need to be elaborated. Also, the Italian public administration has learned to improve its relationship with the most important providers by reconsidering the "contract culture" within the field. The awareness of both users and citizens, however, still needs to be enhanced in order to increase their involvement in advocacy for frail older persons, as well as their ability to control the professionals.

Notes

1   The modernization of the Italian Public Administration received a dramatic push in 1990, the year in which the first of a series of regulations was implemented for the introduction of guidelines for administrative procedures. These guidelines, which aim to improve the relationship between the citizen and the Public Administration, can be summarized as a simplification of procedures, openness, formal standards for administrative actions, and substantial guarantees (involvement).

2   In 1994, the Public Services Charter was promulgated as an instrument for user protection, in the sense of conferring direct control of service quality on the citizen. All the charters of the various departments have the same structure: (a) principles (for example, for health services: equality, impartiality, continuity, right of choice, participation, efficiency and efficacy); (b) tools (adoption of standards, simplification of procedures, information for the user, relationship with the user, obligatory evaluation, refunds); and (c) mechanisms (internal inspectorate, Control Commission to check observance of the charter). Specific local charters are being promulgated on this basis for each sector (one for each health department and Local Board, for example), and not just one national charter as in the UK.

3   To exemplify the backwardness of the Italian situation regarding these needs, we can consider that most basic expression, the right to express one's own wishes. Only very few of the elderly now institutionalized chose their solution voluntarily, and very few had any say in the specific location of their accommodation. It is no longer acceptable to fall back on financial or organizational constraints (lack of funds to provide intermediate solutions between home and institution) as a basis to justify this practice, since it would be possible in many cases to maintain the elderly at home, giving him

or her the necessary support and assistance, at a lower cost than institutionalization. The problem is also "cultural", by which we mean that the criteria that have guided decisions up to now have favoured such a recourse.

4   Projections for 2007 estimate the population of Genoa over 65 years of age as about 160,000. On this basis, we can apply the 1988 value of 2.88% calculated for Northern Italy by ISTAT (Istituto Nazionale della Statistica) as the percentage of these needing assistance in institutions (ISTAT, 1991). This will give us a hypothetical need for 4,600 beds, as opposed to the present 4,100 beds. It must be stressed, however, that the ISTAT data underestimated the existing situation by not counting the numerous small institutions spread throughout the larger cities, which makes this measure a rather conservative one.

5   Regulations in Italy for the protection of the elderly with psychological and/or psychiatric problems have been incorporated within those for adults with disabilities. The resulting serious limitation problem has led to a revision of these regulations, at least partially. The other modalities under study relate to entitlements of protection that, in the opinion of this writer, should not detract from the complex question of the guaranteed right to a dignified life, to assistance and treatment when necessary and, more generally, to recognition of individual rights. In other words, we hope for a system that gives due consideration to the wishes, needs and preferences of the elderly, as well as total protection of his or her rights; this is particularly important and urgent for the elderly in institutions.

References

Ascoli, U. (1996) 'Terzo settore e societa italiana', *Sociologia e professione* 21: 13-30.

Bertin, G. (1994) 'Un modello di valuatazione basato sul giudizio degli esperti', in: Bezzi, C./Scettri, M. (eds.), *La valutazione come ricerca e come intervento.* Perugia: IRESS.

Bond, S./Bond, J. (1982) *Clinical Nursing Research Priorities: A Delphi Survey.* Newcastle-upon-Tyne: University of Newcastle-upon-Tyne (Health Care Research Unit).

Charlton, J.R.H./Patrick, D.L./Matthews, G./West, P.A. (1981) 'Spending Priority in Kent: A Delphi Study', *Journal of Epidemiology and Community Health* 35: 288-292.

Costanzi, C./Ferrari, F. (eds.) (1997) *Progettare la qualità negli istituti per anziani.* Milano: F. Angeli.

Dalkey, N.Y. (1967) *Delphi.* New York: Rand Corporation.

Delbecq, A.L. et al. (1975) *Group Technique for Program Planning: A Guide to Nominal Groups and Delphi Processes.* Glenview, Illinois: Scott, Foreman and Co.

Deming, E. (1991) *L'impresa di qualità.* Milano: ISEDI.

Jacques, E. (1970) *Work, Creativity, Social Justice.* London: Heinemann.

Laboucheix, V. (1990) *Trattato della qualità totale.* Milano: F. Angeli.

Linestone, H.A./Turoff, M. (eds.) (1975) *The Delphi Method: Technique and Applications.* London: Addison-Wesley Publishing.

Mullen, P. (1983) *Delphi Type Studies in the Health Services Management Centre.* Birmingham: University of Birmingham.

Nelisse, C. (1993) 'Aiutare e intervenire: proviamo a chiarire alcune difficolta', *Inchiesta* 23, April-September: 54-63.

Niero, M. (1985) *Metodi e techniche di ricerca per il servizio sociale.* Roma: La Nuova Italia Scientifica.

Oliva, D./Bassanini Setti, M.C. (1996) 'L'accreditamento in sanità', *Prospettive Sociali e Sanitarie* 1: 2-5.

Parasuraman, A.S./Berry, L.L. (1992) *Marketing Services.* Milano: Sperling and Kupfer.

Robertson, A. (1995) 'Definire e valutare la qualità nei servizi socio-sanitari', pp. 105-126 in: Bertin, G. (ed.), *Valutazione e sapere sociologico.* Milano: F. Angeli.

Sackman, H. (1975) *A Delphi Critique.* Lexington, Mass.: Lexington Books.

Sackman, H. (1974) 'A Sceptic at the Oracle', *Futures* 8: 444-446.

Turoff, M. (1970) 'The Design of a Policy Delphi', *Technological Forecasting and Social Change* 2: 149-171.

Zeithmal, V.A./Parasuraman, A./Berry, L.L. (1991) *Servire qualità.* McGraw-Hill.

CHAPTER 17

Some National and Local Quality Strategies in Finland

Riitta Haverinen

1   Quality in the Context of Public-Sector Efficiency

Increasingly emphatic demands for quality management surfaced in Finland from outside the scope of social services, along with the public-sector goals of economy and productivity. Quality management methods were already being applied in the private sector and within various professions. In the context of social services, it was thought that trained personnel, facilities and a sound ethical base would guarantee good-quality services. The discussion on quality issues in the 1990s has revealed the need to scrutinize quality in the social services from various angles.

This article examines the departure point and present state of quality management in Finland in terms of national and local strategies. It inspects national recommendations for quality management in social welfare and health care as a tool to stipulate quality projects in social welfare.

The position and rights of service users have been stressed in legislation, but the perspective had shifted, particularly at the start of the present decade. This shift is in keeping with development of administration within OECD circles and with consumeristic approaches. In view of the present economic crisis, the market concept has been strong enough to amass alternative welfare services into an integrated whole, based on the ethic of the individual (individuality, choice, freedom), on the principle of efficiency (competition, price) and on the mechanism of assessment and development. Within this conceptual framework, the individual is nowadays seen as a free, autonomous actor striving to maximize the quality of his/her life through personal choices (Rose, 1995: 37).

Various administrative reforms have been collected under the concept of New Public Management. One of these is the objective of increasing efficiency in the public sector. In 1990, the Ministry of Finance initiated an "Office for Good Services" project, the aim of which was to award recognition to government offices that were successful in the eyes of service users. The initial assumption was that an official body perceived as functioning well by the client would be successful in other respects, too. A client-oriented government office, it was thought, would be successful in its organizational development, management procedures and personnel policy. All this would culminate in savings. Further, it was thought that good service would not cost more than poor service (*Hyvän palvelun virastot*, 1991).

The Office for Good Services project was to employ the results of management adaptations in order to find new operational models and to implement the principle of providing different services at the same unit by launching trials within municipalities. A citizens' guide to services was also produced. Publications compiled by the project drew attention to criteria for success by importing examples, e.g. from Denmark, Great Britain and Canada. Such features as people orientation, participatory management and innovative leadership were seen as desirable. Central factors were innovation and the search for new, more flexible operational models (*Tuloksena palvelu*, 1993). The Espoonlahti Social Welfare and Health Care Centre participated in this project as the only social welfare organization.

The Office for Good Services project was motivated by the idea that administration can be seen as a service and the citizen as a client. Service agreements were seen as improving the position of service users. Now this was included as a part of management by results.

2   Social Services and the Rise of Demands for Efficiency

Social services have been the object of diverse development projects from the 1970s onwards but have been more systematically targeted since the 1980s. Earlier, it was believed that legislation, national norms and letters of guidance created the prerequisites for achieving high quality in the social services. The real change occurred in the 1990s, with the weakening of the state economy and the rise in unemployment.

Earlier demands for decentralization and a transition from national guidance to an emphasis on room to manoeuvre and information-based management, brought municipalities and other service providers additional latitude. The pivotal change came with the revision of the state subsidy scheme: the new system provided municipalities with both opportunities and decision-making power concerning service provision.

The other vein is the discussion of the position of social service users. This discussion had been intense, even heated in the 1960s and the 1980s; but no real breakthrough had taken place. The discussion on empowerment and its implementation began in the sphere of care for people with disabilities, spurred by a number of citizens' organizations. In any case, no strong client organizations campaigned concentratedly for quality in services. This has been said to reflect citizens' support for the services provided by the welfare state (e.g. Sihvo/Uusitalo, 1996: 37-39). People have been generally satisfied with public social services; the recession, however, has made a dent in the support for these services provided by the welfare state.

At the beginning of the 1990s, quality management models and quality systems derived from business and marketing spheres, as well as from the health care sector, were proposed for use in social welfare. In some of the opinions of policy-makers and administrators, the development of quality in social welfare was "lagging behind"; the sector had few quality projects in progress, and quality systems had not been adopted. This lagging behind stemmed e.g. from the fact that social service personnel shied away from models developed for different services, as well as from special quality management concepts and quality management methods offered from outside sources – even though points of convergence were detected.

The attention paid to user opinions and the priority attached to service users' views in the customer orientation of consumeristic models, were equally echoed in discussions on social services.

The idea of the client as a consumer rang true because it reflected the social welfare sector's decades-long debate on empowering the clients. The background of the concept of the consumer as a skilled and independent individual making choices on markets with options, remained somewhat remote.

Anna Coote stresses that resources may be wasted by creating many alternative services (Coote, 1993: 144-145). The basis of market-place thinking is to relate people only to their role as consumers, although welfare service users are in a more complex relationship with public service, for they are both service users and citizens. The consumer of social welfare services is often facing an economic and/or life crisis where there are only limited service alternatives; in reality, access to services may require queuing.

In social services, the quality received by the client/consumer encompasses not only the concrete service but also the quality of interaction. According to the projects conducted by STAKES, as shown by telephone feedback from citizens, the majority of disappointments and complaints experienced by service users pertain to how they are treated as human beings (Mäntysaari/Aalto/Maaniittu, 1995; Kiikkala et al., 1996). As was pointed out by Wistow and Hardy, it is quite a different issue who washes windows and who washes people (Wistow/Hardy, 1996).

In the social services, the quality system and quality management models coming from business life are recommended for a different context: highly diverse products and services. The services incorporate a societal interest and a heterogeneous consumer group. The purpose of the welfare system is to eliminate avoidable disadvantages and to compensate for those disadvantages that cannot be overcome. Individuals have diverse needs and need more control over their own life. The goal of equity and equal life chances thus points to the further objectives of responsiveness and empowerment. The goal of equity may conflict with the goals of responsiveness and empowerment, but the process of defining and assuring quality provides a bridge between them (Coote, 1993: 145-146).

The spark to quality management has often been the interest expressed by top-level municipal politicians and administrators; the means utilized have included quality policy, practical projects associated with quality and training, and lately client feedback mechanisms as well. Perhaps the austere economic situation is prompting municipal politicians to seek alliances beyond professionals, i.e. with citizens. Many explanations for this are plausible. Municipal agencies dealing with the public trust have been rationalized and cut. Many elected representatives feel that they have little room to manoeuvre.

Municipal politicians may also be interested in the municipality's image and in the commitment to services that raises that image. For top-level management, management by quality seems to be a natural extension of management by results, requiring only a change of concept in a situation where a result-based orientation has already been accepted. Professionals easily support quality management methods, the implementation of which makes their input pivotal. This has long been the case in health care, although in personal social services some small-scale trials and quality projects by professionals have been initiated.

3   National Input in Quality Development

3.1   Task Forces, Projects and Networks as Tools

Trials with various quality management methods and quality systems have been conducted in the health care sector, and reports on these trials have been available for quite some time. Some researchers talk of a second wave of quality management, stressing fitness for use and application of industrial models. There has also been discussion of taking both internal and external clients into consideration, as well as discussion on managerialistic leadership and talk of process analysis rather than external inspection of the service process. Process analysis emphasizes co-operation in the course of the care-giving and service processes (Harteloh/ Verheggen, 1995: 265).

In Finland, the national priority was with quality health care. A national expert group was appointed to this end in 1992 by STAKES. Initially, a joint quality project for social welfare and health care was envisaged; but the need for a separate quality project in the social welfare sector soon became evident, owing to issues of orientation and differences in emphasis with respect to quality.

As a national research and development centre for welfare and health, STAKES had both the legitimation and interest to address quality. It set up a separate quality project for social welfare, as well as a separate expert task force. The idea was to try to find some kind of consensus on how to proceed in social-service quality methods. The goal was to define the quality strategies central to social welfare through discussions with university researchers, development specialists and practical social workers in managerial positions. The idea was also to provide support, training and consultation to local actors in local social-service quality projects, and to address the need for research and discussion on quality in the social services. Yet a spark was needed to initiate this discussion and this came from a publication written by researchers, development specialists and field practitioners in the social services (Haverinen/Maaniittu/Mäntysaari, 1995). The articles brought out the issue's multidimensionality and placed quality into the context of the essence of social welfare, lifting it from the level of task-force discussion.

Local actors also expected more clarity and theoretical framework for municipal-level quality projects. Because soft networking methods were preferred, the national social-welfare quality project set up national networks for social workers and researchers working with the quality projects. As a place for training and for presenting the projects in a discussion forum, the network has inspired the launching of local practical quality projects as well as local training. The network bulletin serves as a dialogue forum for discussing research and development projects from the standpoint of both theoretical and practical issues. STAKES has the role of a facilitator in the national sessions. It also serves as publisher of the bulletin. The forum has served as an arena for peer consultation, clarifying project plans and further inspiring those interested in quality methods. It has also created faith for local project participants in their own ideas and working methods.

3.2 Dialogue with Interest Groups for a National Quality Recommendation

Despite the national quality project, additional means were needed to support local quality development. The idea of a national recommendation popped up as a modern motivator. The Ministry of Social Affairs and Health commissioned STAKES to draw up a national quality recommendation with the purpose of creating a common recommendation for both social welfare and health.

The Ministry's point of departure was that the quality of social welfare and health services must be so good that they not only promote the population's health and independent coping skills, but also satisfy the service needs of the population with the resources available (*Sosiaaliturvan strategiat – viisi vuotta 2000 luvulle*, STM 1995). So, no additional resources for development of quality were forthcoming. The idea of a national recommendation was well-suited to the idea of providing information on innovations and alternatives to be adopted independently by service providers.

The national recommendation was devised to introduce the basics of quality management and to present the various approaches available for local actors to choose from. It was up to STAKES' coordination group to define the content of the recommendation. In several consultations between key actors, it was agreed that the recommendation was to be a national stand concerning the importance of quality management as a supporting method in economically difficult times. The idea was to encourage efforts to enhance quality, to emphasize client orientation, to give examples of quality management methods already experimented with and, finally, to clarify quality concepts vague in many respects in the context of social services.

Moreover, the preparation of the recommendation constituted a new mode of operation. The views prevailing in social, medical and nursing sciences had to be made compatible. That demanded mutual sharing and discussion, hence drawing the terminology to a more abstract level. In addition, the need to address social services and health care with the same recommendation was a real challenge. The collaborative aspect brought in the key stakeholder by addressing the service users in plain language and arguing for different quality approaches. To bring about an extensive discussion and commitment to quality management, external stakeholders were brought into the process. The actual preparation was a process whereby different disciplines, external stakeholders, client associations and non-profit organizations – altogether around 200 partners – collaborated in a process instructive to all participants. It brought up common priorities with respect to important issues, such as seeing the client as a key actor in defining service quality. This came as a clear message from service user associations but was also addressed by social service managers and professionals.

The challenge was that the recommendation had to be written to suit quality projects in very different phases and in social services, health care and non-profit organizations alike. The language had to be common to practitioners, politicians and service users. Consultations with interest groups were the main method used to elaborate the recommendation. The procedure applied in consultations with different interest groups was to seek consensus with respect to the central priorities and issues taken up in the recommendation.

Dialogue was the main means of proceeding with the various interest groups in social welfare and health care. This was based on four different sessions where issues and opinions prepared in advance could be handled. The process required much input from the participants to express their views, because the discussion was at a very preliminary level. Common dialogue and a sincere need to hear the views of different groups, professional organizations, service user organizations and executing bodies clearly showed that the time had come to raise the service user to a central position with respect to defining quality. It was then that the content of the recommendation changed. The need to arrive at a consensus meant that the recommendation was trimmed and brought out a broad range of alternatives that were then presented in the recommendation.

The recommendation, published in 1995 (*Quality Management in Social Welfare and Health*, Stakes 1995), in fact became a general stand on the importance of quality management, central approaches, and concepts of and literature on quality. There was a market-place for the recommendation; it became a best seller among service providers, municipalities and organizations. As the first national statement on social and health care quality, the recommendation tried to avoid possible conflictual issues or taking any stand on the superiority of any quality management method.

The motivating ideas behind the recommendation reflect an attempt to sincerely address quality in social welfare and health and to fit together the ways in which quality is seen in consumerism, science, managerial approaches and the traditional sense. The recommendations are built on a few pivotal principles:

a) quality management is part of everyday work;
b) quality management should be client-oriented;
c) quality management in social welfare and health care should be implemented through providing information.

These principles are stressed through such proclamations as

The future will be client-oriented.

- The client is the expert on the efficacy and quality of the services he or she has received.
- Quality management necessitates client group analysis and employment of analysis results.
- Quality management needs an effective client-feedback system.
- Clients must be able to influence the nature of the information collected.

Quality through collaboration.

- Quality should be everyone's concern.
- The main responsibility for quality rests with the service providers.
- In a quality-oriented unit, genuine participation is possible.
- Regional service chains must be made efficient.
- Quality emerges from well-organized units and work processes.

Introducing quality activities in a working community.

- Each organization should select quality management methods on the basis of its own starting points.

- Quality activities may focus on problems and processes or on the organization as a whole and how it puts into practice methods of quality management.
- The aim is to create a quality system in all social welfare and health care organizations.
- Every provider of services will formulate a written quality policy in 1996.

Knowledge improves quality.

- Quality management requires follow-up and evaluation of activities at all levels.
- Quality development always requires measurement.
- Quality management should be an element of basic and continuing education in social welfare and health care.

The recommendations encompass all social services, whether municipal services, services provided by NGOs or private services. In fact, the recommendation is a presentation of main quality approaches, terminology and literature. Its point of departure is that responsibility for quality rests with the service provider.

According to the recommendation, service providers are encouraged to devise their own quality policy during the year 1996. It was thought that compilation of a quality policy would bring together the service provider's central mission and core task(s) realistically and in a manner fit for implementation. Many of the existing quality policies have concentrated on describing either basic service principles or the ethical background for service provision. It might be essential to emphasize the values on which service provision is based. On the other hand, for follow-up and evaluation, concrete commitments would be really important.

While the national recommendation was initiated from the top down, its formulation process included a bottom-up approach with a great deal of openness. Openness was seen as the key to committing different groups into quality thinking. When the recommendation is up for revision in 1998, we will need to have acquired some experience as to how well diverse approaches and quality management methods function in social welfare. It is important to start new innovative projects to develop quality methods, and to publicize their results with sufficient practical detail to appropriate target groups. Effective forms of cooperation should be found and encouraged both locally and regionally.

4.   Some Evaluative Remarks on the Quality of Social Welfare Following the National Recommendation

Drawing conclusions is far from easy because of the profound changes happening at the same time with quality management discussions. These have to do with scarce economic resources. Anyhow, it can already been seen that the recommendation boosted the number of quality activities in the field of social services. The recommendation helped to break existing resistance towards quality ideology. Quality management and quality systems are no longer seen as a passing fashion but as an important tool in developing the services in a process of promoting quality management nationally.

The national network has increased the flow of information between the actors, improved the self-reliance of participating local actors, and given opportunities for mutual sharing and development of ideas to be adopted and further developed elsewhere. The bulletin has served as a forum for writing about the experiences gained. As an initiator, STAKES has drawn attention to quality issues in several ways. It has collected different stakeholders and organized training and consultation to raise discussion and interest in quality management. It has organized forums for discussion and initiated further development projects. At the same time, the current quality boom is progressing according to its own rationale. What has been achieved is that quality management is now taken seriously as a development strategy in the social service field.

The soft steering method of support and guidance through information is drawn from a national strategy adopted in the 1990s for public administration in Finland. The self-governance of the municipalities, along with framework legislation and different decentralization schemes, guarantee extensive room for the municipalities to manœuvre in. In the context of quality, this means that providers are free to adopt any quality method suitable for them or not to adopt any at all. According to a Nordic report, Finland tends to use information-steering in addressing quality more than other Nordic countries (Socialstyrelsen, 1995). It is important to find out if the tool used really works in the direction hoped for.

The first national recommendation did not include any special incentives or performance reviews. It did, however, address the importance of quality systems, process-oriented quality management, quality improvement, internal or external auditing, quality standards and criteria, quality awards, the importance of follow-up, measurement and evaluation of quality management, user feedback mechanisms, and training and development work.

Most of the ongoing quality projects were initiated in the 1990s before the recommendation was published. Most of the existing quality projects are service-provider-based. Some municipalities have experimented with quality-award criteria for self-assessment (Espoo). One municipality has drawn up local social service charters (Hämeenlinna) to describe the services municipal residents can expect to receive, specifying the background values of services and giving the commitment to provide a service within a set span of time. If this cannot be carried out, the applicant is paid financial compensation. Training for building quality systems has also increased. Some municipalities train their entire staff in basic quality thinking. New projects have emerged. There has been an increase in the number of requests for consultation from local quality projects.

Especially private service providers are adopting quality management as a competitive edge. Some organizations intend to apply for certification. The idea of adapting ISO 9000 standards to social services has been considered but has not led to any concrete breakthrough. ISO standards are experienced as laborious to implement and their concepts as poorly understandable in the field of social services. Practical quality management has proceeded gradually, with a move towards application of quality-award criteria for self-assessment. The work on adopting quality management methods and on application of quality-award criteria for self-assessment that has been under way in the Espoonlahti Social Welfare and Health Care Centre for a few years, realistically illustrates that the system itself must shape its own model even if it holds a particular ideal. Quality-award criteria have introduced a basis for comparison of one's own assessment, even if a quality award as such is not sought.

Although interest in quality management has awakened in social services, methods suitable for the sector's own context still need to be formulated. This is usually a long process, where examples derived from other social service units may be useful. A wide range of quality ideologies, the simultaneous existence of more traditional and new approaches and the rhetoric typical of administration (e.g. client orientation) appear to be present both in the discussion and in practice.

The practical work shows now that in seeking criteria for quality with service users, social service professionals also want to formulate the quality of interaction in the context of their own activity, instead of taking over models applied in other sectors. That social services are different, is a central assumption (Wistow et al., 1996: 28-29) in the spheres of Finland's social services, too. It is difficult to find concepts for elaborating on this assumption. It seems that quality management brings changes into managing systems of services. It is also the managers who have to adopt and profoundly understand quality thinking.

In the boom of quality systems, it seems important to keep in mind that the traditional preconditions for quality – such as facilities, tools and workers' professional education – have become more fundamental, whatever type of quality system is selected. It can already be seen that in difficult economic times, workers with less education and training need to deal with increasingly-difficult client cases, especially when providing services in clients' homes. This calls for profound discussion and quality tool development in social care services.

The quality management recommendation has been in use since the beginning of the year 1996. We can see that the interest in formulating quality systems has emerged. At the same time, there are still some reservations, the basic question being, do quality systems really provide the tools needed in the social service context? However, we lack sufficient information about the ability of quality management systems to solve real quality problems, i.e. have promises been met in practice? In his article herein, Christopher Pollit points out that, to date, quality management systems have worked better in other sectors.

The national recommendation for quality management is to be followed up and reviewed during the year 1997 in order to renew it next year. This will be done in dialogue and collaboration with different key actors and stakeholders. The main interest lies in finding out if this tool really works, what has really changed, has there been interest in adopting quality management tools, and with what results? Has addressing service users created good practices and feedback mechanisms which were innovative? Did quality management tools help to address quality gaps and really improve the quality of services? It seems that, from the point of view of the service users, new innovative quality management systems are emerging in the field of services for people with disabilities initiated by non-profit organizations.

In the practical quality projects carried out in Finland, it has become crystal-clear that building well-functioning quality systems requires much work, training and top management's genuine commitment. Quality management cannot be a separate project run by the quality manager; it must be a model for organizing everyday activities, an organizational model where both the self-assessment of one's own work and rapid service-user feedback have an important role.

In the future, it would be wise to see the selection and practical implementation of quality management systems holistically, including the traditional preconditions for quality work. When services need to be cut, the relevant actors must be sensitive to weak signals originating from the field that deal with threats to quality. This has to be built up into the system whenever possible. Addressing relevant needs is of the utmost importance, whatever quality system is adopted.

Sensitivity is also needed to clarify the potential and shortcomings of existing quality systems and quality management methods with respect to the core of the social welfare context. Follow-up may show whether quality management tools help social services identify quality gaps, as well as whether the methods used can grasp the essence of social services in times of scarce resources. If soft information guidance is to be of sufficient viability as a future tool, then evaluation reports, comparisons and knowledge production on the gains, problems and quality gaps will emerge as most significant.

References

Aalto, Anu-Riikka/Mäntysaari, Mikko/Maaniittu, Maisa (1996) *"On oltava hirveän vahva"*. Stakes, Aiheita.

Coote, Anna (1993) 'Understanding Quality', *Journal of Interpersonal Care* 7 (2): 141-150.

Harteloh, Peter/Verheggen, Frank (1994) 'Quality Assurance in Health Care. From Traditional towards a Modern Approach', *Health Policy* 27: 261-270.

Haverinen, Riitta/Maaniittu, Maisa/Mäntysaari, Mikko (eds.) (1995) *Tulokseksi laatu*. Raportteja 179/95. Helsinki: Stakes.

Hyvän palvelun virastot 1991, Tuloksena palvelu, Valtiovarainministeriö, palveluhanke 1991.

Kiikkala, Irma/Kantola Hannu/Sohlman, Britta: *Meaningful Life*. internet http://www.stakes.fi.

Kunnallisen sosiaali – ja terveydenhuollon tavoitteet ja toimintaperiaatteet. Valtakunnallinen suunnitelma sosiaali – ja terveydenhuollon järjestämisestä vuosina 1995-1998 ja vuosina 1996-1999.

Quality Management in Social Welfare and Health (1995). Helsinki: Stakes.

Sosiaaliturvan strategiat – viisi vuotta 2000 luvulle (1995). STM.

Tuloksena palvelu, palveluhankkeen loppuraportti, Valtiovarainministeriö, palveluhanke (1993).

Pollitt, Christopher (1996) Business and Professional Approaches to Quality Improvement: A Comparison of their Suitability for the Personal Social Services. Presentation in European Seminar "Developing Quality in Personal Social Services", Helsinki 12-14 April, 1996.

Rose, Nikolas (1995) Eriarvioisuus ja valta hyvinvointivaltion jälkeen. teoksessa Risto Eeräsaari, Keijo Rahkonen (toim): Hyvinvointivaltion tragedia. Keskustelua eurooppalaisesta hyvinvointivaltiosta. Tampere: Gaudeamus.

Sihvo Tuire/Uusitalo Hannu (1996) 'Sosiaaliturvamielipiteet lamassa', *Dialogi* 1: 37-39.

Vad de Nordiska länderna sade om kvalited i socialtjänsten våren (1995). Stockholm: Socialstyrelsen.

Wistow, Gerald/Knapp, Martin/Hardy, Brian/Allen, Caroline (1994) *Social Care in a Mixed Economy*. Public Policy Management. Buckingham/Philadelphia: Open University Press.

Wistow, Gerald/Knapp, Martin/Hardy, Brian/Forder, Julien/Kendall, Jeremy/Manning, Rob (1996) *Social Care Markets, Progress and Prospects*. Public Policy Management. Buckingham/Philadelphia: Open University Press.

CHAPTER 18

Quality of Care: On Whose Terms?

Marja A. Pijl

1   Introduction

In this paper, we will describe an innovation in home care in the Netherlands. It consists of giving a budget to persons who are assessed as needing home care instead of offering them services. This innovation was first tried out on an experimental basis in a few areas. Because it proved to be successful, this scheme is now available on a small scale all over the country; but it is still an experiment. The present situation can be considered as the second phase of the experiment. Since April 1996, when this paper was presented, considerable new developments have taken place. After the first phase had been evaluated, the government decided to set certain new rules for the second phase.

We will first discuss the initial experiments and the statements of budget recipients concerning the quality of care. We will then point out which new rules have been introduced by the government and to what extent the government has referred to the quality of care as an issue.

We will next discuss how the different parties concerned – such as the government, the regular home-care organizations, the professional organization of home helps, the trade union, and users' organizations – look at quality of home care.

The personal budget for care is meant particularly to enable care recipients to buy "tailored care": they themselves can decide what kind of care they want and what qualities they seek in their care providers. Do they define quality in the same terms as professionals, or as output-oriented home-care organizations? Or do persons who need long-term care, either living in a family or by themselves and acting as employers, define the quality of care in different terms?

This article will point out that the latter is the case. A consequence of this finding is, that the debate about the quality of care should take a broader focus than has been usual until now: the values – of a rather personal nature – of the care recipients and the members of their households should be introduced into the debate so that they can find their own place among the criteria that define the quality of care.

2   A Personal Budget for Care: Two Experiments

2.1   The Experiment of the Health Care Insurance Council

In the early 1990s, the Health Care Insurance Council commissioned research for an experiment on the personal budget for care.

The normal way of dealing with demands for home care is that the person who needs care applies to a so-called "regular" organization for home care, home help or district nursing. In this context, "regular" means financed on the basis of a national health-care insurance scheme.

A home care organization is an organization that offers both nursing and home help. In many areas, the former home help organization and the district nursing organization have merged to become a single organization for home care; but in other areas, they are still separate. Applicants are assessed by the organization, and the organization then decides how much help or care is needed. The number of hours of home help allocated may be less than the assessment indicates. The applicant may even be put on a waiting list. This depends on the capacity of the organization, due to budgetary constraints. Users of home help have to pay an income-related fee. Persons needing the care of a nurse have a right to receive such care. They must be or become a member of the organization and pay a membership fee, after which services are free.

The experiment with the personal budget for care was conducted and evaluated by the Institute for Applied Social Sciences (ITS) (Miltenburg et al., 1993). It was carried out in two regions in the Netherlands and was aimed at persons who needed home care (i.e. home help and/or nursing) for a period of at least three months. Involved in the experiment were 668 persons.

After a person had indicated his/her willingness to participate, instead of being assessed, he/she was interviewed on the basis of a questionnaire designed by the research team. The outcomes formed the basis of a care plan which was discussed with the participant. This care plan was then sent to the health care insurer, the agency which finances care. If the health care insurer agreed with the care plan, it was authorized.

After this procedure, the participants were randomized over three groups:

- those who received care from the regular home care organization;
- those who could choose between care by the regular organization or a budget;
- those who could choose between care by the regular organization or a budget with the optional facility of using a counsellor.

The health care insurer informed the persons in the second and third group of the choice they were supposed to make. As a result of this procedure, 361 persons received care from the regular organization, 157 persons received a budget, and 150 persons received a budget plus counsellor. Of those who had a choice, 45% decided for a budget, after which the health care insurer made a contract with them.

The amount of the budget was fixed on the basis of the care plan. The gross hourly rates for home help, nursing help and qualified nursing were multiplied by the number of hours that had been allocated in the care plan. From this amount were deducted the contributions that the participant should have paid if he/she had received care from the regular organization. Participants received the budget in advance over a period of four weeks. After four periods of four weeks, there was a reassessment. On average, the budgets amounted to 1,100 Dutch guilders per four weeks.[1]

It was agreed with the regular care organizations that they would give all participants in the experiment who were assigned to their organization all the care indicated in their care plan, so that those participating in the experiment received an equivalent amount of care respectively money.

Clients who received a budget were free to spend it as they saw fit. Only in very few cases was the money spent on anything besides care. Of the clients with a budget, 28% went to the regular district nursing organization to buy help from that organization, and 22% went to the regular home help organization to buy help there. 15% made use of private agencies, 63% employed a private person, and 12% paid a relative, most often a daughter or daughter-in-law. Those who employed a private person were obliged to follow the rules of Civil Law: they had to allow for at least four weeks of paid holidays per full year, payment during the first six weeks of illness with the exception of the first two days, and a term of notice of at least four weeks. If they employed a person for more than two days a week, they had to pay taxes and social insurance premiums. Recipients of the budget were not obliged to account for their expenses.

Some Outcomes of the Experiment

Part of the research in this experiment involved a comparison of user satisfaction between participants receiving a budget and participants receiving regular care (hereafter referred to as "budget clients" and "regular clients").

The researchers pointed out that the vast majority of participants in the experiment had had experience with regular home care prior to the experiment. This means that most budget clients themselves could compare regular care with care provided on the basis of a budget.

I   REASONS TO OPT FOR A BUDGET

A first relevant outcome deals with the reasons why budget clients opted for a budget. The following motives were given:

being able to arrange one's own care	40%
having a say about one's own care	19%
employing the same person regularly	10%
freedom of expenditure	9%
problems with home help	9%
trying out a new system	7%
financial reasons	4%
to prevent going into a nursing home	1%
because of a need for care at night	1%

II   ORGANIZATION OF CARE

An important issue relevant for the success of the budget formula is the way in which budget clients arrange for care. Do they manage to find suitable persons who can do the jobs they want done? More than 90% of the budget clients were fully satisfied with the arrangements they made. Only 9% had had some difficulties during the three months preceding the interview.

The problems mentioned most frequently were lack of continuity because of sickness or vacation, problems in getting care corresponding with their needs, personal problems with the helper, and lack of skills.

III   QUALITY OF CARE

The researchers were aware of the problem that there is no generally-accepted definition of the quality of care. Therefore, they tried to indicate certain concrete aspects of care which they knew to be important from the perspective of the care recipient.

They asked two matched groups of 190 budget clients and 190 regular clients about their satisfaction with these aspects, with regard to both nursing and home help.

As it turned out, the differences in satisfaction were small. Either both groups were equally satisfied, or budget clients were slightly more satisfied. The latter was the case regarding the personal contacts with the nurses and the continuity of nursing care (knowing who comes when and being informed about changes or absence).

Budget and regular clients differed slightly more in their appreciation of home help; but here too, the differences were not great. Budget clients were more satisfied with the amount of help they received and the way in which the tasks were carried out. They consulted more with the helper and they found help slightly more effective. They were less often obliged to explain how things need to be done.

There were, however, very important differences between budget and regular clients in their appreciation of their influence on the choice of help, the time at which help was given, and the amount of help. The budget clients scored considerably better.

Apart from these quantitative data, there are also some qualitative data. A group of 24 persons all younger than 55 and needing both nursing and home help, was asked to participate in a qualitative study. The central question of this part of the research was how the budget affected the life of these persons.

The results were positive. In many cases, they were able to buy more help than they could have gotten from a regular organization on the basis of their care plan. They were able to have a wider range of activities done by their help, and the help performed these tasks better.

They had the same person(s) coming to help them on a regular basis and at times that were convenient. During the experiment, they found out that it was very practical to have not only help at regular hours but also to have help at flexible hours for special activities. This made it possible for them to maintain more social contacts. The pressure on informal carers was also reduced. The relationship between the client and the help was felt to be better because it was more equal. The home helps were less patronizing. These clients said that the budget made them feel better, freer and less dependent.

2.2   *The Experiment of the Home Help Organization in Rotterdam*

The home help organization in Rotterdam would have liked to participate in the experiment of the Health Care Insurance Council, but it was not accepted. The organization decided to set up its own experiment. It involved 25 clients and dealt with home help only, not with nursing. The clients participating in this experiment were assessed as usual, and they received an amount of money which was the equivalent of the gross hourly wage of a home help multiplied by the number of hours for which they were assessed. The clients could use this money for buying assistance wherever they wanted. Any money left over had to be returned. The clients had to show how they had spent the money every four weeks. They were offered an introductory course where they were informed on practical matters and on the rules for employing assistants (as they were called in this experiment). This experiment served to answer two questions:

- Are clients' needs better met with a budget?
- Which questions and which dilemmas need to be dealt with in order to incorporate the budget as a regular provision of the organization for home help?

The outcomes of this experiment were as positive as those from the experiment by the Health Care Insurance Council.

The participants experienced the budget as an instrument enabling them to keep functioning in their social roles. It also improved their social relations with their environment.

Of the 25 participants, 24 were very satisfied with the way in which their assistants carried out their tasks. They arrived in time, did often more than they were supposed to, took the initiative, and participants could ask them to do things differently. A large majority (20) said that things were done better now than in the past, when they received help from the regular home-help organization. Their quality of life improved due to a number of factors.

Some clients were able to buy more help than the regular home help organization would have been able to give for the same amount of money. The tasks that were done were better suited to the clients' needs.[2] They were done at a more convenient time: most activities were done between 8:00 a.m. and 5:00 p.m., but a number of clients also arranged for help to be given in the early morning, the late evening or during the weekend. Most clients arranged with their assistants to work according to a fixed schedule, but many clients kept a number of hours for special occasions when something extra needed to be done. This flexibility was very much appreciated.

Of the participants, 75% had two or more assistants, and as many had one or more persons lined up for replacement.

The majority of assistants were acquaintances and neighbours (49%), relatives (23%), persons unknown to them until they were recruited for this task (20.5%) and friends (7.5%). The relationship with these assistants was of a rather personal nature. In 50% of the cases, the clients made a written contract with their assistants.

The clients had different requirements for different tasks. For activities like accompanying them, clients found it important that their assistants were of the same age, had similar interests and a similar lifestyle. For other activities, these requirements were less important but still appreciated.

None of the clients had assistants who had had professional training for this job. For almost all tasks, clients did not think it necessary to have professional training. They instructed their assistants themselves.

The following criteria turned out to be most important in the opinion of the clients:

- the assistant must be motivated;
- the client and the assistant must know each other fairly well, so that there be a certain trust;
- the assistant must be willing to work outside office hours and to be flexible;
- the assistant must be able to take the initiative;
- the assistant must have a similar lifestyle;

- the assistant must have an understanding of the situation;
- the assistant must be capable.

The clients felt themselves less dependent, more autonomous and more mobile due to the budget. They felt less patronized by their assistants than by regular home helps. Their relationship with their assistants was more equal because of the payment of wages. They were glad that they did not have to feel grateful all the time to their relatives and assistants (*Stuurgroep Klantgebonden Budget,* 1993).

2.3   What Have These Experiments Taught Us about the Quality of Care?

The outcomes of both experiments were quite similar, although the experimental conditions differed. The experiment of the Health Care Insurance Council included nursing and home help; the one in Rotterdam, home help only. The participants in the experiment in Rotterdam had less freedom and received a smaller amount of money. The following is a summary of the main factors that contributed to client satisfaction:

a) The clients themselves decide who is going to help them. It is important for them to be able to choose assistants whom they like and who have a similar lifestyle.
b) It also makes a difference that the same person(s) help them on a regular basis and that they do not have to deal with new helpers every so often (continuity).
c) They can decide about the time when their assistants come. They appreciate some flexibility in the schedule.
d) They can decide which tasks should be done.
e) They can give instructions about how they want these tasks to be done.
f) They can buy more help with a budget than a regular organization would be able to give them. This is either because they buy help that is less qualified, or because they have assistants for not more than two days a week (see Footnote 2).
g) Problems with assistants who get sick or are on vacation seem to have been solved without many difficulties.
h) Clients feel more independent, autonomous and mobile because of the budget.
i) Clients feel that they are less patronized by their assistants and that there is more equality in their relationship with assistants than with regular professional helpers.
j) The burden on their informal network is reduced, and therefore relationships are improved.

3   The Second Phase of the Experiment

It goes without saying that the personal budget for care is a very controversial innovation. Persons who need long-term care and their organizations, such as the National Council of Persons with Disabilities, are very much in favour; but other organizations – such as the trade unions, the regular home-care organizations, or the Equal Opportunities Council – have objections of various kinds. The Declaration of Policy of 1994 by the then-incoming government, contains a paragraph on the personal budget for care. The present government is of the opinion that the budget is an instrument that furthers the emancipation of people who are dependent on care. Therefore, it is to be promoted. In its first policy paper on the subject, the government proposes a change in terminology. Whereas the original name was a "budget for clients" (in Dutch: *cliëntgebonden budget*), it now becomes a "budget for persons" (*persoonsgebonden budget*). The explanation for this change is simple: a person who is entitled to a budget need not be a client of any agency – he or she is a person who needs care. At the same time, a new name for persons receiving a budget had been introduced: they are now called "budget holders".

In July 1995, the Minister of Health, Welfare and Sports together with his Minister of State published a second policy paper in which they announced how they wanted to continue with the personal budget.

They would go step by step in an experimental fashion. The possibility of obtaining a budget would be extended gradually to various sectors of (health) care, beginning with home care and care for persons with learning disabilities. They would not yet give a legal basis to the personal budget. Each year a certain amount of money would be set aside for personal budgets, and the amount would gradually be increased. The effects of the personal budget would be monitored by research, and more data would be collected over a period of two years (1996 and 1997). The model to be used would be the one that was tried out in the experiment of the Health Care Insurance Council; but a number of new elements would be introduced. The most important of these is the association of budget holders. Each person receiving a budget is obliged to become a member of an association of budget holders. This is an entirely new phenomenon. Two such associations have been established since the publication of the policy paper, and more will follow. The money allocated to budget holders will go to their Association of Budget Holders (AoB), except for an amount of HFl. 2,400,- per year, which will go directly to the budget holders themselves. The AoBs must see to it that budget holders make valid contracts with their assistants: they must pay wages to the assistants and pay taxes and social premiums to the Inspector of Taxes. The Inspector must be informed of all wage payments, also to assistants who work not more than two days a week (and for whom the employer need not pay taxes and social premiums). The budget holders must authorize the AoB to make these payments on their behalf. The AoB is responsible to the Health Care Insurer that the budgets be used for care.

This new arrangement guarantees that no money (except the amount of HFl. 2,400,- per year) can flow into the "grey economy".

The Health Care Insurance Council has been asked to develop criteria for the recognition of AoBs.

In the new situation, the budget holder is still the one who decides where he/she wants to buy care; so care providers must offer care that meets the needs of the budget holders, according to market principles. This being the case, the government has less responsibility for the quality of care. Still, the government's policy paper devotes some paragraphs to it with the following content.

- The Inspector of Health Care can examine the quality of the allocation process, i.e. the composition of the assessment committee, the process of decision-making and the complaints procedure.
- The Act on the Quality of Care Institutions applies to care given by organizations (regular or private). In the next paragraph, some more information will be given about this Act, which has been in force since April 1996.
- The Act on Professions in Health Care applies to care given by such professionals as medical docters and nurses (also see the next paragraph).
- A new feature is the obligation of the assessment committee to inform the general practitioner of those budget holders receiving a budget for eight months or longer, where the committee has reasons to believe that they may be neglected.

The second phase of the experiment was started in 1996. As the Minister of State of Health, Welfare and Sports explained to a Parliamentary Commission, it was the Minister of Finance who insisted on the introduction of the AoBs. The Parliamentary Commission did not like the idea but accepted it for fear of cancellation of the entire experiment.

4 Quality of Home Care according to Different Actors

Everyone studying the quality of care knows this is a tricky subject. How is quality defined, and how is it measured? Quality is different from the perspectives of the various actors involved in home care.

In the following paragraphs, a summary will be given of the views expressed by these actors. We will discuss how their viewpoints compare with the factors that emerged as important for budget holders during the first phase of the experiment.

4.1 The Viewpoint of the Ministry of Health, Welfare and Sports

It is part of the present-day philosophy concerning the role of the government that it should operate at a greater distance from the actors in the field. Therefore, the Ministry no longer states specific requirements that home care organizations must meet. The Act on the Quality of Care Institutions and the Act on Professions in Health Care are the two most important instruments of the government to control the quality of care. Both of them are so-called "framework laws", which means that details may be filled in by administrative decisions.

What are, briefly, the contents of these two acts?

The *Act on the Quality of Care Institutions* aims at making sure that institutions (both regular and private) offer "warranted care", i.e. care of sufficient quality which is efficient, effective, client-directed and corresponds to the needs of the patient.

The way in which care institutions are organized must be conducive to warranted care. The institutions must have a quality system which serves to systematically monitor, control and improve quality.

The institutions must publish an annual report on their quality policy, including such items as

* whether and how patients and users have been involved in quality policy;
* how and how often quality has been assessed, and with what results;
* what has been done about complaints and other statements concerning the quality of care.

In other words, it is left to the institutions themselves to set up a quality system. The only guidelines directly referring to the quality of care are the requirements that care must be efficient, effective, client-directed and corresponding to users' needs (*Kwaliteitswet Zorginstellingen*, 1996).

The *Act on Professions in Health Care* was passed in 1993. The professionals concerned are medical doctors, dentists, pharmacists, clinical psychologists, psychotherapists, physiotherapists, midwives and nurses. Of the persons who can be paid out of a personal budget for care, only the nurses are affected by this Act. The quality of care is maintained by the obligation of the professionals to be registered. They must meet certain criteria in order to be accepted for registration. They must renew their registration regularly, and they can be removed from the register in cases of bad practice. The Act also states how complaints about professionals will be dealt with (*Ministerie VWS*, 1995).

4.2   The Viewpoint of the National Association of Home Care

The National Association of Home Care (LVT) is the umbrella of local/regional organizations of regular home help and district nursing. The Association was the initiator of a project on the quality of home care, in close cooperation with other actors. The outcome of this project was a list of criteria for the quality of home care. This list has been used as input for the formulation of membership criteria for the Association.

If local/regional organizations for home care want to join the association, they must meet 13 criteria. Ten of these criteria are explicitly concerned with the quality of care.

What are these membership criteria? Briefly summarized they contain the follow-ing requirements[3] (Working Document of the Association LVT):

1) The corporate body (i.e. the member organization) provides a description of its products in order to make clear to users what is being offered.
2) The corporate body provides users with written information about its products and the terms of delivery.
3) The corporate body can be reached by telephone during the hours when its products are available. The institution must also be sufficiently reachable in terms of physical and non-physical accessibility (e.g. accessibility of information).
4) Products are delivered on the basis of an individual care plan made up in a professional way on the basis of an assessment. There is communication about the plan with the user. From the plan follows an individual care contract, at least in those cases where a substantial care package is given. The conditions for its delivery are incorporated into it.
5) The corporate body makes sure that employees have an adequate level of pro-fessional qualifications.
6) There is a policy and guidelines for hygiene, safety and environment.
7) The corporate body uses the complaints procedure of the Association, which offers the possibility of calling on the Association's Complaints Committee.
8) The corporate body uses the Association's regulations concerning privacy.
9) The corporate body uses a quality system and reports both regularly and pub-licly on its quality policy.
10) The corporate body has made a structural provision for the involvement of clients in policy-making.

4.3 The Viewpoint of the Professionals

The data in this section only relate to the discussion about home help. The view of professionals in nursing is not represented in this paper. It must be noted, however, that nurses have a much stronger professional identity than home helps. The major part of the care bought with the personal budget is not nursing care.

For a few years now, there has been an intensive discussion going on about the professionalization of home help. In this discussion, the professional organization of home helps plays an active role. The following picture of the essentials of home help from a professional point of view, is based on this discussion (see Hornman, 1994; Vulto e.a., 1994; Gremmen, 1995).

The main premise of home help is to maintain and stimulate self-care and self-sufficiency by the client and the household to which he/she belongs, including informal carers.

The nature and the complexity of the situation in which the home help operates is determined by the following factors:

- the characteristics of the person who needs help;
- the nature and the complexity of the care needed;
- the context in which the help is given.

Home helps work in other people's homes and therefore have to take these people's norms and standards into account.

Home help is work involving hands, head and heart. What is done by the hands is well recognized: it is mainly housework and some personal care. What needs to be done by the head and the heart is less visible and therefore less recognized.

The following skills are necessary for a home help, according to research by Vulto:

- Ability to quickly diagnose the mental state of the client.
- Ability to adjust her approach to different persons in different situations with different needs.
- Ability to choose between stimulating or slowing down.
- Ability to tactfully advise.
- Ability to draw a line when the client asks too much and being able to explain the policy of the Home Help Organization.
- Ability to take the initiative for problem-solving or the regulation of emotions.
- Ability to keep a professional distance and, at the same time, be close to the client.
- Being practical in case of crises.
- Ability to structure chaotic situations.

On top of all this, home helps must be able to plan their work, to cooperate with colleagues and supervisors, as well as with representatives of other disciplines who come into the household; they must have an understanding what it means to be ill and what the consequences are of the state the client is in.

In the present discussion, it is argued that such skills as mentioned above should be recognized, included in training programmes, and remunerated financially.

Home helps are faced with at least two paradoxes:

- They want the emotional factors they encounter in the relationship with clients to be more important, and they want more responsibility to decide themselves what to do; whereas the management of home help organizations stresses the rational elements and resorts more and more to standardization of tasks.
- A professional attitude means keeping a distance from the client, whereas the personal attitude of the home help may be to reduce the distance and go further along with the wishes of the client than official instructions allow. Gremmen calls this the "discrepancy between formal professional ethics and relational care ethics".

4.4 The Viewpoint of the Trade Unions

When the personal budget for care was first launched as an experiment, the largest trade union to which employees in home care belong was quick to voice its criticism (*Aaneen*, 1993).

Its main objection was the fear that private persons employing assistants might not be very good employers. Their employees would risk not getting the minimum wage, workers' benefits, paid holidays, paid sick leave, etc. How would disputes between private employer and employees be settled? What would be done about the training and support of these employees? When anybody can be hired to provide personal care, this will lower the quality of care, according to this trade union.

At that time, the trade unions were campaigning for upgrading the profession of home help by pleading for better training, better working conditions and higher salaries. It was obvious that the personal budget for care went against this trend.

Since the introduction of the second phase of the experiment, the trade union's criticism has become slightly milder; but a trade union representative states that they would have preferred larger budgets for the regular home care organizations instead of money for personal budgets. He doubts whether budget holders are able to buy qualitatively good care. The personal budget will reinforce the image of home care being simple housework, work that can be done by anybody, without training (Bouwmans, 1995).

4.5 The Viewpoint of Care Insurers

So far, there have been few publications about the views of insurers regarding the quality of home care. The insurers have not formulated any requirements for care paid out of a personal budget. They want to respect the freedom of budget holders to buy the care they want. Every six months, the budget holders will be reassessed. In the view of the insurers, this offers an opportunity to look at the quality of care. If, at the time of reassessment, it would become obvious that inadequate care has been bought, it is possible to stop the budget. Since the second phase of the experiment will also be evaluated, in the eyes of the insurers it is too early to say anything about the quality of care in relation to the personal budget (personal communication).

4.6 The Viewpoint of User Organizations

As part of the policy on quality of care, organizations delivering care must involve their users. How they do this is up to them. The National Institute of Care and Welfare (NIZW) supports them and helps them implement a quality policy. In this context, the NIZW has commissioned research in order to find out what long-term users of home care consider as criteria for good care. The results of this research have been described by Verhaak and Tjadens (1993).

At the same time, several organizations of patients, of elderly or of persons with disabilities have set up their own projects to measure quality. In the context of this paper, two projects are interesting. One is a project by a national organization of elderly persons that has asked a research institute to develop an instrument by which local organizations can measure the quality of home help and nursing received by their members. This has resulted in a questionnaire and guidelines on how to process the answers. The questionnaire mostly asks for client satisfaction on a number of items (Unie KBO, 1994).

A more fundamental approach has been followed by the National Council of Persons with Disabilities. They, too, have asked for help from a research institute. This institute has developed, in close cooperation with people having long-term experience with home care, a list of criteria that make for good home care; and they then operationalized these criteria into an instrument with which users can rate the quality of care.

For this paper, the list of criteria is relevant. It is no coincidence that the criteria on this list resemble those that have been presented by Verhaak and Tjadens. A summary of this list is as follows (*Gehandicaptenraad*, 1993).

1) Availability and Accessibility
- Home care must be available for those who need it.
- Home care must be financially within reach.
- It must be possible to reach the home care organization by telephone during working hours.
- It must be possible to reach the organization both day and night.

2) The Needs of the Client as the Central Focus
- The assessment takes into account the total need for care. The assessment is made by an independent agency.
- Flexibility must be possible as to the amount of care, the kind of care, and the hours at which care is given.
- The needs of the client must be taken seriously.

3) Continuity of Care
- Care must be given on the basis of an agreement.
- It must be given by the same person(s), and there must be regular replacements.
- The client must have one special contact person within the organization.

4) Independence
- Decisions about the care to be given, the tasks and how they shall be performed, are made together with the client.

- The client has the final say on which tasks will be carried out.
- The client must be able to decide what is being done in his/her own home.
- The client can choose who will help him/her.

5) Knowledge and Skills for Caring

- The help must have the necessary expertise to be able to carry out relevant tasks.
- The help must be able to do the work on his/her own.
- Home care must be given carefully, safely and hygienically.

6) The Attitude of Home Helps

- The help must stick to agreements.
- The help must be discreet and respect the privacy of the client.
- The help must be reliable.
- The help must respect the client's way of life and his/her choices.
- The personnel of the home care organization must have a serviceable and client-directed attitude.

7) The Rights of Clients

- The home care organization must have an accessible complaints procedure.
- The organization must be responsible for the reimbursement of damage.
- The client must be able to see his/her own file.
- On the basis of the assessment, a care plan must be made of which the client gets a copy.

8) Information

- The organization for home care must inform the client about its working methods.
- The organization must inform the client about his/her rights and responsibilities.
- The organization provides information about financial aspects.
- The organization provides written information which is accessible.
- The organization informs the client about the outcome of the assessment procedure and the arguments on which it is based.

5   Whose Quality Prevails in the Personal Budget for Care?

In the second phase of the experiment with the personal budget for care, the essentials of the system have been maintained. The budget holder has the right to decide who will give what kind of assistance in what manner, when and where. This right is extremely important from the point of view of the budget holder, since it contributes to the quality of care according to users' wishes. As long as budget holders spend their entire budget to buy care from private persons, they are not bothered with any other kind of quality criteria than the criteria they set independently. However, as soon as they buy the services from a registered nurse, they have to deal with a professional affected by the Act on Professions in Health Care. Should they buy help from a regular organization for home care, then they will find that the help they receive must meet the criteria set by the National Association of Home Care, as discussed in section 4.2. Should the person turn to a private organization, then this organization must meet the requirements set by the government in the Act on the Quality of Care Institutions (see section 4.1).

So far in this article, little has been said about business and professional approaches to quality (see the contribution by Pollitt in this volume).

In fact, neither of them plays a very important role in the development of the personal budget for care. Some criteria for quality which fit well into the business approach can be found in the criteria for membership of the National Association of Home Care. As has been explained, these criteria have been formulated on the national level. It is well possible that individual member organizations of the National Association of Home Care use additional criteria fitting into one approach or the other, but we have not done any research into that. The criteria formulated by the National Association are very much a mixed bag: all parties concerned can find something to their liking in these criteria.

Private organizations for home care which are not a member of the National Association, must comply with the Act on the Quality of Care Institutions. As it is only six months since this Act has become effective, it is too early to present data on its effects.

In the setting of the personal budget for care, nurses are the only kind of workers who can call themselves professionals. However, many of the trained home helps would like to be recognized as professionals, though this is not yet the case. Therefore, the professional approach has a limited influence.

On the other hand, it is worthwhile to note that precisely those items which turned out to play an important role in the satisfaction of budget holders – such as choosing the person who is going to give assistance, deciding which tasks should be done and how, similarity in lifestyle between helper and budget holder, and equality in the relationship between helper and budget holder – do not fit very well into the business approach and even less into the professional approach. The research on the personal budget for care has illustrated the argument brought forward by Evers (in this volume) that these two approaches do not grasp the peculiarities of care. Evers points to the values playing a role in the family- and community-based networks, as well as in perspectives on common interest and citizenship.

The question may be raised whether it is family values or rather such values as people experience in friendships that are essential to persons dependent on long-term care. Choosing the person who will do the job, taking into account the personality and lifestyle of both the carer and the cared for, and creating a relationship on the basis of equality, are all processes that are more like those occurring between persons who eventually become friends than between family members.

At any rate, values playing a role in personal relationships are essential in caring. Formally, this fact receives little recognition; and the use of strategies to improve quality such as those described by Pollitt does not include these values in the debate about care any more than earlier ones did. If we want to do justice to people who need long-term care, we will have to take these values into account and see how we can give them a proper place. The personal budget for care is likely to enhance such a new approach.

Notes

1   HFl. 1,- = US$ 0.50 (1-7-1997).
2   Two peculiarities of the Dutch system need to be explained here. The first one has to do with the rules for employing someone for work in the household. If such an employee works no more than two days a week, the employer does not have to pay for his/her employee's taxes or social premiums. The employee is supposed to declare his/her earnings for taxation. Of course, many employees are tempted not to do this. In that case, money paid out of the budget flows into the "grey economy". Wages paid on this basis are usually more or less equivalent to the net wages of regular employees. In other words, the employer pays less. The second point requiring explanation is about the way in which regular home help organizations function. These organizations only carry out a certain number of well-defined household tasks. Such activities as working in the garden, taking care of animals, spring cleaning, mending clothes, administrative tasks and accompanying the client on errands outside the home are not done by the regular home help.
3   The requirements are formulated in a terrible jargon. In the translation, I have tried to keep as closely as possible to the Dutch terminology.

References

Aaneen (October 1993). Zoetermeer: AbvaKabo.
Bouwmans, M. (1995) 'De zorgverlener dreigt het slachtoffer te worden', *Trefpunt* 17. Rijswijk: Ministerie van VWS.
Gehandicaptenraad (1993) *Utrecht. Langdurende thuishulp: van knelpunten naar kwaliteit.*
Gremmen, Ine (1995) *Ethiek in de gezinsverzorging.* Utrecht: J. van Arkel.
Hornman, M. (1994) *Terwijl je afstoft kom je heel wat tegen.* Utrecht: STING.
Miltenburg, Th. e.a. (1993) *Experiment Cliëntgebonden Budget Verzorging en Verpleging.* Nijmegen: ITS.
Stuurgroep Klantgebonden Budget (1993) *Klantgebonden budget: een nieuw product van thuiszorg Rotterdam?*

Unie KBO (1994) *'s-Hertogenbosch. Kwaliteitsmeting Thuiszorg.*

Verhaak, P./Tjadens, F. (1993) *Kwaliteit binnen handbereik?* Utrecht: NIZW.

Vulto, M. e.a. (1994) *Thuis bij de cliënt sta je er alleen voor.* Leiden: RU Leiden, Faculteit Sociale Wetenschappen, Vakgroep Vrouwenstudies.

Ministerie van VWS (1995) *Beleidsbrief aan de Tweede Kamer,* 13 juli 1995.

Ministerie van VWS (1995) *De wet BIG.*

Ministerie van VWS (1996) *Kwaliteitswet Zorginstellingen.*

CHAPTER 19

Quality Measurements and Some Unintended Consequences: Can Quasi-quality Be a Consequence of Quality Standards?

Britt Slagsvold

1 Introduction

In the last decade, and especially in the 1990s, the quality of personal services has gained increased attention. Old-age care is a typical example. In this sector, quality management, quality assessments, quality assurance, etc., have been widespread during the last few decades in the USA, and in the 1990s they have gained increased attention in Europe, too.[1] Journals on "quality" are being published, and "quality" is the headline of numerous working groups in all parts of the care system. The efforts to improve the quality of services are many and varied. In the Scandinavian countries, so-called ISO standards on quality in nursing homes have been applied, quality awards have been implemented, quality circles have been formed, and quality committees have been set up.

There are many reasons for this intensified focus on quality, among others an increased academization and scientification of the professions within social services and long-term care.

High quality of services has, however, always been of concern to professionals. What are the new aspects? One is that the *concept* of quality has come into the foreground: it is consciously and constantly reflected upon. Perspectives on quality have become more abstract and theoretically founded, and approaches to quality improvements have become more standardized, universal and based on models and advice given by experts and consultants on "quality".

This new wave of quality attention has also been accompanied by an intensified interest in measures of quality.[2] As instruments, quality measures can tell whether quality is high or low, improving or decreasing, secured or below standards. Quality measures are also tools for making comparisons both between and across time and settings. Quality literature often stresses the importance of setting aims that can be measured and of making continuous measurements.

Quality measures are consequently constantly constructed, presented and applied and have become widespread within health care and social services.

The discussion to follow refers to measures constructed for evaluating quality in nursing homes. Nursing homes should, in this context, be seen as an example: the rationale behind measures, the type of measures used, and the unintended consequences of being measured, all reflect and exemplify topics of general concern to social services and health care.

Measuring quality, on the one hand, and securing and improving quality on the other, are areas where research and practice are closely connected. This can be fruitful but also problematic. Some of the problems that can arise, and which to a considerable extent can be attributed to the close connection between research and practice in quality work, will be addressed in the pages that follow. This discussion will concern validity in two ways: (1) if practice is to be based on research, it is urgent that the research results or instruments be valid; and (2) valid research methods are not necessarily valid methods for practice.

This double perspective on validity of measures and efforts to increase quality raises the question of what I will call "quasi-quality": "Can quasi-quality be a consequence of quality measures?"

The following discussion is organized into four parts.

- First, the quality of old-age institutions is outlined. The definitions of quality and the perspectives on quality within this sector are to a large extent similar to other sectors within the health care and social services.
- Second, a measure of quality applied in a study of nursing homes will be presented. It is an indicator measure on quality (or standard) and is representative of a widespread type of quality measures. I have named this kind of measure "standicator measures". The study on quality in nursing homes raises the question of whether quasi-quality may be a result of invalid quality measures.
- Third, a methodological distinction is outlined between quality aspects that are supposed to form quality, and quality aspects that are thought to *reflect* quality: formative vs. reflective quality indicators.
- Finally, quasi-quality as a consequence of reactive measurement effects is discussed.

2 Quality in Old-age Institutions

For several decades, gerontological researchers have studied quality in old-age institutions and have tried to trace the preconditions for high quality. For research purposes, hundreds of quality measures have been constructed (Slagsvold, 1995).

Since the 1980s, more universal standards for quality in such institutions have become increasingly common, i.e. standardized measures according to which quality in single institutions can be assessed. These universal standards are to a large extent based on quality measures constructed for specific research purposes. The "quality sector" is indeed one where research seems to be applied. When reviewing measures used for research purposes and those used for monitoring quality, the overlap is striking. This may seem quite reasonable, as it is the same quality they are intended to measure. But the practical application of research-based measures of quality actualizes a perpetual challenge in all kinds of research or evaluation, namely the question of the validity of measures: to what extent do quality measures measure what they are intended to measure? The question is central to researchers: if measures are invalid, their results and conclusions will be invalid, too. The question of validity of measures, however, becomes much more urgent if the measures are applied directly when assessing institutions (for instance, closing down homes with low quality according to measurements) or used as guidelines for improving quality in daily care. If the measures of quality have low validity, they may at worst harm or reduce quality.

What do we know about the validity of quality measures in old-age institutions? The answer is, very little. A huge number of quality measures have been constructed, but very few researchers have in fact tried to validate them. And those few studies that have done so, directly or indirectly, seem to reveal that the validity seems distressingly low with regard to distinguishing between homes with high and low quality (Geron, 1991; Clark/Bowling, 1990; Slagsvold, 1995; Schwarz et al., 1994; Booth, 1985).

It may seem surprising that there have been so few attempts to validate measures with such widespread application. There are probably several reasons for this, of which three are suggested here.

First, applied research projects often have too low budgets and tight time limits within which to do adequate methodological work.

Second, and probably more important, is that measures of quality have high "face validity". The content of these measures seems so obviously reasonable and plausible that the need for time-consuming validation of measures seems unnecessary to both practitioners and planners. The quality measures are evidently so plausible that researchers, too, seem to rely on face validity, in spite of the general and well-known warnings against the danger of plausibility in research (for instance Montgomery/Borgatta, 1987; Lazarsfeld, 1959). Very few have, for instance, asked "dumb questions" concerning the importance of single rooms in nursing homes: it seems self-evident that the availability of single rooms is an important aspect of quality. Consequently, the proportion of single rooms is widely applied as an indicator of quality, even though this indicator has not been properly validated. The few empirical studies which have focused on the relationship between single and shared rooms and residents' well-being do, however, reveal ambiguous results; some even find positive effects on well-being in sharing rooms (Kayser-Jones, 1986; Gallagher/Walker, 1990).

The third and probably most important reason for not doing adequate methodological work lies in the difficulties of actually validating measures of quality. Which other measures or criteria on quality should they be validated against? What in fact is quality in old-age institutions?

In professional literature, few have attempted to give an adequate definition of quality in old-age institutions. If quality is explicitly defined, the definition tends to be either very general and abstract (for instance, "good, flexible and individualized services", or "meeting the resident's needs"), or detailed and trivial, defining quality operationally (for instance, "resident's representation on the board", "routines for continence training", "be given choices as to when to have a bath", "proportion of single rooms", etc.). While the general definitions tend to focus on clients' or patients' needs and be related to outcomes, the operational definitions tend to focus on services and input.

It does, however, seem self-evident that quality in nursing homes must have implications for well-being among clients in some way or another. In high-quality institutions, clients should be more satisfied than in institutions with low quality.

The difference between quality of *care* and quality of *life* is sometimes underlined in the literature on institutional quality: high quality of care (or services) may be secured, but quality of care is not the same as quality of life.[3] The distinction between quality of care and quality of life is, however, problematic for populations of seriously-dependent elderly people. They are dependent on others for expending their resources and for organizing "arenas", and long-term benefits are of little relevance to most of them. If services do not contribute to their well-being within a rather *short* period of time, quality of care cannot be said to be really high.

Saying that quality of care should *contribute* to quality of life, does not mean that quality of care is the most important factor influencing the quality of life of dependent people (physical and mental health, bereavement, family relations, etc., are more important); but high quality of care should at least make a positive difference in the quality of life of those concerned.

Measures of quality of care should therefore ideally be validated against the residents' quality of life in some way or another. The most obvious way would be to validate measures of care quality against residents' own evaluations. User satisfaction, as a method of assessing quality among dependent people, does, however, raise a number of serious methodological problems. Most of these "problems" contribute positively to expressed contentment.[4] The rather constant proportion who express contentment more or less independent of their life circumstances, implies that consumer evaluations are not valid criteria against which to validate measures of quality of care.

3   A Study of Nursing Home Quality and the Validity of Measures

The intention for presenting a study of nursing home quality here is twofold. First, a typical quality measure is presented. It is the structure and rationale behind this measure that is typical and of primary interest here. It is this kind of measure, "quality measure", or "standicator measure" refers to in the discussion to follow.

Furthermore, the results of validating this measure are of more general interest and are the point of departure for raising questions concerning measurement-induced quasi-quality.

The aim of the study to be presented was to analyse the relationship between nursing home size and quality. Which differences could be identified? Why and how does size possibly influence quality?

The "which" question indicated using a standardized quantitative quality measure; the "why and how" questions indicated gathering qualitative information. A combination of methods was chosen and applied in a strategic sample of nursing homes. Altogether, 19 wards in five small homes and four large homes were studied both with an extensive quantitative measure on quality of care, and by participant observation.

The dimensions of quality to be measured were chosen with reference to need theories, governmental regulations and guidelines, and theories on welfare.

The main dimensions of quality studied were: 1) medical and somatic care; 2) rehabilitation; 3) activity; 4) social contact; and 5) autonomy. The first two dimensions refer to the medical aspects of care; the last three, to psychosocial aspects. The problem of quasi-quality first and foremost concerns the psychosocial aspects.

3.1   The Quantitative Quality Measure – A Standicator Measure

Each quality dimension was measured by a set of indicators. The quality dimension "autonomy" will be used as an example in the following. The quantitative measurement of autonomy consisted of 12 indicators, of which most are included in several other measures of quality (for instance, Bland, 1992; Booth, 1995; Evans et al., 1982; Gjerberg, 1995; Geron, 1991). The indicators referred to options provided (for instance, choosing when to go to bed), restrictions imposed on daily life (for instance, alcohol consumption), formalized influence (for instance, representation on the board), and opportunities for privacy (for instance, keys to rooms and cabinets).

In analyses of the quality dimension "autonomy", indicators were added to an index. Each nursing home was assigned a score on autonomy (as well as on each other quality dimension) according to the assumption that the more registered options and influence, the higher the autonomy.

The quality measure used in this study is typical for studies on quality in old-age institutions, and on quality in personal social services more generally. Some of the typical traits are the following:

- Quality dimensions and items are carefully chosen after studying the literature. There do, however, exist very many measures on quality. Taken together, the number of indicators used is extremely large, and almost all the indicators seem highly plausible. However, the quality measures have to a very small extent been validated against other criteria for quality of care. Consequently, one is free to choose among these many plausible indicators and to compose a quality measure of one's own. Our measure on autonomy was similar to, but not identical with, many other measures on autonomy.
- The quality measurement builds on a simple input-output model or production model of quality.[5] It is, however, not primarily the *product* that is evaluated. Indicators of output (results) are few, if any. Most of the indicators are on the *input* side; some input indicators concern resources and organization (the structural level); but most of them concern what is done (the process level). Our measurement of autonomy consisted exclusively of indicators on input; restrictions imposed, options, influence, and opportunities provided – none of the indicators were on the output side.
- When analysing the data, it is usually assumed that the relationship between indicators and quality is additive and monotone (the more the better).

This type of quality measurement is widespread, and will be referred to as "standicator measures". That is a hybrid concept made up of "standard" and "indicators". A standicator measure has the following general characteristics:

- It builds on indicators that are *supposed* to be related to quality or clients' well-being.
- It primarily consists of items that refer to what the services "have" (the structural level) or to what is "done" (the process level). This implies that the items refer to aspects that can be manipulated.
- It builds on items that can easily be registered.
- It builds on registrations that can easily, or naturally be quantified (counted).

The concept *standard* refers both to (1) quality and (2) "making alike", i.e. to conformity. This double reference fits this kind of measurements. They are supposed to measure quality (or standard) at the same time that they define quality or standard, and thereby may contribute to standardizing institutions or to making them alike. In other words, the concept "standicator measure" has an insidious connotation.

When raising the question of whether quasi-quality may be a consequence of quality measures, the reference is to such standicator measures.

3.2 Participant Observation

Quality of the nine nursing homes was also evaluated by participant observations. The observations were intended to highlight questions of why and how size may influence different dimensions of quality. In this context the observations are, however, primarily used as criteria for evaluating the validity of the standicator measures used in the study.

In each nursing home, two psychologists participated as nursing aides from one to three weeks and made observations independently of each other. The same quality dimensions that were measured by a standicator measure were also observed. Notes were taken in an observation guide. Besides, each ward (or nursing home) was given an observational quality score ranging from 0 to 7, or from very poor to extremely good, on each quality dimension. The interrater correlations were high, ranging from .79 to .97.

3.3 The Validity of Standicator Measures

In this way, we had two quantified evaluations of quality, one standicator score and one observation score.

- The *standicator scores* refer primarily to input, and to information that is easily registered and naturally quantifiable.
- *Observational scores* are closer to output or results, i.e. to clients' and staff's observable behaviour: respect shown, choices given and used, mutual interaction, emotional behaviour and expressions, reactions, initiative, requests, activity, etc., and to the institution's social "atmosphere".

The observational scores are taken as sufficiently valid, and are used as criteria for testing the validity of standicator measures.[6]

The two measures were compared in different ways. They were both supposed to measure the same quality dimensions, but they mostly revealed divergent results.

- Correlations (range correlation) between standicator scores and observational scores were around zero for all the quality dimensions on the psychosocial aspects of quality. For the quality dimension "activity" and some of the subdimensions ("differentiation of care" and "information"), the correlations were slightly negative.

- Comparisons of the relationship between size and quality gave different results, depending on whether it was measured with standicator measures or with observations. Using "autonomy" as an example, *standicator scores* indicated that there was no relationship between institutional size and autonomy, whereas *observation scores* indicated a consistent relationship; all the small homes were observed as giving more autonomy than any large institution.
- Comparisons of indicators registered by standicator measures and observation indicated that the staff did not necessarily do what they said they did (for instance, let the residents choose when to get up in the morning, or walk with the residents).[7]
- Observations also revealed that several indicators seemed to be rather irrelevant to the residents (for instance, to choose when to have a bath, or being given opportunities for extra meals).

First and foremost, however, the standicator measures were invalid because relevant aspects of quality were not included.

Observations revealed, for instance, that having autonomy (being offered influence, choices and control) really did seem to be of *great* importance to the resident's well-being. But the kind of autonomy and influence important to them was to decide *what* to decide, *whether* to decide and *when*: e.g. to have the coffee heated, to have somebody help them make a telephone call or get the eraser for the crossword puzzle. Relevant autonomy was an autonomy that was individualized, flexible, and contextual. The standicator measure did not register individualized influence and control but rather only a number of formalized choices.

The conclusion drawn in this study was that, with the observations as criteria to appraise validity, the standicator measures on psychosocial aspects of quality which had been constructed were invalid. The standicator measures did not measure what they intended to measure. They did not catch the kind of autonomy, activity or social contact that was relevant to the resident's well-being.

The standicator measure presented above is a typical one, but only one. What about other quality measures? Are they more valid? It seems unlikely. Few have tried to validate their standicator measures with data on clients' well-being as a reference. The few studies that directly or indirectly highlight the validity of quality measurements indicate that the validity is disappointingly low (Bowling et al., 1993; Geron, 1991; Davies, 1991; Clark/Bowling, 1990; Booth, 1985). A review of the literature reveals that low validity probably is a common problem with standicator measures.

4 Quasi-quality as a Consequence of Invalid Standicator Measures

The standicator measures presented above did not discriminate between the good and the bad nursing homes. Homes being rated as good with this measure, might just as well be bad, and vice versa. The homes rated as good with the standicator measure might be said to have quasi-quality: they just *seemed* good, i.e. they were good only in the measured way.

That is a problem to both researchers and planners. They may be misinformed by standicator measures. I shall illustrate this with an example:

> I did a minor observation study in a small ward for 12 short-term residents at a nursing home called Anguhill. It was the very best ward I had ever observed. The atmosphere there was very caring, warm, empathic, and individualized. The routines, meals, and activities were to a very large extent adapted to the residents' wishes and former habits.
>
> Among the residents were two old immigrants who did not speak one word of Norwegian. These two were located near the centre of the ward. The aides frequently visited them as they passed, smiling, touching them, making nice comments they could not understand, and trying to guess their wishes. There seemed to be a mutual, non-verbal contact and confidence between the immigrants and the aides.
>
> The Norwegian residents seemed more gentle and cheerful than I usually observe in nursing homes: they were more talkative and took more social initiatives. Without being asked they expressed their contentment and told me they called the aides "The angels, the angels at Anguhill". Some of them had been there before, and they always hoped to return to this ward if they should have another stay.
>
> This ward at Anguhill was, however, closed down because the planners found it was below standards. The ward did not have satisfactory care plans, activity programmes or quality assurance programmes, nor did they give priority to rehabilitation and training programmes.
>
> According to standicator measures, this ward had low quality. The consequence was closing it down.

In this case, invalid standards of quality rather directly harmed the clients. The indicators of quality applied in this case referred to "quality of care" as standicator measures do, but the measure of quality did not catch those aspects which contributed to "quality of life" of the residents. This case also raises the question of whether "quality of care" as defined by the standicator measures, and "quality of life" of the clients, may be in some cases in conflict and difficult to combine. Standicator measures may even contribute to levelling the services to standards set and to "cutting away" the very aspects which characterize the excellent institutions.

5   Formative vs. Reflective Indicators

Before discussing how standicator measures may more indirectly create quasi-quality, a methodological distinction between two types of quality indicators will be outlined: formative vs. reflective indicators.

- *Formative indicators* are indicators assumed to form a phenomenon. That means they define what the phenomenon consists of, or at least important parts of it. Returning to the standicator measure of "autonomy", the possibility to choose when to go to bed, etc., can be regarded as important parts of what autonomy in nursing homes *is*. The challenge, then, is to include the most relevant aspects of autonomy in a standicator measure. With formative indicators, one does not measure the complete quality dimension, but the most relevant parts of it should be included. Formative indicators of quality may be used as guidelines for practice. They define aspects that will contribute to quality: if we provide these choices and possibilities to influence, then "autonomy" will increase.
- *Reflective indicators* are intended to reflect a more general phenomenon. Indicators of outcome are always such reflective indicators: improvements in health status, low mortality rates, large discharge rates, etc. may reflect high quality in nursing homes. Standicator measures may, however, also be (or be regarded as) reflective indicators. Low consumption of sedatives may, for instance, reflect a caring and warm milieu; or low catherization may reflect satisfactory somatic care. The indicators of autonomy outlined above may, however, also be seen as reflecting, or mirroring, an environment giving autonomy in many *other* ways than those being measured. If residents are given choices and influence on those 12 aspects included in the study above, one assumes that the behaviour and atmosphere *more generally* give "autonomy" to the residents.

If indicators are primarily reflections of autonomy, then using them as guidelines for practice will not in and of itself contribute to quality or to residential well-being. To manipulate reflective indicators will only give quasi-quality.

The distinction between formative and reflective indicators of quality is important but easily forgotten. In most studies on quality of services, the distinction between formative and reflective standicators is not drawn. In some of the studies where the distinction is indicated, researchers seem to refer to indicators as reflecting quality when the measures are outlined on the first few pages. That means the indicators are *not* carefully chosen as the most important aspects, but they are chosen as indicators that can *reflect* quality more generally. When the results are discussed and the consequences for practice are outlined on the last few pages, the indicators are, however, referred to as guidelines for practice: that means that they are referred to as *formative* indicators. Spector and Takada (1991), for instance, change the meaning of "use of urinary catheter" from an indicator supposed to reflect the staff's orientation (an assumed causal relationship between staff orientation and functional decline) to a formative indicator suggesting that catheters should be used sparingly (interpreting the results as a causal relationship between catheter usage and functional decline).

Of course, it is even more difficult for the practitioners and planners using this literature than it is for researchers to keep this distinction in mind and to detect the discrepancy. It may even be difficult to know whether quality indicators are formative or reflective without doing careful research. Evidence of relationships between input indicators on the one hand (as, for instance, appropriate care plans, community involvement, use of sedatives, prevalence of catheterization, choosing bathing day, number of activities, etc.), and some other criteria of quality on the other, do not tell whether these indicators merely reflect more general attitudes or situations, or whether they are formative and can be used directly as guidelines to increase quality.

It sometimes appears "dumb" to professionals and planners to question the formative character of indicators, because it seems so obvious that, for instance, integrating children from the community into the nursing homes should contribute to the residents' quality of life in some way. Some studies, however, indicate that "importing children" in some instances may rather detract from quality, without the staff even recognizing it (Slagsvold, 1995; Seefeldt, 1987).

Above, it was suggested that "quasi-quality" can be a consequence of invalid quality measures. If invalid indicators of quality are used as guidelines for practice, the well-being of the residents will not increase. But the organization will seem good – it will have an appearance of quality. But it is good only in the measured way.

The discussion of formative vs. reflective indicators implies that invalid measures are not the only way to achieve quasi-quality. Quasi-quality can also be a consequence of quality measures that are valid for research purposes. Quality measures may give correct evaluations. They can be valid as measurement but *invalid as guidelines*.

If the indicators reflect quality in a valid way, it does not follow that quality is improved if these reflections are used as guidelines. In some cases, the contrary may even be true: using reflective standicators as guidelines for practice may actually detract from quality and reduce the well-being of residents.

6   Quasi-quality as a Consequence of Reactive Measurement Effects

The discussion of quasi-quality as provided here is tied to two well-known methodological issues: (1) the issue of valid measurements, which has been discussed above; and (2) the issues of reactive measurement effects, which will be discussed in this section. Reactive measurement effects refers to the fact that measurements can influence the behaviour that is measured, most often in undesirable ways.

When raising the question of possible harmful effects of being measured, there is little empirical research to draw on. There are, however, other authors who have more theoretically raised the question (Vladeck, 1988; Eliasson, 1996; Wærness, 1996). The problem of quasi-quality is, however, well known from other settings. We know it in grotesque form from the old Soviet state. There are also examples from warfare and from police work (Etzioni/Leham, 1967; Campbell, 1979). In those settings, it is documented that setting criteria for measuring success, productivity or quality can pervert behaviour and influence priorities in meaningless and unfortunate ways.

The problem and the possibility of quasi-quality is probably a universal phenomenon. There is no reason to expect that health care and social services are exceptions.

Donald Campbell (1979) has formulated two kinds of laws, or postulates, relevant to the concept of quasi-quality. He talks about quantitative social indicators and the corruption pressure they can impose:

> The more any quantitative social indicator is used for social decision-making, the more subject it will become to corruption pressure, and the more apt it will be to distort and corrupt the social processes it is intended to monitor. (Campbell, 1979: 85)

The first postulate says that measures will twist priorities and behaviour in the direction of what is being measured. This postulate might be said to refer to quasi-quality as a consequence of *intentional* behaviour.

The other postulate says that being measured may also distort and corrupt social processes. This postulate refers to quasi-quality as a result of *unintended* social consequences.

These two postulates are points of departure for suggesting some of the ways in which quasi-quality may be created.

6.1   Measurements May Twist Priorities and Behaviour in the Direction of What Is Being Measured

6.1.1 Cheating

The simplest form of measurement-imposed quasi-quality is plain cheating: that is, to change practice in accordance with indicators even if they are known to be of little importance to the clients' well-being. The indicators easiest to follow will probably be most subject to this kind of "creaming". The risk of being tempted to cheat will probably be higher if incentives are tied to quality scores.[8]

6.1.2 Interpreting Measures of Quality as Recipes for Quality

A more common and more sympathetic motive behind measurement-induced quasi-quality, however, is probably a genuine ambition to be good, and to do good. This motivation does, however, often have a vague aim, because it is tied to a vague conception of what quality actually is and how it can be created.

There is a strong and widespread ambition among care workers to offer high-quality services, to assure, and to develop quality. This ambition often seems to be accompanied by an amazingly high state of readiness to accept suggestions of what quality might be and what might be done to develop it. Many care workers seem to be hunting for guidelines to increase quality.

In such a situation, it is not surprising that there seems to be a large but somewhat uncritical readiness to accept suggestions of how to develop quality. And in such an atmosphere, standicator measures, consisting of simple indicators, can easily be interpreted as guidelines and translated into practical actions. Standicator measures can be interpreted as recipes for good quality. As outlined above, indicators are sometimes meant to be formative ingredients in such a recipe (Chambers, 1986). The quality measures are, however, seldom validated and the indicators are seldom carefully chosen as important parts of such a recipe. The indicators may in fact be reflective, with questionable relevance as guidelines.

6.1.3 Professionalism

Yet another reason for seeing indicators as guidelines may be that they give care work a kind of professionalism and rationality. The everyday activities in caring becomes more scientific, therapeutic, and purposeful. Perceiving housework as "activity therapy", taking a walk with residents as "rehabilitation", organizing small talk as "group activity" or changing it to "reminiscence groups", etc., may contribute to making trivial care work seem more professional. The prevalence and frequency of different activities can even be counted and used in an assessment of quality.

6.1.4 Harmful Effects?

Plain cheating, following harmless advice, and feeling a bit more professional is not likely to increase the well-being of the residents. But can it do any harm? It does not necessarily do harm, but it may; and it is important to be aware of that.

Quality measures may harm quality by twisting priorities as already mentioned. Activities with minor effects on well-being may expel activities with more impact. Time and money are scarce goods. They always have alternative applications.

An example may be extensive care plans in nursing homes. They are used as indicators of quality and as guidelines for improving quality. Filling them in, reading them, and continually updating them takes time. Several authors have questioned the priority this work is given in nursing homes. Few have tested the relationship between care plans and residents' well-being. Another example might paradoxically be quality assurance programmes in nursing homes. How much do they contribute to the residents' well-being, and in what ways do they detract?

It may also harm well-being if *reflective indicators* are used as guidelines: for instance, if the consumption of sedatives is reduced directly without reducing the need for it. Low consumption may reflect a positive and stimulating environment. But reducing the consumption of sedatives, without changing the environment and thereby reducing the need for it, may do harm if the consumption is not disturbingly high beforehand. In daily care, it is often more difficult to distinguish between input and output, between formative and reflective indicators, than we assume.

To sum up so far, standicators may set the agenda for what should be given priority in quality work. They make some aspects of care visible and disregard others. Standicator measures may reduce sound scepticism and expel individual judgement. The indicators are all so plausible, and quality is such a vague phenomenon.

But standicator measures and quality are not the same. Standicator measures have a form: they are built on assumptions and refer to aspects that can be formalized and manipulated, that can easily be registered and easily counted. Quality that contributes to residential well-being is much more than that. Giving priority to guidelines that fit standicator measures will not necessarily increase quality. It may even reduce it.

6.2 Standicator Measures May Distort Social Processes

6.2.1 Giving Medical Aspects Precedence

Quality in nursing homes has two main aspects, a medical and a psychosocial aspect. To a large extent, the medical aspects do fit the rationality behind standicator measures. Medical qualities can be formalized, planned, and measured.

But the psychosocial aspects are of a different kind. They do not fit the standicator format. This difference in the nature of the two quality aspects may contribute to giving priority to the medical tasks. Since the medical tasks fit the standicator rationality best, they may be given precedence in modern professionalized care, at the cost of more important psychosocial aspects.

6.2.2 Instrumentalization of Psychosocial Aspects

The standicator measures and the simple input-output model they build on, may also delude practicians into treating the psychosocial aspects of care as if they were simple input-output connections. This may contribute to a kind of formalization and bureaucratization of the psychosocial or "homely" aspects of care.

The input-output model can change relational behaviour into intended means and planned guidelines instead of spontaneous and mutual interaction. The standicator measures supply the care workers with guidelines for action, but not guidelines for *inter*actions; how to adjust to the *resident's* answers or reactions.

To meet other persons' social needs intentionally, by means of planned measures, can create quasi-relations and quasi-autonomy; and it may be experienced as such by the residents who are exposed to it (Slagsvold, 1994). Use of standicator measures may lead to a relationship between residents and care workers that is artificial and alienated.

In the study on nursing home quality presented above, we found discrepancies between standicator-measured quality and observed quality on *all* the psychosocial dimensions. Some of these discrepancies are explained by the fact that we *observed* spontaneous interaction and mutual actions and reactions between residents and staff, while we *registered* formalized and planned contact. The relationship between staff and residents is an important aspect of quality – perhaps the most important, if quality means residents' well-being. Standicator measures, and the simple input-output rationality they build on, do not capture this quality. On the contrary, the standicator measure can impair the preconditions for mutual, spontaneous, individualized and affirming relationships.

6.2.3 Homogenization of Care

Standicator measures may also do harm if they contribute to reduced heterogeneity among old-age institutions. They may contribute to making the institutions or services more alike; so the variance may disappear. This may be positive if we could be sure that it was the worst institutions that disappeared. But homogenization might also make the best disappear, like Anguhill did. A homogenization of old-age institutions and of services may, at the same time, remove the best examples, the good institutions from which we could learn in the future.

7   Summary and Concluding Remarks

Quality measures may have unintended consequences for quality. It is quasi-quality as an unintended consequence which has been focused on here.

The discussion of quasi-quality has been tied to two methodological issues which are often regarded as scientific and methodological problems, with only abstract relevance for practice. The two issues are valid measurements and the reactive measurement effect.

The first question concerning valid measurements refers to the trivial but important question of whether the measurements are actually measuring what they are intended to measure – in this case, aspects that are relevant to residents' or clients' well-being. There are hundreds of quality measures in the care literature, mostly of a standicator type. Few of them have been validated, and there seem to be good reasons why we should be seriously sceptical as to the validity of this type of quality measures. Achieving high quality according to these measures may only mean having quasi-quality, quality in a measured sense.

The second issue of reactive measurement effect refers to the fact that measurements can influence the behaviour that is measured, by twisting priorities and distorting social processes.

The reason for focusing on the *practical* question of quasi-quality and for tying it to methodological issues, is to highlight why and how quality measurements can create reactive effects, not only distorting validity but also harming actual quality.

If quality measures reduce the well-being of the residents, it is not only a scientific problem, but also a problem of practical importance.

The issues of measurement-induced quasi-quality may be seen as part of what may be called a "mutual vulgarization of both science and practice"; a carry-over of an atomistic approach from research to practical concerns, one which sacrifices scientific-methodological work in order to adapt research instruments to practitioners' assumptions. This issue has, in much more general terms, been called an "engineering mentality" within social research, which may be seen as part of a modern consciousness. Measures of quality may be seen as a prototypical example of such tendencies towards modernity.

Measuring quality is becoming increasingly popular, and quality evaluations have become more and more widespread. There are no good alternatives to standicator measures, as far as I can see. So what do we do?

There is at least one suggestion for researchers and one for practitioners:

1) *For the researchers:* Thorough work ought to be invested in validating standicator measures, using a diversity of methods from observational studies to experiments: what do standicator measures measure, and what do they *not* measure?

2) *For the practitioners and planners:* A serious and sound scepticism is needed with regard to quality measures, as well as some knowledge of the unintended effects which the use of such measures might have on priorities and social processes.

What we can hope for is that being aware of the possibility of quasi-quality may in itself reduce the likelihood that quasi-quality will be created.

Notes

1   For example: Chambers, 1987; Lemke/Moos, 1987; Fleishman, 1989; Bond et al., 1989; Morris, 1990; Geron, 1991; Phillips, 1991; Spector/Takada, 1991; Cherry, 1991; Bland et al., 1992; Zinn et al., 1993; Spri, 1993; Timko/Moos, 1991; Wilde et al., 1993, 1994; Gjerberg, 1995.

2   It is probably a mutual relationship between widespread quality attention and quality measures. Interest in quality actualizes a need for quality measures, but the existence of quality measures also contributes to focusing attention on quality.

3   The argument concerning quality of care vs. quality of life is parallel to arguments central to welfare research, where the distinction between welfare and well-being is stressed (Ringen, 1995): Welfare means having opportunities through adequate resources to available arenas where resources can be applied. A high level of welfare cannot be the same as well-being. Well-being is a subjective experience, influenced among other things by preferences and expectations. It should not be the objective for direct influence by, e.g. the authorities.

4   Elderly, dependant people express contentment with little; they tend to give socially-acceptable answers (Diener, 1984) and to make downward comparisons (Crocker/Major, 1989; Heidrich/Ryff, 1993). They are reluctant to complain (Carp/Carp, 1981; Connidis, 1984). In old-age institutions, those who can be interviewed are not representative of the institutionalized population. The rather constant proportion of elderly who express satisfaction with different life circumstances raises the question of whether life satisfaction is to a large extent related to personality traits (e.g. Hanson/Carpenter, 1996; McNeil et al., 1986). These and some other psychological mechanisms contribute to positive evaluations and represent serious methodological problems concerning user evaluations (f.i. Larson, 1978; Doyle/Forehand, 1984; Horley, 1984; George, 1979; Zinn, 1993; Slagsvold, 1985).

5   Donabedian (1966) has outlined an input-output model which is often referred to. Davies/Knapp (1981) have refined this model with reference to long-term care.

6   It might, of course, be questioned which of the two measures are most valid. The assumptions of the high validity of the observation scores are based on high interrater correlations and on "what we saw with our own eyes".

7   An example: in 89% of the wards, the head nurse reported that they walked daily with inhabitants as part of the rehabilitation programme. In only half of these wards did we observe such training, only once, with one resident over the space of at least one week.

8   In Norway, where we have few of these kinds of incentives, I believe plain cheating would be rare. In one study from the USA where a quality-incentive programme was validated, "cheating" did, however, seem to be one of the consequences of being quality-measured (Geron, 1991). It was those parts of the programme which were of the "standicator type" which invited cheating. In this study, indicators of a "homelike environment" were (among others) having stimulating items like fish bowls or tanks and plants. "Participation" was assessed by counting residents participating during two predetermined times of peak activity; "community participation" was assessed according to the time residents spent involved in community activity. Being assessed by these indicators of quality contributed to some unintended changes in some of the nursing homes; renting fish-tanks and plants before being surveyed, establishing two

structured activity periods, structuring group outings in the community, and in addition imposing considerable extra paperwork for documentation.

References

Ammentorp, W./Gossett, K. D./Poe, N. E. (1991) *Quality Assurance for Long-term Care Providers*. London: SAGE Publications.

Bland, R./Bland, R./Cheetham, J./Lapsley, I./Llewellyn, S. (1992) *Residential Homes for Elderly People. Their Costs and Quality*. Edinburgh: Her Majesty's Stationary Office.

Bond, J./Bond, S./Donaldson, C./Gregson, B./Atkinson, A. (1989) 'Evaluation of an Innovation in the Continuing Care of Very Frail Elderly People', *Ageing and Society* 1 (9): 347-381.

Booth, T. (1985) *Home Truths. Old Peoples Homes and the Outcome of Care*. Aldershot: Gower Publishing Comp. Ltd.

Bowling, A./Formby, J./Grant, K. (1993) 'Factors Associated with Mortality in National Health Service Nursing Homes for Elderly People and Long-stay Geriatric Wards in Hospital', *International Journal of Geriatric Psychiatry* 8: 203-210.

Campbell, D. T. (1979) 'Assessing the Impact of Planned Social Change', *Evaluation and Programme Planning* 2: 67-90.

Carp, F. M./Carp, A. (1981) ' "It may not be the answer, it may be the question" ', *Research on Aging* 3 (1): 85-100.

Chambers, L. W. (1986) *Quality Assurance in Long-term Care: Policy, Research and Measurement*. Paris: World Health Organization, International Center of Social Gerontology.

Chambers, L. W. (1987) 'Promoting Long-term Care Quality Assurance: Strategies Used in Europe and North America', *Danish Medical Bulletin*, Special Supplement Series 5: 21-28.

Chambers, L. W./Blum, H. M. (1988) 'Measurement of Actions of Care-providers in Long-term Care', *Journal of Clinical Epidemiology* 41 (8): 793-802.

Cherry, R. L. (1991) 'Agents of Nursing Home Quality of Care: Ombudsmen and Staff Ratios Revisited', *Gerontologist* 31 (3): 302-308.

Clark, P./Bowling, A. (1990) 'Quality of Everyday Life in Long Stay Institutions for the Elderly. An Observational Study of Long Stay Hospital and Nursing Home Care', *Social Science and Medicine* 30 (11): 1201-1210.

Connidis, I. (1984) 'The Construct Validity of the Life Satisfaction Index A and Affect Balance Scales: A Serendipitous Analysis', *Social Indicators Research* 15: 117-129.

Crocker, J./Major, B. (1989) 'Social Stigma and Self-esteem: The Self-protective Properties of Stigma', *Psychological Review* 96(4): 608-630.

Davies, A. D. M. (1983) 'Quality of Life for the Elderly Long-stay Patient', *Ageing and Society* 3 (3): 396-403.

Davies, B./Knapp, M. (1981) *Old Peoples Homes and the Production of Welfare*. London: Routledge & Kegan Paul.

Diener, E. (1984) 'Subjective Well-being', *Psychological Bulletin* 95 (3): 542-575.

Donabedian, A. (1966) 'Evaluating the Quality of Medical Care', *Milbank Memorial Quarterly* 44 (2): 166-206.

Donabedian, A. (1978) 'The Quality of Medical Care. Methods for Assessing and Monitoring the Quality of Care for Research and for Quality Assurance Programmes', *Science* 200: 856-864.

Doyle, D./Forehand, M. J. (1984) 'Life Satisfaction in Old Age', *Research on Aging* 6 (3): 432-448.

Etzioni, A./Lehman, E. W. (1967) 'Some Dangers in "Valid" Social Measurement', *Annals of the American Academy of Political and Social Science* 373: 1-15.

Evans, G./Hughes, B./Wilkin, D./Jolley, D. (1982) 'Analysis of Daily Practices', pp. 237-341 in: Goldberg, E. M./Connelly, N., *The Effectiveness of Social Care for the Elderly. An Overview of Recent and Current Evaluative Research*. London: Heinemann Educational Books.

Fleishman, R./Bar-Goria, M./Ronen, R./Mendelson, R./Bentley, L. (1989) 'Improving the Quality of Service in Long-term Care Institutions for the Elderly', *World Health Forum* 9: 327-335.

Gallagher, E. M./Walker, G. (1990) 'Vulnerability of Nursing Home Residents during Relocations and Renovations', *Journal of Aging Studies* 4 (1): 31-46.

George, L. K. (1979) 'The Happiness Syndrome: Methodological and Substantive Issues in the Study of Social-psychological Well-being in Adulthood', *Gerontologist* 19 (2): 210-216.

Geron, S. M. (1991) 'Regulating the Behaviour of Nursing Homes through Positive Incentives: An Analysis of Illinois' Incentive Programme (QUIP)', *Gerontologist* 31 (3): 289-300.

Gjerberg, E. (1995) *Kvalitet i sykehjem? En analyse av sykehjemmene i Oslo slik avdelingssykepleierne ser det*. Oslo. Arbeidsrapport nr. 2: Folkehelsa.

Hansson, R. O./Carpenter, B. N. (1994) *Relationships in Old Age. Coping with the Challenge of Transition*. New York: The Guilford Press.

Heidrich, S. M./Ryff, C. D. (1993) 'The Role of Social Comparison Processes in the Psychological Adaption of Elderly Adults', *Journal of Gerontology: Psychological Sciences* 48: 127-136.

Horley, J. (1984) 'Life Satisfaction, Happiness, and Morale: Two Problems with the Use of Subjective Well-being Indicators', *Gerontologist* 24 (2): 124-127.

Kane, R. A./Kane, R. L. (1988) 'Long-term Care: Variations on a Quality Assurance Theme', *Inquiry* 25: 132-146.

Kayser-Jones, J. S. (1986) 'Open-ward Accommodations in a Long-term Care Facility: The Elderly's Point of View', *Gerontologist* 26 (1): 63-69.

Larson, R. (1978) 'Thirty Years of Research on the Subjective Well-being of Older Americans', *Journal of Gerontology* 33 (1): 109-125.

Lazarsfeld, P. F. (1949) 'What is Obvious?', *Public Opinion Quarterly* 13: 378-380.

Lemke, S./Moos, R. H. (1987) 'Measuring the Social Climate of Congregate Residences for Older People: Sheltered Care Environment Scale', *Psychology of Aging* 2 (1): 20-29.

Mc.Neil, J. K./Stones, M. J./Kozma, A. (1986) 'Subjective Well-being in Later Life: Issues Concerning Measurement and Prediction', *Social Indicators Research* 18: 35-70.

Montgomery, R. J. V./Borgatta, E. F. (1987) 'Plausible Theories and the Development of Scientific Theory', *Research on Aging* 8 (4): 586-608.

Morris, J. N./Hawes, C./Fries, B. E. et al. (1990) 'Designing the National Resident Assessment Instrument for Nursing Homes', *Gerontologist* 30: 293-307.

Phillips, C. (1991) 'Developing a Method of Assessing Quality of Care in Nursing Homes, Using Key Indicators and Population Norms', *Journal of Aging and Health* 3 (3): 407-422.

Ringen, S. (1995) 'Well-being, Measurement and Preferences', *Acta Sociologica* 38 (2): 3-14.

Schwarz, C. E./Ozminkowski, R. J./Hoaglin, D./Cella, M./Branch, L. G. (1994) 'Can a Survey Influence Quality of Care in Nursing Homes? The Impact of the New York Quality Assurance System on Resident Deterioration and Adverse Outcomes', *Journal of Aging and Health* 6 (4): 549-572.

Seefeldt, C. (1987) 'The Effects of Preschoolers' Visits to a Nursing Home', *Gerontologist* 27 (2): 228-232.

Slagsvold, B. (1985) 'Inadequate Living Conditions and yet Satisfied in Old Age', in: *Ageing – Living Conditions and Quality of Life*. NGI-rapport 5/85 ed. Oslo: Norsk gerontologisk institutt.

Slagsvold, B. (1994) 'Helhetlig omsorg – er det mulig og "naturlig"?', in: Helset, A./Nygård, Å. M./Seim, S./Utne, T., *Alderdoms vekst. Festskrift til Eva Beverfelt*. Oslo: Norsk gerontologisk institutt.

Slagsvold, B. (1995) *Mål eller mening. Om å måle kvalitet i aldersinstitusjoner*. Oslo: Norsk gerontologisk institutt.

Spector, W. D./Takada, H. A. (1991) 'Characteristics of Nursing Homes that Affect Residential Outcomes', *Journal of Aging and Health* 3 (4): 427-454.

Spri (1990) *Starta kvalitetssirklar i vården*. 1990 2; SPRI-rapport 265. Stockholm: Hälso- och sjukvårdens utvecklingsinstitut/Spri.

Timko, C. T./Moos, R. H. (1991) 'Assessing the Quality of Residential Programmes: Methods and Applications', *Adult Residential Care Journal* 5 (2): 113-129.

Tropman, J. (1987) 'Introduction to "Quality of Long Term Care" ', *Danish Medical Bulletin*, Special Supplement Series (5): 1-2.

Vladeck, B. C. (1980) *Unloving Care. The Nursing Home Tragedy*. New York: Basic Books Inc. Publishers.

Vladeck, B. C. (1988) 'Quality Assurance through External Controls', *Inquiry* 25: 100-107.

Wærness, K. (1984) 'The Rationality of Caring', *Economic and Industrial Democracy* 5: 185-211.

Wilde, B./Larsson. G./Larsson, M./Starrin, B. (1994) 'Quality of Care. Development of a Patient-centred Questionaire Based on a Grounded Theory Model', *Scandinavian Journal of Caring Science* 8: 39-48.

Wilde, B./Larsson, G./Larsson, M./Starrin, B. (1995) 'Quality of Care from the Elderly Persons's Perspective: Subjective Importance and Perceived Reality', *Aging Clinical Experience Research* 7 (2): 140-149.

Zinn, J. S./Lavizzo-Mourney, R./Taylor, L. (1993) 'Measuring Satisfaction with Care in the Nursing Home Setting: The Nursing Home Resident Satisfaction Scale', *Journal of Applied Gerontology* 12 (4): 452-465.

List of Contributors

Steen Bengtsson, Senior Researcher at the Danish National Institute of Social Research in Copenhagen, and Associate Professor at the University of Roskilde (Denmark)

Peter Beresford, Open Services Project; Reader in Social Policy at Brunel University, West London, and a member of Survivors Speak Out

Jonas Bjelfvenstam, Director of The Quality and Strategic Tender Documentation Department in the City of Stockholm's Executive Office, Stockholm

Rosemary Bland, Lecturer in Social Work at the University of Stirling, Scotland; currently on secondment to the Social Work Services Inspectorate of the Scottish Office

Karen Christensen, Sociologist; Researcher at the Centre for Social Research, Bergen (Norway)

Carla Costanzi, Sociologist; Manager at the Social Services Department of the Genoa Local Administration, Genoa

Suzy Croft, Open Services Project; Social Worker with St John's Hospice, London

Monica Dowling, Lecturer in Evaluative Research, Royal Holloway College, University of London

Clare Evans, formerly Founder and Director of Wiltshire Users Network, an independent user controlled organization; presently Coordinator of the National Leonard Cheshire User Empowerment Project

Adalbert Evers, Professor for Comparative Health and Social Policy at the University of Giessen (Germany), and one of the Directors of the Institut für Sozialforschung, Frankfurt am Main

Tessa Harding, Head of Planning and Development at Help the Aged, United Kingdom, London

Brian Hardy, Senior Research Fellow in the Community Care Division, Nuffield Institute for Health, University of Leeds

Riitta Haverinen, Researcher at the National Research and Development Centre for Welfare and Health (STAKES), Helsinki

Barbara Klein, Head of the Market Focus Unit at the Department of Public Health of the Fraunhofer IAO, Stuttgart

Kai Leichsenring, Head of Programme at the European Centre for Social Welfare Policy and Research, Vienna

Mikko Mäntysaari, Head of Research and Development at the National Research and Development Centre for Welfare and Health (STAKES), Helsinki

Sturle Næss, Research Assistant at the Department of Sociology of the University of Bergen (Norway)

Maria Oppen, Senior Sociologist at the Research Unit II "Technology–Work–Environment" of the Wissenschaftszentrum Berlin für Sozialforschung (WZB)

Marja A. Pijl, Freelance Researcher in Social Policy, The Hague

Christopher Pollitt, Professor of Government at Brunel University, West London, and currently Visiting Research Professor at the Public Management Centre, Katholieke Universiteit Leuven

Marketta Rajavaara, Researcher at the Research and Development Centre of the Social Insurance Institution of Finland, Helsinki

Britt Slagsvold, Senior Research Fellow at NOVA / Norwegian Social Research, Oslo

Gabriëlle Verbeek, Project Leader of the Programmes "Empowerment of Clients" and "Quality Improvement" at the NIZW / Netherlands' Institute for Care and Welfare, Utrecht

Kari Wærness, Professor at the Department of Sociology of the University of Bergen (Norway)

Gerald Wistow, Professor of Health and Social Care and Head of the Community Care Division at the Nuffield Institute for Health, University of Leeds